2 95 ƒ/

JET STRESS

...WHAT IT IS & HOW TO COPE WITH IT

JUDITH GOELTZ

DISTRIBUTED BY
TONY B. ENTERPRISES
130 Clifford Terrace
SAN FRANCISCO, CALIFORNIA 94117
415 / 564-8844

published by

INTERNATIONAL INSTITUTE OF
NATURAL HEALTH SCIENCES, Inc.
7422 Mountjoy
Huntington Beach, CA 92647

DEDICATION

For Sam & Robin, In Appreciation
of their support

PREFACE

When I received this manuscript on jet travel I was immediately interested, because I have travelled long distances by air all my life and can appreciate the need for such a book.

Indeed, stress and fatigue that accompany jet travel are much overlooked, crucially important topics. There may be other health problems which aviation medicine must face, but there can be no doubt about the fact that flight crews, attendants and passengers are exposed to an unusual amount of stress.

I am not competent to make recommendations concerning the sociologic measures to be taken or the improvement in instrumentation that may minimize the risk of aviation and space travel, as my past experience has been to research the fundamental mechanisms of stress reactions in general. I expect, however, that this book will not only help people withstand flying better, but will also encourage general awareness of the seriousness of the problem of jet stress so as to create public pressure for more research in this area.

Some remarks on general principles of stress management may be in order. Each of us is born with a certain amount of vitality, which is gradually used by stress; this is the key; I believe that if this were widely recognized our concept of aging and living would be considerably altered.

The essential aspects of a code of behavior which I have adopted to cope with stress in order to achieve health, long life and happiness, are as follows:

1. Find your own natural stress level, the level at which you can comfortably advance toward your own selected port of destination.

2. Be an altruistic egoist. There is a natural instinct in all human beings to look after themselves first. Yet the wish to be of some use, to do some good to others, is also natural; we are social beings, and everybody wants somehow to earn respect and gratitude. Being useful to others gives you the greatest degree of safety, because no one wishes to destroy a person who is necessary.

3. Earn thy neighbor's love. This is a contemporary modification of the adage "Love thy neighbor as thyself" It recognizes that all neighbors are not lovable and that it is impossible to love on command.

This book is quite indispensable for all those who may attempt to cope with the problems of air travel. Judith Goeltz has succeeded in presenting a well-balanced book, a volume written with uncompromising integrity.

HANS SELYE, M.D.

FOREWORD

Ms. Judy Goeltz has produced a most intriguing and thorough book on a very complex subject. As she has frequently experienced the uncomfortable and adverse effects of circadian dysrhythmia, her study of the field and her writing on it are characterized by authenticity. Many uninformed travelers have rushed by air to a distant land, anticipating the immediate effective accomplishment of their mission, only to discover that "jet lag" has produced sub-par mental and physical performance. As the author points out, fore-knowledge of circadian rhythms and the effects produced when these are disturbed, can prevent desynchronosis. Information is provided on methods of preventing these adverse effects. This book is commended to all those who expect to travel long distances by air, whether passengers on business or pleasure flights or flight crew members.

Stanley R. Mohler, M.D.
Professor and Vice Chairman
Director, Aerospace Medicine
Department of Community Medicine
Wright State University School of Medicine
Dayton, Ohio

INTRODUCTION

I flew for a major international airline for five years. I suffered from chronic fatigue. I could not get enough sleep. Energy was a long-forgotten luxury.

I never felt well. Upper respiratory infections plagued me. So did mouthfuls of canker sores. I was a regular patient of six doctors, all specialists. I ate medicine and aspirin like food but never felt any better. Finally one internist adamantly advised, "Quit flying. I've never seen a stewardess who was well."

So I did. But I didn't get any better. Finally, three years later when my E.N.T. specialist gave me up as hopeless I heard of a doctor who was able to help me. He was an innovative professional who changed my diet and boosted my tired body with supplementary nutrients.

I got better. So much better, in fact, that I spent the next several years studying alternative approaches to health care that are routinely frowned upon by many of the more "oxthodox" doctors. I moved to a farm where I raised my own food and animals, all by natural methods. I wrote a book to help others make the transition from the average American diet into natural, whole foods.

One day a friend, Mardi Feather, called me. Mardi is still flying for an international airline and her father, Dr. James E. Crane, is a leading aerospace doctor. "Judy, we have to do something!" Mardi exclaimed. "It's getting worse than ever. We are exhausted all the time. The ozone is burning our lungs. We can't sleep. We're sick most of the time. There must be some way to conquer this fatigue problem. Will you help me write a book on it?"

Together we checked medical libraries and poured through aerospace medical journals. When she got involved in another project I continued. By now we realized that not just flight attendants and pilots were suffering from the amount of traveling they had to do in jet planes, but anyone who traveled a lot could use some help.

I interviewed airline doctors and FAA-examining physicians. I wrote to experts whose research we had read. I attended conventions, sent out letters of inquiry and questionnaires and made phone calls. A pilot working with his union on the problem of pilot fatigue offered me invaluable information, direction, materials, advice and help.

Gradually the enormity of the problem became evident. We were dealing with more than just crossing time zones and jet lag. We were dealing with many stresses that added up to fatigue in anyone who traveled al lot by jet.

We are also dealing with a subject that few people know much about. Some research has been done on some isolated areas but never in real-life situations have all the stresses involved in flying been studied together. No one has applied the concept of stress to what was happening to us when we fly.Not the experts, not the airlines, not the unions or government or aerospace doctors.

Jet stress is a new concept. This book will tell you what it is. It will attempt to present some solutions to cope with it-- some backed by strong medical opinion and experience, some unorthodox, some speculative. Anything that might work for someone is included. The more technically-inclined can refer to notes at the end of each chapter for documentation and further details.

At times we seem to wander off-course somewhat. Actually we do not. Before any of us will make a change we must really want to. We must be convinced that such a change is for our benefit. If we don't understand the problem or its solution we aren't likely to be convinced that change is worthwhile. For that reason this book is quite comprehensive, so you will have a background for understanding.

I hope this book will help you. I also hope it will make you more aware of the serious need for more research into jet stress and pilot fatigue, for better FAA guidelines on how long aircrews may work and how much rest they need, and for acknowledgement of this fatigue factor in airline disasters. Jet stress and accompanying fatigue are quietly-ignored areas of tremendous importance to the lives of every one who flies. Airlines, government agencies, and even unions will take a serious look at these problems only when you demand they do so.

JET STRESS:
What It Is And How To Cope With It.

A Travelers Guide to Dealing with the Physical Effects of Flying

TABLE OF CONTENTS

Chapter One

What's It All About?

Jet lag. An oft-repeated word. A commonly-accepted fact of jet travel. A condition many of us shake our heads about knowingly but few really understand.

Most think of jet lag as what happens to us when we cross time zones. We don't really understand what it is that crossing these time zones does to the body, but we know that we feel more tired than we should, and we don't sleep or work as well when we arrive at our destination.

Jet stress is much more than jet lag. It is the cumulative effect of all the conditions or stressors, minor and major, that affect us when we travel on a jet airliner. Many of these conditions are not obvious to the passenger. Even the pilots and flight attendants are not fully aware of some of them. Noise, vibration, exposure to ozone and dehydration and an atmosphere with lower than normal amounts of oxygen strain our bodies. There is even the possibility that air ions within the cabin may affect how well we feel while we are on the plane, and how well we work.

But the major problem comes because our body's circadian cycle--the 24-hour rhythmic patterns our bodies normally operate within--is upset. Every part of the body--the cells, organs, tissues and glands--works in a cycle characteristic to itself. Each cycle has a rhythmic pattern of its own, and seems to be governed by its private, internal clock. (Possibly there is one central clock governing the individual clocks but one hasn't been found yet.) We are all familiar with the monthly menstrual cycle of women. There are also many cycles or rhythms that repeat themselves daily--about every 24 hours--and these are what we are referring to when we talk about the body's circadian cycle.

Crossing time zones upsets these cycles. So does traveling or working when we would normally be sleeping. Even taking a north/south flight where we don't cross any time zones makes us susceptible to jet lag because we are making our bodies work when they expect to rest and sleep. This throws the body's cycles off-pattern. It jars the internal clocks governing these daily cycles. The body reacts by trying to reset these biological timepieces while it meets the unscheduled demands we are placing on it. We are not as coordinated. We don't think as clearly. We don't remember as well. We don't sleep as well.

The body is so remarkable that when we impose this strain on it, it is usually able to respond and readjust quickly, depending of course on our age and overall health. With a few nights of good, natural rest we seem to be back to normal. The problem comes when, for some reason, we don't get that rest. Then we get back on an airplane and the strain of the second flight is greater than the first. The effect is cumulative. Eventually fatigue sets in.

Take, for example, what the pilot encounters. His work day may begin in late afternoon or evening, when he would ordinarily be slowing down and going to bed. Six, 9 or even 20 hours later he arrives at his destination, after crossing many time zones. He tries to land the airplane when his body is in its lowest cycle, when it thinks it should be sleeping. It is less able and less willing to respond to the demands put on it. Once in his hotel room the pilot is fatigued and wants to sleep, but local time is noon. The sun is high in the sky, people are active, talking, working, socializing--everything around him tells him he should be active and doing things.

If he does manage to get some sleep, he will probably awaken just about time it's getting dark outside. Now his body is ready for breakfast and some exercise, but everything in his environment tells him he should have dinner, relax, and go to bed. So he has dinner and goes back to bed. Sleep comes, if at all, late--probably around 3 or 4 in the morning, his normal bedtime at home. Just as he is half-way through his sleep cycle, trying to rest & rejuvenate, the 8 o'clock wake-up call comes and he has to get up and go to work. He has had 24 hours of rest, but not enough rest has come. He begins work tired.

The flight attendant has an even greater problem. While his schedules and trips are similar to the pilot's they are generally more strenuous since they do not have as much protective regulating of schedules by the FAA. There is seldom a relief crew--extra crew members to relieve the heavy work-load on a long, tiring flight. If the flight attendant does get a chance to rest there is seldom a place to do so. Flight attendants will sleep on the floor between rows or seats in order to get rest on a long night flight.

Most importantly, according to Dr. Frederick Leeds, former Medical Director for Pan American World Airways, San Francisco, the flight attendant is the only person on board who does strenuous physical work at cabin altitudes of 6,000 to 8,000 feet, and who walks many miles.

We used to joke about "walking to Tokyo tonight." But it isn't a joking matter.

Authorities have compared the work of the flight attendant to that of a young housewife with children, or a building or steel worker. The work is difficult because it is so sustained. Combine this with the other factors of jet stress and we see a very demanding job devoid of the glamour commonly associated with it.

I was fired for canceling out on a trip because I was too fatiqued to continue. We reported in the evening for an all-night flight from New York to Argentina. Towards early morning we had to make an unscheduled stop in Paraguay to pick up extra fuel since the winter weather was so bad around Buenos Aires that we would have to be prepared to circle the airport, if necessary, before being cleared to land. Refueling took longer than usual since the workers weren't at the airport at that early hour. We had to wait for them to arrive. The refueling stop and the need to circle the Buenos Aires airport added hours to an already long "duty-day".

When we finally landed we flight attendants were not functioning adequately. We had spots before our eyes. We couldn't think. We nearly forgot to remove the emergency slides from the doors. Some were crying. We were clumsy.

In essence, had there been an emergency, which is the primary reason for a flight attendant, we would not have been able to handle it properly.

The pilots got off and went to the hotel for rest. Their trip was over. A fresh cockpit crew arrived at the airplane and we were expected to go on with them to Montevideo, Uruguay.

This is normally a short flight of less than an hour. That day, though, we were going to have to circle the Montevideo airport for an unknown period of time because the same bad weather conditions were there. We also had a couple of hours of transit time in Buenos Aires before departure.

We looked forward to at least 3 more hours of duty before we could walk off the airplane. One stewardess was crying from exhaustion. We canceled, refusing to take the flight on to Montevideo because of fatigue, with the accompanying inability to perform in case of an emergency.

The freshly-rested captain and crew couldn't understand why we should be tired. Neither could the company. We were suspended from flight and deadheaded home the next day. We were fired, and only through efforts of the union and a supporting letter from the original captain were we reinstated.

The public sees the lives of flight attendants as glamourous and exciting. They are unaware of the heavy professional duties involved in the job or what the continued exposure to jet stress does to their bodies.

It is not unusual for a passenger ending his San Francisco to London flight to ask the flight attendant who "walked" and worked his way there, "Now do you go on from here?" To one who understands, the question is absurdly ludicrous.

Yet to most people the aircrews flying them around the world seem to be attractive, sophisticated young people who embody sexual charm, technical knowhow and the thrill of world-wide travel. The job does have some of that. But take a look at those who have been flying for 10 years or more and you will see that the job has taken its toll, especially on the crews flying long range, international flights.

An authority noted, "Crew members are often, perhaps due to their basic physical fitness and public relations image, thought to be supermen or women who should not be susceptible to such stresses. Or alternatively that they should bear them bravely as an inevitable consequence of their chosen occupation. But such attitudes do neither a service to air safety and efficiency, nor are they in line with current enlightened social and industrial practice." (Sleep Patterns)

A former stewardess with a leading American interntional carrier resigned at age 30 after flying for 8 years. She said it took a full year after quitting before she felt the fatigue and weariness leave her body before she "felt normal".

Another wrote this open letter to her former coworkers: "After nine and a half years as a stewardess, I have resigned. I couldn't take the exhaustion anymore. It left me no time for the rest of my life--I was too busy getting my health back for my next trip.

"The physical and emotional stamina required to do the job is mind-boggling to those who dwell on land. A toll is being taken on our physical and emotional well-being. All through flight service health is breaking down and love relationships are breaking up. Gone is the laughter and gaiety that once filled a jet winging to some exotic port of call.

"Flying is basically one of the loneliest jobs a person can take. It requires great amounts of inner strength."

Such repeated exposure to stress from jet travel can lead to illness and even early death.[A] While no one really knows this to be a fact there are several studies indicating that this is likely.

While the effects of jet stress are not so obviously dramatic on the frequent travelers, they do affect them in the same way. But even more crucially, the acute and cumulative fatigue that we know is experienced by both pilots and flight attendants can jeopardize the passenger's life.

Commercial airline accidents and fatigue seem to be correlated. A special report by Channel 5, KPIX-TV, San Francisco, pointed to four fatal crashes where crew fatigue could not be ignored, including the Pan Amercian crash on take-off in Tahiti, the 1977 crash of a cargo plane belonging to Fleming International Airways, the Pan Am/KLM crash at Tenerife, the Canary Islands, when the KLM plane took off without clearance and flew into a Pan Am 747 taxiing on the runway, and a cargo flight in Santa Cruz, Bolivia.

Spanish authorities strongly suggested that fatigue may have been involved in the worst air disaster ever when the Pan Am 747 and KLM 747 collided on the runway at Tenerife in 1977. The KLM pilot had been flying a very long schedule and was apparently hastening to take-off before his duty-time limits would prevent his flying that next leg of his trip. Tired and under pressure, he made a serious error in judgment.

French investigating authorities felt that the Pan Am crash in Tahiti, which occurred on the second leg of a flight pattern that began in New Zealand and was to end in Los Angeles, was partly caused by fatigue, "Occasioned by long flights in the course of the preceding 24 hours . . . perhaps to the regulations in force." The pilots, they pointed out, had been flying multiple night flights, crossing multiple time zones and having short layovers for days preceding the crash.

Investigators of the cargo flight crash in Santa Cruz found fatigue to be a major factor. The crew has only 2 hours and 45 minutes of rest after working for almost 24 hours, before they were again in the airplane. Nevertheless, they were operating within duty-time regulations of the FAA.

The Channel 5 special report concluded that present FAA regulations may have caused "almost 40% of all U.S. carrier accidents in the past 10 years."

With such high stakes one would assume that there must be a lot of study, research and concern going on in the areas of fatigue and stress in flying, with the goal of lessening these problems.

That doesn't seem to be the case. Safety has long been a major interest to commercial airlines and their aerospace medical doctors, but it is safety as it relates to sudden loss of compression in the cabin, what to do in case of a crash, how well seat belts work, what the best body position is when a take-off is aborted, how long it takes to get everyone out of a plane in an emergency, how to handle passengers suffering from smoke inhalation, how to prevent fires--in other words, the obvious crisis situations. The subject of fatigue and how it relates to performance has not been delved into to any extent.

Neither the FAA nor the National Transportation Safety Board (N.T.S.B.) consider fatigue an important component of air disasters. The N.T.S.B. checklist used in investigating crashes includes 83 separate human factors. Fatigue is not one of them.

FAA regulations dictating how long a pilot or flight attendant can be on duty and how much rest must follow are woefully inadequate, to say the least. Virtually unchanged since they were first formulated in 1934, they are so confusing and vague that FAA personnel responsible for administering them admit they almost defy interpretation. There are over 1000 pages of amended regulations which have been spot-amended with special exemptions, made in response to economic pleading and pressures from airline management.

While it is true that the FAA is in the process of developing new duty/rest regulations, these new proposed guidelines still fail to take into account strong research evidence that the body is not a machine that can sleep at will. Researchers have made strong attempts to convince the government that the body will sleep only when it is in a sleep cycle, and to expect it to be able to sleep at any other time is fallacious, foolish, and unscientific. Nevertheless, the new regulations propose that a pilot be on duty a certain number of hours, after which he is allowed a certain number of hours of rest before he returns to flight. When those rest hours occur in the 24-hour day is irrelevant to these so-called authorities.[B]

Even the airline doctors themselves don't concern themselves too much with fatigue among crews. When asked how they would combat it they suggested eating well and getting enough rest. This is good advice, but most of us don't know what is involved in eating well. Nor do most doctors, since medical schools don't teach nutrition. And getting enough good rest while flying is nearly the impossible dream.

These suggestions do not explain nor get to the root of the problem.

What's it all about? It's not about a bolt falling off a wing of an airplane. It's about fatigue. The problem is serious. Jet stress and accompanying fatigue concern our health, and possibly, our death.

NOTES FOR THE PROFESSIONAL

A. The official stance of the Air Transport Association is that pilot fatigue is not a common occurence in the airline pilot, and that the same age-bracket of pilot is healthier than his contemporary in the general male population.

Still, Dr. Charles F. Ehret, researcher in chronobiotics, feels that every time the circadian cycle of the cell is reset, whether by drug or a natural cue from the environment, we risk tumor-producing damage to the gene machinery of the cell.

Dr. Aschoff of the Max Plank Institute in Germany found that insects flown once a week between Europe and the United States have a shortened lifespan by 25%.

Dr. Martin C. Moore-Ede, chronophysiologist at Harvard Medical School, reported that studies or organisms ranging from Drosophilia to mice show that repeated time-zone shifts constitute a significant stress which can cause a reduction in life span.

An Iberian Airline study noted, "In a major airline company most pilots live only 6 years beyond their retirement of 60; some only live 1 or 2 years more." *(Sickness and Incapacitation)*

Dr. Hans Selye, world-reknown stress researcher and President of the International Institute of Stress at the University of Montreal, explains that each of us is born with a certain amount of adaptive energy and vitality which is gradually used by stresses. True physiological aging is not determined by the time elapsed since birth, but by the total amount of drain on this vital supply.

While Dr. Frederick Leeds, retired flight surgeon and medical director for Pan American World Airways, points to statistics that show that the commercial pilot lives to be as old as his non-flying counterpart, he says he would not be surprised if other studies were done which show that there is a life-shortening affect--especially if such studies where done on flight attendants.

B. Present proposals fail to take into account present-day knowledge of the functioning of the human body. Dr. Martin C. Moore-Ede of Harvard Medical School, a leading researcher in circadian cycles of the body, charges that these new proposals lack any awareness of the prominent circadian (day/night) variations in wakefulness, alertness and psychomotor performance that have been well-documented in man over the past 20 or more years.

"It treats the human body as a machine which will benefit from a given number of hours rest at whatever time of the day they are provided. It totally ignores a considerable body of scientific evidence showing that capability for sleep and recuperation is highly dependent upon the previous schedule of the individual over the previous week." Otherwise, "a severe problem of 'desynchronosis' may then occur with serious impact on alertness, a reaction time and other important parameters." *(Air Line Pilot, May, 1979)*

Dr. Elliot Weitzman, chariman of the Department of Neurology, Albert Einstien College of Medicine, has shown that rest periods are not readily useable for sleep when they occur at inappropriate times in the circadian cycle of the body. He agrees with Dr. Moore-Ede, warning that "is has been repeatedly documented that the time of the subject's biological day is a very important contributor to critical function of inattention, decreased vigilance, judgment and performance", and that the "apparent lack of (this) will continue to contribute to potential flight hazards to the passengers and crews." *(Air Line Pilot, May, 1979)*

Dr. John R. Beljan, dean of the School of Medicine at Wright State University in Dayton, Ohio, made these comments regarding the new, proposed FAA duty and flight-time regulations, "It appears to me that (they) are in desperate need of expert medical input from (FAA) Air surgeon staff. As it is presently constituted and proposed, I see it as unworkable and scientifically unfounded. Nowhere do we see any considerations of time-zone translocation or dislocation, or an appreciation for nocturnal schedules of human beings on diurnal patterns, which is the normal mode of our society." Ignoring these factors "might compromise air safety." *(Air Line Pilot, May, 1979)*

Dr. Moore-Ede has advised the National Transportation Safety Board to completely document the exact times of sleep and wakefulness, duty and off-duty, and mealtimes for the previous ten days of the pilots involved in accidents. This would tell what phase of their circadian cycle the pilots were in when the accident occurred, to help determine if trying to operate an airplane when the body is in a low phase of its cycle can contribute to poor performance that causes accidents.

Chapter Two

Conditions Inside the Airplane Cabin That Affect Us.

Much of the jet stress we experience when we fly comes from the stressors we find inside the airplane itself, conditions of the airplane environment like noise, high and low vibration, reduced atmospheric pressure, extremely low humidity, the occasional presence of ozone gas, and possibly an insufficient number of negative air ions in relation to positive air ions.

IT'S NOISY

We are all familiar with the noise inside an airplane. Scientifically defined, noise is a discordant sound that results from nonperiodic vibrations in the air. To most of us, noise is unwanted sound.

Noise levels within the Boeing and Douglas aircraft correspond roughtly to the noise of intense auto traffic or a machine shop.[A]

Dr. S. R. Lane Reported to a meeting of the Acoustical Society of America that "Babies and children, in particular, and adults should not be exposed to the noise levels inside commercial aircraft. the passenger cabin noise levels during flight equal or exceed even the inappropriately high level limits which have been shown not to protect hearing and health. Studies have shown that airline pilots have above normal hearing loss."[B]

Boeing Aircraft refutes Dr. Lane's statements, claiming, "Travellers are not being exposed to hazardous noise levels inside passenger cabins of modern jets."[C]

How much sound can we tolerate and what damage can it do? Everyone agrees that too much noise leads to hearing loss but there the agreement stops. We have to consider not only the intensity of the noise but how long we are exposed to it, and how often.[D]

In general the noise within the cabin falls within the 78 dBA to 96 dBA range. We should be exposed to sound levels in excess of 70 to 80 dBA as infrequently as possible, according to Dr. E Granjean of the Swiss Federal Institute of Technology. A leading laboratory specializing in hearing aids found that the human ear normally tolerates sound level to about 85 dBA, but beyond that the auditory nerves are usually damaged. With 90 dBA we begin to get permanent destruction of hearing nerves.[E]

Hearing ability decreases. Not only do we lose the ability to detect sound quality may be poor. Pitch, clarity and loudness may all be distorted. We may hear sounds that are only moderately loud that to us appear much too loud--a case of auditory recruitment.

After exposure to noise, hearing loss or impairment may be only temporary, lasting minutes or days. Ringing in the ears, called Tinnitus, is a danger signal that a small percentage of hearing has been lost. This may be temporary or permanent. Even when we think we have recovered from temporary hearing loss we may suffer residual, permanent effects on the ear and hearing.[F]

What we do know is that the major cause of hearing

damage--nerve deafness--is related to prolonged exposure to excessive noise.

Continued exposure to high levels of noise can cause hearing loss. Noise can permanently damage the inner ear, resulting in permanent hearing losses ranging from slight impairment to nearly total deafness. it can also cause temporary hearing losses, but repeated exposures can lead to chronic hearing losses.

Noise does not affect only hearing. Balance and vision can be altered by noise. Eyes don't accommodate as quickly to focus clearly on near and distant objects when there is a high noise level. This is not a serious problem for the passenger except where it may affect the ability of the pilot to do his job well.

Noise can affect the pilot's performance in other ways. Noise hinders productivity, lowers intellectual output, and affects performance.[G] Quality of work is affected. However, the simpler the task and the better trained we are for it the less likely that noise will influence how well we do it. Also a steady continuous noise is less likely to disrupt us than short, intermittent noises or random bursts of noise.[H]

Noise can contribute to fatigue. Air Force aerospace doctors find that excessive noise makes us more fatigued and less able to cope with unexpected or difficult situations. Even 11 dBA exposure makes us use more energy to maintain the same level of concentration that we would have with less noise.

While we aren't sure how it works we do know that noise causes stress to the body. We have measured the body's physical response to stress when it is exposed to brief sounds over 80 dBA. When some of the noise is removed, stress levels on the body lower. Happily for the jet traveler, when the sound becomes predictively repetitive, as it is in an airplane, the physiological signs of stress diminish.

How much noise is required to produce this stress, lowered productivity and performance, hearing impairment and fatigue is not known for a certainty, and the variables are many. But we must remember that we are not considering just noise in the airplane. It is not the only stressor affecting us when we fly. There are others, and while noise, in and of itself, may not be a dreadful stressor by itself, combined with the others we encounter it must be seriously considered.[I][K]

THE DRY AIR DEHYDRATES US.

We aren't accustomed to the very dry air inside an airplane. It's the kind of air we find in a hot, arid desert. It irritates our eyes and mucous membranes of the nose, makes our throats dry and scratchy, the skin itchy, and the hair dry with more dandruff. We may get static shocks and sparks.[J]

Airplane cabin air is normally pressurized at a 5000 to 7000-foot altitude, giving it an humidity of around 12%, with a range of between 3% to 16%. What moisture there is comes from people inside the plane when they breathe out water vapor.

The best relative humidity for working is around 35%, plus or minus 10%.[K] Researchers warn that "the low humidity in the fuselage of jet aircraft is an environmental situation which may lead to a performance decrement in the crew and discomfort to the passenger." Performance is affected since there is less volume of blood in the body when the body is dehydrated. This means that less oxygen and blood sugar reach the brain.[L]

Researchers feel that dehydration is a major cause of jet lag. It contributes to fatigue and slows our ability to recover. Cigarette smoke and alcohol compound the problem.[M]

We can tell when we are dehydrated because we get thirsty, and because our volume of urine decreases and becomes more concentrated. To counter this we are advised to drink large amounts of juices or water, but not coffee, which makes us lose even more fluid. For every cup of coffee we drink we will probably lose 1 to 1½ cups of fluid from the body.

THE TEMPERATURE IS UNCOMFORTABLE

Because the air is so dry, the temperature of the cabin becomes uncomfortable. While the actual temperature may remain constant, when the humidity varies so does our comfort. If the cabin temperature is raised the total flow of air throughout increases, which takes even more moisture out of the air and the people. This makes us even cooler, and we loose even more fluid through the skin and lungs.

Temperature may affect our performance. The only available information thus far comes from a review of all the literature in this field of study done by the Air Force. They concluded that we work best at 70 degrees Farenheit, and when it is warmer or colder than this we can expect to perform less well.

HYPOXIA OCCURS

The cabin is usually pressurized to an altitude of from 5000 to 7200 feet. Since this atmospheric pressure determines the amount of oxygen we can have each time we breathe, we are getting less oxygen than usual into the tissues of our bodies. This condition is called hypoxia-- lowered oxygen.

How seriously hypoxia affects the passenger and crew on a commercial airliner has not been established. One study concluded that it would not seriously trouble healthy people. Another study done on healthy, young subjects found changes occuring in the body showing strain on the heart. We also need to ask what the former researchers considered "serious" health problems and to consider that not everyone who flies is healthy.

Hypoxia also occurs to a limited degree when we stay awake during normal sleeping hours. This time, approximately between midnight and 6 in the morning, is called the "back side of the clock". There is less oxygen in the blood, naturally, than during daytime hours, meaning that less oxygen reaches the brain. This, in turn, affects our ability to think and make decisions.[N]

There is also less oxygen available for breathing because of cigarette smoke, which produces carbon monoxide, polynuclear hydrocarbons, ammonia, and ozone.

Carbon monoxide, which is also produced within the human body, is toxic to us because it unites with that part of our blood that carries oxygen, the hemoglobin. The hemoglobin carries the carbon monoxide rather than the oxygen, so less oxygen reaches our cells. What's more, it inhibits our using the oxygen that remains in the hemoglobin. The signs and symptoms of hypoxia are the same as those of carbon monoxide poisoning.[O]

We can see that hypoxia occurs from more than one source, and while any one of them might be minor, added together and then added to the other conditions in the cabin, it can adversely affect us. This is especially true of those with heart conditions and of the working crew members.[P] Of special concern is the affect of decreased oxygen supply on the functioning of the brain of the pilot of the airplane.

OTHER POLLUTANTS IN THE AIR

There are other pollutants which may contaminate the aircraft cabin from outside. Usually these come from exhaust gases emitted from the power and air conditioning units that keep the plane functioning while it is on the ground*, from the hydrocarbons escaping during refueling, and from other aircraft engines. In the cabin itself we have pollutants from the galley and the toilets, including smoke fumes and biological pollutants.

OZONE GAS MAY BE PRESENT

Probably the most serious contaminant that comes into the airplane is ozone.

Ozone, or O_3, is a bluish, unstable explosive gas or a blue liquid, which is a more active form of oxygen, O_2. It is found in the earth's atmosphere below 30,000 feet in varying concentrations. At this earth-level ozone concentrations are normally around 0.03ppm (parts per million) in non polluted areas, rising to values higher than 0.10ppm is such polluted cities as Los Angeles and Tokyo. The greatest concentrations of ozone is found in the ozonosphere, at altitudes from 80,000 to 100,000 feet.

What we are concerned with as air travellers are the finger-like streaks of ozone that reach down into the

---

* The jumbo jets don't require such outside support systems, but it has always amused me to watch a Boeing 707 or DC-8 approach the terminal. In the sky they are majestic, powerful, graceful, dignified creations of man, beautifully streamlined for their purpose. But once they touch the ground the clock strikes twelve and these Cinderellas become heavy, lumbering masses of metal, awkwardly waddling to the terminal where a variety of life-giving machines rush up to meet them and "I.V." them to keep them from expiring in the foreign atmosphere at ground level.

altitudes we are flying. We have no satisfactory, reliable method for predicting where or when these "fingers" will occur, since vertical air currents constantly change the distribution, pattern position and magnitude of peak concentrations of ozone. Such variations depend upon the weather, the time of the day, the season of the year, and what degree north or south the airplane is flying. In the Northern Hemisphere the ozone is more concentrated in March and April.

Ozone is a very labile or changeable substance. It is harmful because of the oxygen atom that remains when ozone, O_3, breaks down into oxygen, O_2. It is this oxygen atom, O, that is so highly reactive.

Man seems to be more sensitive to ozone than animals, and in sensitive individuals concentrations as low as 2.0 ppm may cause severe irritation within less than one hour. It seems to affect the surface of the wet, soft tissues of the respiratory tract. It isn't able to penetrate so does not go into the blood. Apparently it decomposes completely in the respiratory tissues of the lungs.

Symptoms range from being simply symptomatic, to being irritants, to becoming severe irritants as ozone concentration increases. Injury begins in the throat. With longer exposure and higher concentrations the tissues of the lungs, especially the alveoli where the air we have breathed in passes into the blood, are injured. Eventually edema results, harming lung function. Edema will occur at concentrations above 4.0 to 5.0ppm for only 1-hour exposure to ozone, but even lower concentrations of 0.6 to 0.8ppm can bring on edema. Q

Acute and repeated lung injuries resulting from inhaling of ozone bring on physiological, biochemical, immunological and pathogenic* changes. There is a decrease

*Capable of causing disease

in both the vital capacity and the reserve capacity of the lungs. * R

Exposure to ozone at 0.4 ppm starts irritation in the eyes, ears and nose. Eyes tear, vision blurs, the throat becomes scratchy and dry. We feel chest pain. We begin to cough. Often depression, headache, general body pain, accelerated heart rates and fatigue are felt.* *

Ozone exposure can also reduce our immunity to respiratory infections, impair our sense of smell, make night vision poorer, make it harder to concentrate, and make us more lethargic. S

How serious is this for the flying public? Is there a health hazard?

Ozone was first detected in the DC-8 aircraft in 1962. Most of the subsequent studies were done during the 1960's in preparation for the supersonic Concorde. Interest died when the ozone problem was successfully controlled in the Concorde, to be renewed again with the advent of the Boeing 747SP, a shortened, longer-range version of the Boeing jumbo-jet 747.

NASA* * * became interested when passengers began to complain of dry, burning nose and throat, substernal chest pain, headache, fatigue and coughing. They found that these complaints coincided with high levels of ambient atmospheric ozone in the cabins of the aircraft they had equipped with their GASP system.

As early as 1962 average ozone concentration within a Boeing 707 was found to be several times the maximum

---

* Vital lung capacity is the amount of air we can eliminate from the lungs after taking the biggest breath possible. Reserve lung capacity is the volume of air which is always present in the lungs and can be removed only by surgery.

* * While some of these symptoms may be due to the very dry air of the cabin, in one test all symptoms disappeared as soon as the ozone was removed.

* * * National Aviation and Space Administration

permissible limit of 0.1ppm recommended by the American Conference of Governmental Industrial Hygenists. This same limit has been set by OSHA and other government agencies as well as the Anglo-French Concorde Aeromedical Group.[T] Concentrations of 0.3 to 0.4 ppm were found on a 1966 study. This was slightly higher in the cockpit than in the passenger compartment.

In the 1970's several studies confirmed the presence of high ozone concentrations in cabin air. The threshold of 0.1 ppm for breathing air was surpassed about 75% of the time during 8 to 10 hour flights between Copenhagen and Seattle. Maximum concentrations of 0.4 ppm occurred for 4 hours, with 0.6 ppm for 1 hour. On some of these flights more than 1.0 ppm entered the cabin for periods of 1 hour.[U]

The FAA claims that ozone will be mostly destroyed when it passes through the airplane's pressurization system so that only about 20% of the ozone coming into the engines will actually enter the cabin. Douglas Aircraft, in private communications with Bischof, stated that no ozone destruction is expected in the bleed-air system because, in spite of the high temperatures which could possiblly break the ozone, O_3, down into oxygen, O_2, the ozone doesn't remain in contact with these high temperatures long enough for the breakdown to occur. [*]

As early as 1963 the FAA began studies on ozone and determined that should it exist in airplane cabins in greater concentrations than 0.2 ppm for significant periods of time it would be dangerous to health and would have to be destroyed. Yet nothing was done for years to remedy the

---

[*]   After a survey of the literature available on ozone, the United States Air Force School of Aeromedicine concluded that ozone is reduced by 50% by the time it enters the cabin, but that this still leaves a critical concentration of ozone in the air we would be breathing, according to EPA standards.

problem. If anything, airlines and government alike played down the problem. Even today ozone studies eminating from the FAA state that concentrations of 0.2ppm won't produce negative effects on any system of the body, in direct conflict with their statement in 1963.

The ozone problem is finally being admitted. Airlines, aircraft manufactures and the military are experimenting with ways to lower ozone concentrations in the cabin, using heat and catalytic filters. Presently Pan American Airways is the only carrier with any ozone filtration system aboard its aircraft. Needless to say there is great cost involved, not only in the research but in the system finally built into the airplane itself.

With constant pressure from flight attendants unions and specifically the I.U.F.A.*, the FAA published a Notice of Proposed Rulemaking on Ozone. Aircraft will have to meet OSHA standards of 0.1 ppm time-weighted average and a 0.3 ppm threshold limit value. To meet these standards filters are being placed on the Lockheed 1011's ordered by Pan American.

In the meantime ozone can be a serious problem. How serious depends upon many variables. As we have seen, time of year and length, altitude and location of flight are important. But there are other variables.

For the professional traveler we are not talking about a one-time exposure but repeated exposure. Other stressors concommitant with flying are present. Age and health of the individual are variables, as are the time of day and body cycle we find ourselves in when the ozone is encountered. While present exposures may not be highly harmful in a

---

* International Union of Flight Attendants/Pan Am. It was this group who first complained of ozone and were called a bunch of "hysterical women."

laboratory situation, the traveler is not a "pure" environment with only the stressor of ozone to contend with. What may be relatively harmless in the laboratory is a cumulative stress effect.

AIR IONS MAY ADVERSELY AFFECT US

Air ionization is just beginning to be recognized as something which affects our health, sense of well-being and performance. Some scientists feel that this is a valid area of concern inside commercial airplanes. Since this is a fairly new subject for most, let's begin with some background.

Air is made up of molecules with positive electrical charges called protons and negative electrical charges called electrons. These exist in a balanced state. When the molecule loses or gains an electron an air ion is created, and with it air electricity.

An air ion is an electrically-charged particle. It is a molecule or group of molecules with an unbalanced number of electrons. We are especially interested in molecules of oxygen and hydrogen which are ionized by the action of ultraviolet and other radiations from the sun and space, by emissions from radioactive substances near the surface of the earth and by air turbulence or friction.

These air ions occur in three sizes: small, medium and large. We are concerned with the small air ions that are absorbed by living matter. These seem to be very necessary to life itself. So important are they for growth that bacteria, plants, and even small mammals have withered and died when placed in an air environment entirely free of air ions.[V] Apparently we need them to absorb enough oxygen in order to live. "The human race was developed in ionized air," says James B. Beal, who worked with NASA to deter mine the optimum environment inside space capsules for our astronauts. "Nature used the ions in developing our biological process."

A proper balance of air ions is critical to our physical and emotional well-being.[W] They influence physiological processes. Tissue changes can be seen in the hypothalamus, the adrenal, pituitary and throid glands, which alter water balance, thirst, appetite, sexual behavior, sensitivity to pain,[X] psychomotor performance and adaptation to stress.

Air ions affect respiratory infections as well. A virus or bacteria is positively charged. They attach themselves to the healthy target cells which are negatively charged. If negative air ions are present they change the electrical charge of the virus or bacteria, making them temporarily inactive. But when there aren't enough negative air ions or when there are too many positive ions, this doesn't occur and the cell can't resist the infector as well.[Y]

We need both positive and negative air ions. In nature there are usually more positive than negative, in a ratio of 3 to 1. This ratio is as important for our health as the total number of ions present. It is this ratio we are concerned with inside the airplane. Too many positive air ions nor not enough negative air ions produce biochemical changes in the body that can cause feet and ankles to swell, reduce our ability to perform, and produce irritability, headaches, fatigue, quickness of temper, and irrationality -- symptoms of air ion sickness. This may also be the cause of air sickness for some people.[Z] Of greatest concern for the traveler is the adverse effect of insufficient negative air ions on the pilot's performance and on fatigue.

Not all studies done on how air ions affect performance reach the same conclusion.[AA] There are several reasons for this, among them the fact that motivation is important. People vary, also. Not everyone is observably affected by air ions. It depends upon individual sensitivity. Generally speaking, one-third are affected but not aware of symptoms which can be objectively measured even though they are not subjectively felt. Another one-third are highly sensitive, often reacting violently to varying degrees. Another one-third are virtually immune to the ions as long as their bodies are healthy.[BB] Older people, children, and people under stress are susceptible.

In the airplane we are concerned mainly with having the proper balanced ration of air ions. It takes days for the lack of ions to affect us, but a balance change can cause immediate symptoms. Some researchers have found that the cabin of airplanes contains an overabundance of positive air ions and not enough negative ones.[CC]
This lack of negative ions may be caused by friction produced as the airplane moves through the air. A positive charge is set up on the outer metal skin of the plane which attracts negative air ions to it. The aluminum body acts like a giant magnet drawing the negative air ions inside to the outside, while repelling the positive air ions within the airplane, where they remain to build up.

A build-up of positive air ions can also come from the air conditioning system of the airplane where there is friction in the ductwork. Electrical systems and stray electrical fields tend to produce positive air ions rather than negative ones. Clothing, carpeting and upholstery other than cotton, especially synthetics, create a positive potential.

Smoking and frying food appreciably lower both positive and negative ions. Smoking absorbs the negative ions leaving an overabundance of positive ions. The number of ions present will decrease with the amount of breathing done by the passengers and the amount of moving about the ions do.

In 1972 FAA scientists remarked that "Atmospheric ions

can affect the health, well-being, efficiency, emotions and mental attitude of human beings. The particular effect varies with the polarity and size of ions. Negative ions are being called 'happy ions' whereas positive ions are being called 'grouchy' ions.

"Ionization of the atmosphere in aircraft may be an important factor in the health and comfort of the passenger in commercial aviation and in the effective functioning of commercial . . . pilots," they continued. They recommended a survey of existing levels of atmospheric ionization in passenger cabins and cockpits of commercial flights taken at cruising altitutdes.[DD]

While air ionization has been recognized as very important consideration in our space capsules,[EE] the FAA has not followed up on their recommendation for further research on air ions inside commercial liners. In spite of this they reject suggestions that ion levels in the airplane might represent a danger. But others feel such a danger may exist.

Insufficient negative ions in the cockpit of the airplane could contribute to air disasters since they seem to affect pilot performance and to produce fatigue. Dr. E. Stanton Maxey, himself a pilot, points to the crash of the now-famous Easter Flight 401 that fell into the Everglades in Florida. The flight recorder showed an audible alarm had gone off at 1700 feet to warn the pilots that the plane was too low. Neither pilot responded to it and a surviving crew member reported, "there was never any alarm or concern in the cockpit." As Dr. Maxey sees it, two superb pilots had simultaneously quit seeing and hearing the instruments, which fits into laboratory evidence that upsetting the ion count and balance causes, at the very least, a lack of vigilance and a slowing in reaction time--like being "slipped an electrical mickey."[FF]

It is these instances of aircraft accidents where the pilot, usually with excellent qualifications and long experience, suddenly seem to stop thinking for awhile--not blacking out in the physical sense but experiencing a temporary slowdown or shutdown of normal reactions and thought processes, which Dr. Wallach feels have not received satisfactory explanation from investigators. He believes that an increased positive-air ion balance may cause this mental fuzziness,* manifesting itself as sleepiness or fatigue.GG

The truth is that no one seems to really know much about air ions or how and if they in fact affect the pilot and passenger alike. Medical departments of major airlines and researchers at aircraft companies and government agencies appear unconcerned about their potential health and safety effects. Those questioned reported that no studies and no information is available regarding negative air ionization within the airplane cabin. Many weren't aware that the field of air ionization existed. Retired NASA researchers who discovered the importance of these air ions in space capsules are reticent to speak out because the subject is so controversial (and political) within government circles.

We should find out just what the optimal dose of air ions of each charge will do in each set of circumsances. While we know that air ions are biologically important to us we still need to discover how to apply air ions in preventive and therapeutic medicine in order to provide the best environment possible inside the airplane, and especially inside the cockpit.

If we do find that negative ions improve our use of oxygen, then generating negative ions within the cabin of the airplane could increase both passenger comfort and pilot performance by reducing hypoxia, suggests Dr. Bruce

---

* Such mental fuzziness could also come from fatigue, disruption of the normal body cycles, or from entering into an altered state of consciousness similar to hypnosis.GG

Rosenberg, engineering research psychologist formerly with the FAA. He wants to see a survey made of the existing levels of atmospheric ionization in both the passenger compartment and cockpit "to determine whether ionization has any long-term deleterious effects and whether the use of artificial ions in the airplane environment can be beneficial for pilots and passengers."

In the meantime passengers may suffer swollen ankles, air sickness and sluggishness or irritation. Such reactions are short-term and not serious.

What is serious is poorer pilot performance and the fatigue that improper ion balance may cause. For the most part the pilot is able to perform his job well in spite of such detrimental effects on his mind and body because he is so professional and highly trained. But a compilation of such stresses on the individual, and repeated exposure to such stresses can take its toll. If there is a condition within the aircraft that can improve performance and prevent health deterioration it should certainly be studied and corrected. If this same condition can lead to serious accidents it should have top priority.

We know that the airplane environment produces fatigue in people even when no time zones are crossed. Noise, temperature, cabin pressure and atmospheric quality as well as vibration appear to have a cumulative effect.[HH] While any one of these factors, even if major, can normally be countered with a good rest after exposure, even the minor stressors which may fall into the "normal" or "safe" category can add up to a total stress far in excess of any single one of them. [II] Repeated exposure increases the problem.

More research is needed and it's needed in environments that are realistic. Most studies have been done under laboratory or test conditions rather than real-life, inflight conditions. Such test conditions are often removed from the reality of flight, failing to include enough essential elements of the real-life situation. The difference that exists between the laboratory and the real world, one writer remarked, is as great as the difference between man and ape.

The airplane environment presents us with a number of moderate stressors which have a cumulative effect on us. Repeated exposure enhances these effects. Yet the worst stress on jet travelers results from the disruption of our normal body cycles.

NOTES FOR THE PROFESSIONAL

A. Noise is measured in decibels. The power level of noise doubles with approximately every 10 decibels so that 90 dBA is twice as loud as 80 dBA. The actual intensity of the sound doubles with every 6 decibels, is 3 times as great with a 10 decibel increase, and is 10 times greater with an increase of 20 decibels. A food blender or heavy truck at 25 feet produces noise at 90 dBA. Heavy traffic at rush hour produces noise at 80 dBA.

The following noise levels are found within these aircraft, broken down by area:

	DC-8	DC-10	Boeing 707
cockpit	87	93	78
front cabin	86	82	80
forward galley	95	90	* *
rear cabin	87	88	* *
rear galley	89	95	* *
rear door	96	86	78

B. An unfunded study reported by Dr. S.R. Lane at the 86th Meeting of the Acoustical Society of America found that noise during cruise in the Boeing 727 and 737, the Lockheed L-1011, and Douglas DC-10 is in the 85 to 100-plus dBA range.

C. Boeing Aircraft data shows noise in the 80 dBA range in the passenger cabin during short flights of around an hour or so, where the airplane flies at around a 20,000-foot altitude. But cabin sound levels during long-range flights are typically in the mid-to-upper 70 dBA range, according to their findings.

D.   Aram Glorig found in his studies that continuous exposure at work to noise levels of 80 dBA or less produced
no risk of hearing handicap. Yet a paper presented to the
Acoustical Society of America by E. Granjean of the Swiss
Federal Institute of Technology in Zurich, Switzerland, indicated that if the noise is frequent and regular enough
there is clear evidence that noises of 80 dBA can contribute
to inner ear damage and eventual hearing handicap.
Theoretically, he claims, if we are exposed to noises greater
than 70 to 80 dBA often enough and long enough we could
develop hearing loss as we get older. We can tolerate many
brief exposures in excess of 80 dBA, according to his
research, if these exposures occur infrequently. He concluded, "It seems desirable to have as few sources as possible that expose people to . . . sound levels in excess of 70 to
80 dBA."

Hock Laboratories of Portland, Oregon, specializing in
hearing aides, feels that the human ear normally tolerates
sound level to about 85 dBA, but beyond that our auditory
nerves are usually damaged. With 90 dBA we begin to get
permanent destruction of the hearing nerves.

Temporary hearing loss has been induced by long exposures to levels as low as 5 dBA and lower, and these
hearing losses have required recovery periods of up to 24
hours.

Recommendations from studies done at Wright-
Patterson Air Force Base in Ohio suggest that if we are exposed to noise at 65 dBA or 75 dBA for longer than 16
hours, we should be able to rest from that noise for at least
the same length of time. Long exposures above 90 dBA
should be avoided.

E.   The outer ear, eardrum and middle ear are almost
never damaged by intense noise. But when we are exposed

to intense enough noise for a long enough time, changes occur in the inner ear receptor called the organ of Corti. Here the hair cells which carry sound vibrations to the auditory or hearing nerves are destroyed, and sections of the organ of Corti itself are destroyed or collapse.

F.   Some 10 million Americans suffer some degree of permanent Tinnitus, according to James Miller of the Central Institute for the Deaf.

Hearing inpairment has been defined as a deviation or change, for the worse, in either the structure or function of the ear. Any injury to the ear, or any change in hearing threshold level which places it outside the normal range constitutes a hearing impairment.

G. Results of laboratory tests on whether and how noise affects performance have been variable and contradictory, mostly because there are so many concurrent factors, such as age, motivation, health, individual mental and emotional states, individual attitudes towards noise, absence or presence of other factors besides noise which could increase or decrease its impact on us, novelty of task performed, difficulty of the task, repetitiveness of it, length of time task is performed, experience and training.

H. Short, intermittent noises, random bursts of noise or noise we are not familiar with will have a greater effect on us than noise we are accustomed to. Work that involves a series of steps where we can't relax our attention and tasks that require vigilance will be more affected by noise. More errors are made. We are less accurate. We take longer to react. The more complex the task the more likely noise will affect it negatively. The more trained and automatic the actions required the less likely noise will affect them.

I.　When there is an additional mental or physical stress, human health might be endangered by even lower intensities and shorter exposure times than the 95 dBA level, according to Ger Jensen of Ruhr University, Bochum, Essen, West Germany.

J.　We also experience insensible sweating--sweat that is evaporated so quickly that it is invisible. This usually occurs when the temperature is below 90 degrees Farenheit in a dry atmosphere.

K.　The range of 25% to 45% was established by the United States Air Force School of Aerospace Medicine.

Studies on the Concorde aircraft concluded that the lowest relative humidity that was acceptable was 30%. Yet relative air humidity measured 5% in a Quantas Boeing 707 flying at 30,000 feet for 4 to 6 hours. The French reported relative humidity of 15% in a DC-8 with a full passenger load.

L.　The effect of dehydration on the brain's ability to function is aggravated between the hours of midnight and six in the morning--what pilot's call the "back side of the clock". Individuals tested while flying at standard airplane altitudes showed a 40 to 60 % drop in vigilance.

M.　Both Major James R. Wamsley of the Aerospace Medical Branch of SAC and Dr. Charles Barron, Medical Director at Lockheed aircraft and instructor at the University of Southern California have found that dehydration contributes to jet fatigue.

N.　In the first study oxygen pressure was found to be never less than 2.29 pounds per square inch (psi), and on occasion reached 3.03 psi. Researchers concluded this could not seriously trouble the passenger or decrease the physical performance of HEALTHY crew members. (Emphasis mine)

Yet investigations by Kirchoff show that an oxygen deficit of 14%, as we find in the modern passenger airplane, combined with a medium workload for only ten minutes a day, would cause considerable strain on the heart, increase the pulse rate, the respiratory rate and volume and the blood pressure. What oxygen there was in the body was not used as efficiently. This study was done on young, healthy subjects.

O. Some consider the amount of carbon monoxide resulting from smoking to be insignificant, but the *Jounral of Occupational Medicine* reported a study that warned that while air crew members may be exposed to lower concentrations of carbon monoxide than some other workers, their risk is greater because of the other effects of stress that are related to the job, which work synergistically* with the carbon monoxide.

A test at the Insitute of Environmental Stress at Santa Barbara found that performance decreased when carbon monoxide increased in the body, and decreased even more when the amount of oxygen available to the body was momentarily lessened. Interestingly, when both lower oxygen and increased carbon monoxide were provided, performance didn't deteriorate. Researchers suspect that this might have been due to the body's normal reaction to stress. If this is so, then after long periods of exposure to this condition the body would reach a stage of exhaustion and

---

* Synergistic refers to different items that, when they work together, have a greater effect than would the sum of thier individual effects when working by themselves.

we would expect to see a considerable decrease in performance. (see chapter on Stress).

P.   During nightime hours body functions slow down
even when we try to stay awake. Blood pressure and blood
volume drop. Heart rate decreases, which means less oxygen goes to the Central Nervous System. There is a drop
in the exchange of oxygen and carbon dioxide in the lungs.
This all means less oxygen reaches the brain.

Q.   Acute effects of ozone toxicity on man are well known.
Investigations of Scheel and Griswold explain that when
ozone enters the lungs it reacts with the proteins of the lung
tissue, causing severe irritation of the cells, and changing
the ability of the cell wall to allow the passage of fluids.
Eventually these fluids build up, causing tissues to swell and
resulting in edema.

R.   When the lungs are exposed to ozone fibrous tissue
builds up in the alveolar ducts and bronchioles of the lungs,
which carry the air into the lungs and diffuse it. As these
tissues become fibrous the reserve capacity of the lung is
reduced.
    Human subjects exposed to 1.5 to 2.0 ppm for 2 hours
experienced dryness of mouth and throat, constrictive pain
under the breastbone, and a decreased ability to concentrate. For the next two weeks they complained of fatigue, a
general feeling of ill-being, and a persistent effect on their
coordination and speech. Respiratory function tests showed
a decrease in lung vital capacity.

S.   Mice exposed to ozone had a higher death rate from
respiratory infections. It took less exposure for them to get
the illness, those who got ill survived a shorter length of

time, and more of the test mice died than did the mice in the control group.

Clamann and Bancroft report a definite impairment in sense of smell, as well as note the strong oxidizing characteristic of ozone.

Lagerwerff has shown that human subjects exposed to 0.2 to 0.5 ppm for several 3-hour periods suffered poorer night vision, and one third complained of lethargy and difficulty in concentrating on their work.

T. Occupational Safety and Health Agency set the limits for "safe" exposure to ozone at 0.1 ppm for an 8-hour period. The Federal Register of 1971 gives EPA (Environmental Protection Agency) guidelines for exposure. "There will be significant health effects when photochemical oxidants reach 0.4 ppm when averaged over 1 hour.

U. In 1972 Preston of the British Airways Medical Services stated that it was only on rare occasions and for periods of 10 minutes or so that cabin levels of ozone would reach 0.2 to 0.5 ppm under the worst atmospheric conditions, so passengers and crew would not be harmed in any way.

Yet Bischof reviewed flights between Copenhagen and Seattle during the spring of 1971. In contrast with FAA studies he found considerably large ozone concentrations over longer periods of time. Concentrations exceeding 0.1 ppm entered the commercial flights on polar routes during these spring months about 75% of the flight time, which was 8 to 10 hours. Maximum concentrations of 0.4 ppm occurred for 4 hours, with 0.6 ppm for 1 hour.

L. Machta and W. Komhyr confirmed these results in their studies in 1973. Fabian and Pruchnievicz found high ozone concentrations on Copenhagen/Seattle/Copenhagen flights during springtime that compared with those reported in Bischof's work. They concluded that an airplane cruising in the lower or upper troposphere can have a cabin concentration of ozone that exceeds 0.1 ppm 10% of the time, while values greater than 1.0 ppm may enter the cabin for periods of 1 hour.

In March of 1977 ozone was measured on a KLM DC-10 flight from Amsterdam to Toronto and back to Amsterdam. While IATA (International Air Transport Association) threshold limit is 80 to 100 ppb, concentrations on the flight from Amsterdam were 150 to 300 ppb at passenger level inside the airplane, and reached 300 to 580 ppb near the ceiling. This occurred for about 70% of flight time. On the return flight concentrations at passenger level were 330 to 420 ppb.

V.   Animal tests by D.A. Lapitsky resulted in the conclusion that without air ions we couldn't absorb oxygen in the quantities need to live. Tchijewsky tested mice, rats, guinea pigs and rabbit in totally deionized air. They died within two weeks. He concluded that death was due to the animals inability to utilize oxygen properly.

W.   Based on research by Dr. Felix Gad Sulman, School of Applied Pharmacology in Jerusalem.

X.   Dr. Albert Paul Krueger, world-reknown biometeorologist at Naval Biological Laboratories, U.C. Berkeley, California, found the air ions influence the body's control mechanisms and chemical reactions. They also have a direct effect on the brain, bones, blood, spine, liver reproductive organs and menstrual cycle.

Dr. Charles Wallach reports studies done on rats and rabbits. When placed in deionized air the rats died within 4 days and the rabbits in 1 week. Cause of death was believed due to an affect on the calcium and potassium in the body. The ion deprivation interfered with potassium and calcium metabolism, which in turn affected muscle activity. When the heart muscle was affected, death ensued.

He points to the experience of 3 astronauts who returned to earth so weakened they were unable to walk. NASA scientists feared some terrible space disease. In a few days they spontaneously recovered, and the cause of the disability was determined to be interference with calcium/potassium metabolism due to ion deprivation.

Y.   Dr. Charles Wallach, author of *Updating the Ion Controversy*, feels that a therapeutically-high negative air ion concentration will bring infections under the control of the body's natural immune system faster than any form of medication. Some hospitals use ion generators in their operating rooms and burn wards for this purpose.

Infections already present become more inflamed when there is an overabundance of positive air ions. Mice infected with respiratory virus and kept in ion-depleted air got ill more quickly, more often and survived less often than those left in ion-sufficient air. Most of them died, and they died more quickly than the controls.

A Swiss bank experimented with ionizing the air. Those who worked in the ion-depleted environment, comparable to what we find in most American office buildings, took 16 days sick leave for every 1 day taken by the workers in the ionized air.

Z.   Dr. Krueger postulates that sufficient negative air ions seem to stimulate the action of an enzyme that then oxidizes the neurohormone serotonin, thereby removing it from the body. Too many positive air ions, on the other hand, seem to block the action of this enzyme while at the same time apparently releasing serotonin.

Serotonin is normally found in a certain balance in the body, but when more than normal amounts reach certain parts of the brain, symptoms of air ion sickness can appear.

Dr. Charles Wallach explains that when this ratio of 3:1 positive to negative air ions shifts, many of the body's metabolites of biochemicals such as serotonin, prostaglandins, catacholamines and thyroxin are affected and thrown out of balance. This produces symptoms. For example, of the 32 prostaglandins in the body, two of them, the alpha and the beta, affect the blood vessels.

When the positive ion balance increases, more alpha prostaglandins are released which relax the blood vessels. When more than usual are released the smooth muscles relax, which means the arteries and veins relax. Blood pressure becomes sluggish. Feet and ankles may swell.

Work by Halcomb and Kirk showed that people working in an environment of negatively-ionized air* reacted more quickly and took longer before they tired and performance diminished. Works of Speicher, Wofford, Harrington and Smith agree with this finding. They also found people more active in a negatively-ionized air. Their work demonstrated that ionization of the air is important in our environment because it affects how well we can perform a task requiring vigilance, as a pilot must do. A summary paper on man's reaction to an ionized air environment, prepared by the Department of Health, Education and Welfare, shows that too many positive ions can immediately reduce our performance.

Dr. Charles Wallach feels that the over-abundance of positive air ions in relation to negative ones may be respon-

---

* Negatively-ionized air refers to air where the ratio of positive to negative is a least 3:1, if not 3:2 or better. It does not mean the absence of positive air ions.

sible for the swelling of feet and ankles that so often occurs while flying. While gravity plays some part it is not significant. If gravity were the sole cause then wrists would also swell. Further, this swelling is experienced by about a third of the passengers, which is the same ratio of general population that would show sensitivity.

Up to half of the air sickness suffered while flying can be traced to air ions, according to Dr. Wallach. One of the symptoms of an overbalance of positive ions is nausea. Subclinical oxygen deprivation, a minor hypoxia, can also cause nausea. Both may be present. Usually air sickness occurs a couple hours into flight--again symptomatic of an ion-sensitive reaction.

AA. Studies done in 1960 to 1962 by W. Dean Chiles at the Behavioral Sciences Lab for the United States Air Force showed no effects of ions on performance of the type they tested. They neither affected attitudes nor vigilance behavior.

Bruce L. Rosenberg, engineering research psychologist formerly with the FAA, explains the contradictions. Studies on air ions and how they affect performance show varied results because there is a difference between the tasks tested, because we do not know enough about the physical characteristics of artificially generated air ions, and because we haven't controlled the variables that interact with air ions.

BB. To break it down further, 5% are acutely sensitive. These people dislike air conditioning, are irritated by tobacco smoke, are highly reactive to approaching storms, and become agitated or short of breath in close or "stuffy" rooms. Another 20% are clinically sensitive to ions. Moderate changes in the ionic environment cause the symptoms, which are often observed by those around them as modified behavior. Fifty per cent are subclinically sensitive. Symptoms they feel are mostly subjective. They feel less alert, less efficient at their tasks. They are prone to fatigue, respiratory infections and cardiovascular deterioration. Another 20% are barely affected, and the remaining 5% are essentially not affected at all.

CC. Dr. Charles Wallach has taken ion count studies on airplanes and found a definite decrease of negative air ions. A former NASA researcher involved in analyzing the environment within space capsules for our space program worked in the field of air ions. He believes there is a high concentration of positive air ions inside the airplane, with very few negative ions--a situation he feels affects the performance of those working inside the aircraft.

DD. The FAA report further stated, "The atmosphere is our most precious natural resource. Since we all breathe air from the day we are born until the day we die, and since atmospheric ions have been shown to exert significant effects on living organisms, the fact that there is relatively little ongoing research concerning their physical nature and behavioral, physiological and biochemical effects seems appalling.

"An atmosphere that is predominantly negatively ionized, that contains an excess of negative ions, improves the process of oxygenation of the blood and excessive positive ions may interfere with the oxygenation of the blood."

EE. In 1966 Nefedov and Anismov concluded that prolonged stays in positively-ionized or deionized air is detrimental. They recommended the alteration of both positive and negative air ions for long-term use in the closed environment of pressurized cabins. NASA researchers previously mentioned also found air ionization important for space capsule environment.

FF.   Dr. Maxey also suggests that changes in the electrical force field in the cockpit could have induced currents in the central nervous system, especially the brain of the pilots, at frequencies tending towards trance states. He speculated in aeronautical journals that since humans did evolve to function in a certain low-strength electrical field we might possibly be affected by certain fluctuations in that field.

In support of this thesis he points to a study commissioned by the United States Air Force involving installing a device in the cockpit that generated electrical fields similar to those found over open land. Pilots using this equipment were less fatigued and had faster reaction times than pilots operating under ordinary conditions.

GG.   "The impairment of normal brain function by increased positive ion balance probably occurs far more frequently than is generally realized amoung drivers and pilots; often manifesting itself as sleepiness or fatigue. It is not an unfamiliar phenomenon, nor an uncommon one. However, when this effect is suddenly and substantially aggravated by passing through a meterological 'shower' of pos-ions, the results can be disasterous."

HH.   Dick Stuphen, hypnotist and researcher, explains in his article, *"Unrecognized Altered States"* how easy it is to go into an altered state of consciousness while driving down the road. He believes many car accidents occur because the driver is lulled into an alpha brain wave state. This same thing could happen to the pilot, especially at night when the body wants to sleep and the brain waves want to slow down for sleep. One might also consider looking into possible vibrations that would be comparable to brain waves in an alpha state which would induce the brain to match them, thus pulling the brain down into this semi-sleep stage.

II.   This synergistic effect is explained by Dean and McGlothlen in *Longterm Aircrew Effectiveness*. They caution that the interacting effects of stressors, however mild, when considered together may add up to a total stress far in excess of any one of the single effects. We can't look at how we might perform under a single stress and then predict how we will perform when there are many stress factors present.

The Pilot's Physiological Index warns that the addition of a second major factor or two or more moderate factors can be excessively fatiguing, expecially for the crew.

Chapter Three

The Body's Daily Cycles and Internal Clocks

OUR BODIES WORK IN CYCLES

The greatest stress of flying comes from disrupting our normal 24-hour pattern of work and rest, and from crossing time zones. This is what people call "jet lag".[A]

Our bodies do everything in cycles. We know that there are times of the day and of the month when we function better than we do at other times. Like most living things there is a time structure within our bodies that has many rhythms, ranging from cycles per second to cycles per year to cycles of a lifetime.

What we are most interested in here are the cycles that occur approximately every 24 hours and are therefore called circadian cycles. The word circadian derives from Latin meaning "about a day". While in some people these cycles may take as long as 48 hours to complete in most of us they occur every 24 hours, more or less.[*] These cycles can be reversed, shifted, lengthened or shortened to some extent,

---

[*] Actually most people would have a cycle closer to 26 hours if they were allowed to "free run", that is, if they were free of outside influences such as light and darkness which influences them to fit into the 24-hour day.

but they can't be radically changed, and they can't be eliminated. Changes that do occur take time--they are not achieved instantaneously. If they were we wouldn't experience "jet lag".

Most of us are accustomed to living in a 24-hour cycle of work and sleep. As body temperature rises during the day we find that we function better.* Most of us reach a plateau between noon and nine o'clock at night. That's when we work the best, with the period between two and four in the afternoon being optimum. Around ten at night we begin functioning less well, and we hit a dead point between three and six in the morning. This period of time between midnight and seven in the morning is called the "backside of the clock" by pilots, meaning that time when it is hardest for them to function and when they are least likely to do well at what they are trying to do.

Around six in the morning hormones from the adrenal gland start pouring into the blood stream getting us ready to awaken and begin the day. Urine production increases. The night was spent eliminating wastes from the body and resting. Now as daylight comes all systems start to wake up and prepare us for the day's activities.

Each part of the body has its own cycle. The pulse, body temperture, blood pressure, excretion of various substances into the urine, chemical constituency of the blood, work capacity of the kidney, liver, intestines and endocrine glands--each has its own 24-hour phase or oscillation.* *

These body cycles or clocks are influenced by two

---

* Deep body temperature appears to be an indicator of performance. When body temperature rises, performance improves.

* * Body temperature alone is the result of 5 different interdependent cycling systems. There are some authorities who believe that upsetting the cycles of the stomach and liver can result in actual organic disorders like gastric ulcer or gastritis, not uncommon complaints of frequent travelers.

sources. One is outside the body, or exogenous, and includes parts of our environment like light and darkness, temperature, geophysical forces like the tides, and our own regular eating, sleeping, working and exercising schedule, as well as social activities. These environmental and sociological conditions are regulators that keep us in phase with the 24-hour day and the world around us.

But when we remove all these externals we still continue with internal rhythms, regardless of the environment. Such rhythms are called "free running". Without cues from the environment, the body sets up its own biological day that is closer to 26 hours. This tells us that such rhythms are not simply a reflex reaction to the world outside but rather that the body possesses several internal clocks that determine, control, and synchronize it's many different internal rhythms. There may also be a central master biological clock, perhaps in the pineal gland or the hypothalamus, that synchronizes these clocks and thus the functions of the body.

Once we establish our own individual internal rhythms these biological clocks continue to function. The rhythm we establish is peculiar to each of us and may vary differently from each of us. But the rhythm is there and the environment can only influence its frequency.

Just as a precision watch has many parts intricately and accurately timed to work together, so the body needs the proplerly-timed meshing of all its functions in order to work well and efficiently. Nearly every metabolizing structure of the body, even those at cell and subcellular levels, has its own daily, biological rhythm.

If the cell of an organ is not in its normal circadian cycle, the organ itself cannot function well. The cycle of the cell must be compatible with the cycle of the organ. Each organ, as well, has its own biological clock that transmits its own particular vibrational frequency to the cells of that organ. When the cells receive this particular frequency they perform certain duties.

This keeps the cells of the liver "locked to" the liver organ, both in frequency and in cycle so liver cells will not "cross talk" with the stomach or stomach cells. The correct cells get the correct message, allowing them to maintain stable functioning of their own organ.

These messages, going from the biological clock of the organ to the cells of that organ, generate electromagnetic fields that we can detect.

We can see the complexity of the problem occuring when body cycles are altered. These biological clocks are oscillating subsystems, properly timed to work in a mutual way. If they get out of synchronization or if there is a change in the environment which causes them to shift into a new phase, these internal clocks become confused. Organs and cells desynchronize from one another. They receive confusing messages and so work improperly and at the wrong time.

Gradually they will resynchronize, though not all at the same time and not quickly. Brain rhythms rephase within 5 days, respiratory rate within 11 days, and potassium excretion rate takes more than 25 days after making the body shift 12 hours from its accustomed cycle. Slowly all systems become locked into a new rhythm. The clocks are reset.

SLEEP LOSS AND SLEEP DISORDERS

One of the most prominent complaints resulting from disruption of these circadian cycles is poor sleep and lack of sleep. Captain Frank Hawkins of KLM has done some detailed studies for the International Air Line Pilots'

Association on sleep and sleep disorders. He found that the major cause of fatigue among long-range flight crews is sleep disturbance and deprivation, which he inextricably links with desynchronization.

The sleep process consists of 2 kinds of sleep: non REM (or orthodox or "S" state) sleep and REM (or paradoxical or "D" state) sleep. NonREM sleep is divided into stages according to specific brain wave patterns that occur within each stage.

NonREM sleep begins with Stage 1 which is the transition from wakefulness to sleep and usually lasts from half a minute to 7 minutes. State 2 is the first, bonafide sleep stage and lasts 30 to 40 minutes. This is followed by Delta sleep, sometimes divided into Stages 3 and 4 according to the number of delta waves present. Delta, or Stages 3 and 4, is the deepest sleep, characterized by delta brain waves.

In Delta sleep it takes a very loud noise to awaken us. Muscles are relaxed, breathing and heart rate slows, temperature declines and blood pressure drops. We stay in this stage for a few minutes up to an hour, depending on how tired we are. Then we move back "up" into Stage 2.

After a few minutes in Stage 2 REM, or Rapid Eye Movement, sleep begins. In this REM stage we show some characteristics of being awake along with others associated with sleep in the non REM stages. For example, brain waves indicate that the mind is active as though it were in transitional State 1. Heart rate and respiratory rate are relatively high and variable. Eyes move about rapidly, yet muscles are very relaxed, especially in the neck and chin area. This is the stage where we actively dream.

Since REM can't be classified as either light or deep sleep some scientists have decided to describe the three separate levels of consciousness as wakefulness, sleep and the REM state. The first REM stage of the rest cycle normally lasts

about 5 minutes, after which we move back into nonREM
Stage 2 sleep.

Thus we complete the first sleep cycle of the 4 or 5 we will
experience in a normal night's sleep. Each such cycle normally takes 90 to 110 minutes to complete. As the rest
period continues we spend less time in deep Delta sleep
while REM periods become more intense, sometimes
lasting up to one hour.

Quantity of sleep is important. The amount each of us
needs varies, but the optimal amount any one of us needs is
very narrowly limited. Sleep in excess of that amount or less
than that amount can lower our efficiency.[B]

Quality of sleep is as important as quantity of sleep. Sleep
patterns as well as the sleep cycle itself must be maintained.
While each of us varies in our sleep pattern we are very consistent in our own, individualized pattern, which we may inherit genetically. We suffer more when these patterns are
altered than we do when we don't get enough sleep. [C]

Sleep is itself a body rhythm. We will sleep even when we
aren't tired when the body's sleep cycle occurs. The body
becomes prepared to go to sleep psychologically,
physiologically and chemically. No amount of presleep will
change that in-bred system. * This means that both the
quality and the quantity of the sleep we get is very dependent on what phase our bodies are in when we sleep. Trying to rest or to sleep when the body is not in a normal
sleep/rest cycle simply will not bring the restfull, revitalizing
sleep we need.

It's difficult to measure how sleep loss affects us but we do

---

* So important is this cycle that men were tested where the amount of sleep was kept
constant but the sleep period was displaced by 2 to 4 hours. Both vigilance and calculation
task-performance decreased, and mood was adversely affected.

know that when we don't get enough sleep or when sleep is constantly interrupted we get moody, irritable and depressed. It's harder to concentrate and we tend to hallucinate and to become more susceptible to infection. Appetite changes. Muscle coordination decreases, vision blurs and body rhythms become erratic. We think more slowly. We react more slowly. Errors are made in simple, routine actions like getting on or off the elevator, or turning right when you mean to go left.

Poor sleep affects our appearance and behavior. We become less motivated, which influences our discipline and professionalism. We become more complacent, accepting standards below those we would normally require. Overall deprivation of good sleep can make us feel detached from reality.[D]

Sleep loss and sleep disturbance are major, subjective complaints of transmeridian air travelers and a common complaint among professional airline crews. They find it difficult to get to sleep, they awaken often during their sleep-time, and they wake up too early. Sleep comes in a series of fragmented, nap-like episodes, with more changes of the sleep stages.[E]

When the body is forced to reset its internal body clocks and cycles many things happen. We experience psychological and physiological problems. We become more nervous and irritable, we develop more emotional and behavioral problems, and we tend to get sick more often. We don't do our jobs as well. [F]   But the most serious offspring of forcing our bodies to alter their normal cycles is the inability to get good and sufficient rest--sleep loss.

The professional traveler forces these cycle changes within his body in two ways. Much flying is done at night when the body wants to sleep. We force it to work as though it were in an awake/work cycle instead of its normal sleep/rest cycle. This is difficult enough to a one-time, one-night basis.* But the businessman, entertainer, diplomat or lecturer on tour, and the crew members often force this change on a repeated basis for several days in a row. It's obvious why they become so tired.

To make a complex problem even more complex the jet traveler usually crosses time-zones, which disrupts the body cycles in the same way that staying awake when the body prefers to sleep does. Cues coming to us from our environment change, and change rapidly. It doesn't matter that time zone lines are artificially set. The distance covered is real and our bodies react accordingly.

This is what we commonly think of as jet lag. The insomnia, stomach and intestinal upset, lowered physical and mental activity is due to disrupting our body's cycles and will last until the body can resynchronize. We must reset our body clocks to fit into the new time zone we find ourselves in.

This resetting or resynchronization takes awhile to occur, and each body function takes a different length of time to recycle itself. Each follows its own clock or oscillation, moving gradually through a number of transient cycles. It may take from 2 to 10 days to get the sleep/wakefullness cycle resynchronized. Deep body temperature patterns can take from a week to 13 days to reestablish themselves.** Psychomotor functioning can take up to ten days to return to normal. Intellectual and personality traits recycle more quickly than physical impairments. Adrenal gland and electrolyte excretion may remain out-of-phase for as long as 24

---

* Teleky recommended that schedules should not be shifted any more frequently than once a month.

** Deep body temperature appears to be related to performance.

days after crossing 9 time zones.

On the average we can assume that recycling requires one day for every time zone crossed. How much we adapt and how long it will take depends upon how many time zones we cross. It takes longer to recover from crossing 8 time zones than crossing six.

Speed of travel doesn't alter this. The same length of time is taken to recycle after six time zone crossings regardless of how fast those zones were crossed.

It is easier to travel west than it is east. This may be due to the fact that our circadian cycles are closer to 25 or 26 hours long when allowed to "free-run". Thus it may be easier to delay or lengthen the cycles than to shorten or advance them.

The body returns to normal more quickly upon returning home than it does outbound. An FAA study found it took 5 days on the outbound trip to rephase to local time but only 36 hours after the home-bound trip. They also learned that we don't perform as well in the morning after traveling east, or in the evening after traveling west.

It is also easier to travel north and south where no time zones are crossed so we only have to rephase the sleep/rest cycle.

On a round-trip the layover time can affect how much we have to rephase. A short layover with just enough time to rest during a normal body-rest cycle is better than a long layover. You return home quickly so that the body has not really had time to phase out of the home cycle. But laying over for a couple of days gives the body time to begin recycling to the new location. Then it must rephase again upon returning home. A quick round-trip is preferrable.

In any case the body cannot be set like a watch. It is internally synchronized and will resynchronize at its own Biological speed, though there are great individual variations accordng to age, general health and social situations.

HOW PERFORMANCE IS AFFECTED

How well we perform is affected when we cross time zones or force the body to change its internal clocks by working when it wants to sleep. Even staying in a new time zone for only 24 hours make us do less well for at least one day after returning home. We are less capable both physically and mentally during the transition period.

Sleep loss occuring during the rephasing cycle--even a moderate loss of sleep--will affect our performance. We miss more signals. We have occasional lapses of alertness* often associated with "Microsleeps"--involuntary and inter- mittent periods where we go to sleep for a brief time with our eyes open. We don't realize we are microsleeping. Any information coming to us will not register in our short-term memory bank. We don't realize that we aren't performing well.**

In general, during rephase we perform inconsistently. We are not as capable nor as motivated. Tasks requiring vigilance and monitoring tend to break down rapidly. We become unreliable.

FATIGUE—THE FINAL RESULT

After repeated, extended exposure to stress, fatigue sets

---

* Such lapses can occur after losing 5 hours of sleep in one night, or only 1½ hours on 2 consecutive nights.

** A first officer of a commercial liner reported glancing over at the captain during lan- ding and finding him asleep. This microsleep occured when the plane was 500 feet from the ground.

in. There is no adequate definition of fatigue but it could be defined as the adverse psychological and physiological influence on performance and our sense of well-being.

Stress-producing fatigue can come from many sources, among them temperature, humidity, color, light intensity, noise vibration, odors, gases, barometric conditions, ozone, protracted immobility, illness, and advanced aging. [G] But the most severe stress results from lack of sleep during body rephasing when we cross time zones or stay awake during a normal sleep cycle. The number of night flights and the number of time zones crossed are important. Also important is the number of 24-hour layovers we have after an evening arrival, which would mean we would sleep the night of arrival but be unable to get proper rest the next day before flying. *

Acute fatigue requires only a good night's sleep for recovery. If we could find a way to get that sleep the traveler would have many fewer problems with jet stress. But for the frequent traveler this fatigue becomes cumulative, with the result that the individual cannot think or react as quickly as he should. He is less attentive. Perception slows down and is often impaired. We lose motivation and start to perform below par both physically and mentally.

Of course the flight crew is more affected by this than the traveler since their schedules tend to be very erratic and repetitive. We also must consider that fatigue that comes from continuous working has a different effect on how we perform than does fatigue that comes from not getting enough good sleep. Pilots and flight attendants are subject to fatigue from both sources. [H] When this fatigue sets in the crew members operating the plane you are traveling in

* Dr. Stanley Mohler, *Pilot's Physiological Index*

experience the same problems the passenger has, plus extras. They tend to forget. The flight attendant may forget where he is on the checklist for landing. They react more slowly. For the most part they are not aware of these changes or that they are not performing normally or up-to-par.

Fatigue is considered an important factor in airplane crashes by many involved in flying.[1] From the foregoing description of how fatigue affects us it is easy to see how this might be true. Yet there is insufficient research to explain exactly what happens to crew members when they fly and how seriously they are affected. We have no data on human physiology and performance in the actual, working environment. There is very little study done on people over 40 years of age, and especially on women. Most tests are done in laboratories using young, healthy and rested subjects, and testing only one or a few factors. The real-life complexities of flight conditions have not been replicated.

So far we can only speculate on exactly what happens with pilots until they are studied in their natural home and work environment. The very fact that pilots perform so well is due to their intensive training and their professionalism, believes Dr. Charles Winget, Ames Research Center, NASA. "Pilots in general are super professionals and do their jobs in an exceptional manner, and the engineers have designed machines that are super at their jobs also."*

DOES THIS AFFECT HOW LONG WE LIVE?

A final, important question that needs to be answered is

---

* Private correspondence

if the constant rephasing of our circadian clock affects how long we live. Premature aging has been reported in pilots by an FAA examiner. Life-spans of experimental animals were shortened from chronic circadian disruption. While human reactions are not always the same as the animal's, it is possible that we will react the same as they do when our body rhythms are frequently shifted. Leading Edge reported that "current research is showing us that the life span is definitely shortened as a result of circadian desynchronosis, and we don't know why!" *

Many crew members, both flight attendants and pilots, feel that flying ages them prematurely. Yet there are no statistics available from the airlines or the insurance companies to document the health and deaths of these professionals. If such exist they appear to be guarded from the public. Another possibility is that when a crew member becomes disabled he is laid off and is not longer listed in health statistics as a crew member. He becomes lost in general population statistics.

For now we don't know what the long-term effects of continual, repeated body rhythm disruption are. One of the world's leading experts in sleep and sleep-related disorders, Dr. William C. Dement, after examining the pilot we mentioned earlier who had lost all circadian rhythm, asked, "Did the body give up after having too many major circadian disruptions? If it did, what are the long-range consequences?" * *

So many questions to ask. So much to be studied.

What we do know, however, is that the aircraft environment and circadian cycle disruption produce stress on the

---

* Article by William Price, *"Task Force on Pilot Fatigue"*.

* * William Price, *"Report of Attendance at Sleep Research Clinic."*

body which affects each of us to varying degrees. To be able to cope with jet stress we need a basic understanding of what stress is, how our bodies respond to stress, and what we can do to make them strong enough to minimize any negative effects occuring from such stress.

NOTES FOR THE PROFESSIONAL

A. The extreme fatigue we feel when flying must be explained by more than prolonged exposure to noise, vibration, reduced atmospheric pressure and the other discomforts of a long flight, according to Carruthers writing in the British medical journal *Lancet.*

B.   Dr. Peter Hauri wrote in *Current Concepts,* "A person has insomnia if his inability to sleep interferes chronically with efficient daytime function, regardless of how many hours he sleeps each night."

Significant fatigue occurs when we fail to recover subjectively after sleep on two successive sleep periods, according to Atkinson in *Long Term Air Crew Effectiveness.*

C.   We suffer when we lose either nonREM or REM sleep. NonREM deep Delta sleep seems to be related to recovery of the musculo-skeletal structures. REM sleep seems related to psychological recovery. We consolidate and integrate information accumulated while awake. We store this information, converting what we have just learned into stable, long-term memory. Information already stored in the memory banks is retained in long-term memory. It has been likened to the librarian who, at the end of the day, picks up all the books used during the day, properly consolidates them and puts them back on the storage shelf for future use.

REM sleep also appears to be explorative, contributing to divergent thinking, towards helping use adjust to new situation.

Since more time is spent in REM sleep towards the end of the sleep session, an abbreviation of normal sleep time may cause us to suffer from REM deprivation. Lack of enough

REM sleep produces symptoms of irritability, poor judgment, inability to make decisions and difficulty in remembering.

Captian Hawkins has stated that it is more important to
maintain these sleep cycles than it is to get enough hours of
rest. Distrubance may be worse than deprivation. But, he
warns, distrubance on top of deprivation becomes very
significant.

D.   Dr. Carlton Fredericks in *Psychonutrition* makes a
connection between sleep loss and mental disease, explain-
ing that sleep is needed for the body to regenerate cells.
Without sufficient sleep brain cells cannot reproduce for lack
of energy. He feels this universal depleting of brain cells as a
consequence of lack of sleep has been neglected in the
study of mental disease and should be the subject of
research.

E.   Such irregularieties of sleep hours and fragmentation
of the sleep period have been impressively demonstrated in
studies on air crews operating world-wide. Professional
flight crews have known for some time that they sleep less
on a trip than they do at home. This has been confirmed by
studies. A BOAC study found that the first 3 nights of night
flights brought a constant loss of 5.5 hours of sleep per
night. After that the number of hours of sleep loss varied
with the individual. All continued to have a steady rise in
sleep loss.

F.   Most research on the effects of altering circadian
cycles has been done on shift workers like nurses, factory
workers and air traffic controllers. What was found was that
people who have to shift their work/rest cycles pay an excessive physical and psychological price. They developed

emotional and behavioral problems. Ulich reported 36% to 50% of those he studied developed bad tempers and become more nervous and irritable.

Night workers tend to get sick more often than day workers. They miss more work and have more serious illnesses. Those working fixed night shifts were still healthier than those required to rotate shifts constantly.

When a shift worker doesn't have time to readjust his body cycles before he is shifted to a new cycle, he shows signs of fatigue, inadequte sleep patterns, nervousness and less-than-satisfacotry work performance.

G.   Dr. Stanley Mohler, former head of the FAA Office of Aviation Medicine sumarized these causations in *"Fatigue in Aviation Activity"* Such stressors can be objectively measured and are well-documented. A british report showed that long-term effects of high temperature, low humidity and hard work load may have long. subtle effects on human beings and fatigue. But they emphasized that the biggest problem, especially for the airline crew member, is the inability to get enough sleep at his destination, particularly after crossing time zones.

H.   The FAA studied a trip pattern of pilots flying for an American international carrier. The Hong Kong pattern involved considerable night flying and crossing numerous time zones. All the pilots experienced sleep abnormalities. Subjectively they reported being tired. They had trouble doing simple mathematics without error. They had trouble remembering things that had just happened, like remembering the full names of crew members. They felt they got irritated more easily.

By objective measurement they got less total deep sleep while away than at home. They were in a constant deadapt/readapt situation, never having the chance to stabilize to the time of the place they were resting. In effect, they were not synchronous with any time zone. The more days he was away from home, the more tired the pilot became.

A pilot flying for the above airline was tested in 1976 at a sleep research clinic in California and found to have no circadian rhythms. The doctors in charge claim that nothing of this sort has ever before been recorded.

I.   There have been indications that some of the major accidents in civil aviation were caused by fatigue due to circadian cycle dysrhythmia, according to Captain Frank Hawkins of KLM.

Dr. Karl Klein of the DFVLR Institute of Aviation Medicine* agrees. He condcluded from his studies that a pilot's schedule should consider the length of the flight, the number of landings that will be made, and the time the flight departs. A flight that departs so that the pilot must be landing when his body is at its lowest efficiency can be dangerous. The added stress on his body increases the fatigue factor so that he will be less likely to perform as well on the next flight. Fatigue accumulates.

He further recommended that the layover on a round trip be as short as possible but long enough to allow a rest time during the body's normal rest cycle and long enough to provide time for recreation. After returning home there should be enough rest time for the body to return to its normal rhythm.

Klein and his associates also suggested that persons be excluded from air crews who are sensitive to circadian cycle disruptions. There are substantial differences among people as to how well they adjust to these disruptions. Twenty-five

* Bad Goedsberg, Germany

to 30% have few or no difficulties adjusting to occasional, sudden cycle displacement but another 25% to 30% can't adjust at all. They also recommended an age restriction for air crews of bewteen 45 and 50 years of age, since adjustment becomes more difficult with age.

Dr. Stanley Mohler, presently Director of Aerospace Medicine, Wright State University, feels that both flight and rest time for pilots should be scheduled according to a formula like the one devised by the International Civil Aviation Organization in Montreal, which boasts membership in 116 countries. This formula, according to Lloyd Duley, chief of the medical section, has good results in lowering fatigue. (See Appendix)

Chapter Four

Just What Is Stress?

Most of us think of stress as emotional upset or nerves. Stress is more than nervous tension. Plants and lower animals with no nervous systems react to stress. Stress is the body's response to any demand, physical or emotional, which helps us maintain life. Simply leaving a warm room to walk into the cold, winter air is a stress. Eating is a stress, Breathing air is a stress.

Not all stress is bad, as we can see. Stress can be good (eustress) or bad (distress). It is a necessary and unavoidable part of life.

What stress is, and how it affects the body, has been the life work of world-reknown researcher, Dr. Hans Selye, Currently Professor and Director of the Insitute of Experimental Medicine and Surgery at the University of Montreal, Dr. Selye has identified what he calls the "stress syndrome"—those changes that occur in our bodies when they are stressed.

BODY CHANGES CAUSED BY STRESS

Three distinct things occur in the body when there is

stress. The adrenal glands enlarge and discolor, the lymphatic gland, crucial to the immune system, shrink intensely, and numerous, blood-covered stomach ulcers appear. There are also changes in the chemical composition of the body which are characteristic of the body meeting stress. Together these changes are called the "stress syndrome" A

These changes occur in a well-defined sequence which Dr. Selye has classified as the General Adaptation Syndrome, or the G.A.S.

The first reaction to stress is a noticeable alarm reaction. Since we can't maintain a continuous state of alarm we either get rid of the stress, rendering it harmless, or it gets rid of us and we die. If we survive this Stage One we will advance to Stage two.

Stage Two is the stage of resistance. The body seems to return to normal. Symptoms experienced during the initial alarm reaction disappear. We mistakenly believe the problem has been overcome. But if the stressor is not removed, or if the condition is not corrected, eventually Stage Three appears.

Stage Three is the stage of exhaustion. Symptoms felt in Stage One reappear. By now the body is in trouble. Disease, formerly lying latent, can be triggered in this exhausted body. Allergies seem to appear out of nowhere. The weakest part of our body breaks down. We are tired. We get sick easily. So-called degenerative problems appear.

How much stress will affect any one of us depends upon many things--heredity, personality, diet, personal habits, job requirements and such. These factors are preexisting conditions. It is impossible, says Dr.Selye, to distinguish between these preexisting conditions and the effects stress itself has upon us. Any or all of these preexisting conditions can be present but in themselves are not likely to make us ill. The final, decisive, eliciting factor, he says, is usually stress.

No one will argue that jet travel puts stress on the body. We can easily measure the body's response to this stress by the increase of hormones from the adrenal glands that appear in the urine in response to that stress, attempting to counter the stress and protect us from it.

The stress of flight was not so great in the days of piston aircraft. With the advent of the faster, more sophisticated jet planes flying at higher altitudes, aerospace doctors noticed their pilot-patients becoming more fatigued and their health deteriorating. They attributed this to the switch-over from piston to jet aircraft.

One of the first doctors to delve into this phenomena and the creator of the term "jet lag" was Dr. James Crane of New Canaan, Connecticut. In response to his questionnaire to pilots' wives, one woman described her husband, now flying jets, as "living in a state of exhilarated exhaustion".

Such hyperactive exhaustion really describes the jet pilot and flight attendant when they return from a trip. The jet stress they encounter on a routine basis produces sleep loss, nervousness, irritability, hyperactivity, emotional swings, and fatigue--all symptoms of exhaustion. The adrenal glands have been overworked trying to combat the stress and they tire, unable to work efficiently. This, of course, happens to everyone who travels often and long distances. It is exaggerated in the flight crews.

STRESS – INDUCED HYPOGLYCEMIA

When the adrenal glands become tired a condition called hypoglycemia, or "low blood sugar" can occur. The Department of Health, Education and Welfare estimate that nearly

one out of every 2 Americans suffer from hypoglycemia
because of the Average American Diet where large quantities of refined white sugar and flour are eaten. B Many suffer from this condition without realizing it, so accustomed to
feeling tired all the time that they consider it a natural part of
life.

Symptoms of hypoglycemia are numerous, various and
not necessarily definitive. They include fatigue, drops in
energy, depression that lasts, headaches, allergies, rapid
beating of the heart, inner trembling, hunger soon after
eating, blurred vision, mental confusion, sudden phobias,
fainting, cold hands and feet, insomnia, waking after a few
hours of sleep and being unable to return to sleep, falling
asleep when you don't want to, feeling old when logically
you know you're not, crankiness, irritability, nightmares,
and just not feeling right.

People who are hypoglycemic may not suffer from all
these symptoms, but if they have a number of them doctors
recommend they take a 6-hour glucose tolerance test performed by a competent physician who knows how to interpret the results. C

As we can see, many of the symptoms of hypoglycemia
are the same as the symptoms of body exhaustion, which is
the condition of the body of the untreated hypoglycemic. It
is Stage Three of the Stress Syndrome.

Hypoglycemia can be acute, occuring suddenly and
lasting only temporarily, or it can become a chronic condition. It represents an abnormal response to sugar. The level
of sugar in the blood is lower than it should be. This
response can be caused by an immediate stressor or by not
eating when the body is tired and the adrenal glands are no
longer functioning as they should. In such a case the condition usually disappears once the stressor is removed or
adapted to.

With continuing stress on the body hypoglycemia can become a chronic problem. The body reaches Stage Three trying to resist the stressor(s) and can no longer cope. The adrenals cannot meet emergencies. They cease to regulate our blood sugar levels adequately.*

With 1 out of every 2 Americans already suffering from this condition, the chance that you have it if you are a professional traveler is even greater. The likelihood is even greater for the pilot and cabin attendant. Some airlines have recognized this problem and occasionally accidents have been attributed to low blood sugar experienced by the pilot.D

The craving for carbohydrates, especially for refined sugar products (those using some form of white sugar) is symptomatic of a drop in blood sugar levels. This is a common occurence for flight personnel towards the end of many hours of flying. If you get a craving for sweets towards the end of a flight you may be hypoglycemic, if only temporarily.

To counter this doctors recommend drinking fruit juice, eating protein-rich snacks in couple-hour intervals, and avoiding smoking, soft drinks and coffee.E Fruit and other complex, natural carbohydrates or a protein snack will reduce this craving for sweets by raising the sugar level of the blood.

So will foods made with refined, white sugar, but they do it differently. White sugar and white flour are "pure" foods. That is, they are simple in their composition and therefore foreign to the natural order of the body. When they hit the blood stream it is as if a bolt of lightening had struck the body, causing a message of alarm to go to the adrenal glands to protect the body from this threat. The adrenal

---

* This condition is sometimes called adrenal cortical insufficiency.

glands send adrenalin to the pancreas, telling it to excrete more insulin into the blood to counter this sudden, rapid rise in blood sugar.

It does this quite efficiently--often too efficiently. The insulin makes the blood sugar level drop again, but this time it drops below where it was before the white sugar was eaten. Nervousness, hunger and irritability reappear.

The cycle is vicious. The sequence and consequence must be understood. We want to raise the blood sugar levels slowly so the rise will be longer-lasting, avoiding extreme elevations and drops. Complex, natural carbohydrates like fruits and nuts, and protein snacks will do this best. White sugar, in whatever form, will not.

Untreated, chronic hypoglycemia can develop into diabetes. United Airlines doctors rank diabetes as third in causes for grounding pilots.[F] Both diabetes and hypoglycemia are related to stress that prevents the body from metabolizing carbohydrates normally.

OTHER CAUSES OF STRESS FOR THE JET TRAVELER

How much stress you experience as a traveler is dependent on what time your flight departs and arrives, what direction you are flying in, how long your flight is, what food and/or liquor you consume during flight, and your travel experience. State of mind, anticipation, familiarization and training can alter the effects of stress. [G]

Sudden changes in climate and adverse weather conditions, including turbulence, are stressors.

Changing cultures can produce stress. There may be little or no friendly, social contact. The general philosophy and customs of the culture may be foreign to you. You may have to follow unusual or different customs and eat unusual foods. Dr. Selye has found that stress produced by social pressures can be measured objectively in the body by changes in its production of stress hormones. According to Dr. Selye, relocation and travel, in and of themselves, are stressors.

Vibration is another stressor. Vibrations are felt through the somaesthetic receptors while sound is heard.[H]   Air sickness in some people may be caused by vibration, when the very low-frequency, high-amplitude vibrations act perpendicular to a horizontal plane, passing through the ear openings and the external corners of the eyes, causing motion sickness.

The closeness of the aircraft environment can be a stressor, stimulating the adrenal glands to overactivity. Body chemistry can be upset.[1]   Dr. Selye has found that crowding will produce the typical signs of G.A.S. in the bodies of both man and animals, including a special tendency toward formation of peptic ulcers and sensitivity to infection.

Pilots can suffer from another stressor--sensory deprivation. On long night flights pilots sit for hours in a darkened cockpit, lit only by numerous small, red and white lights. Air rushing by the outside of the plane can be heard, lulling the mind into trance-like states. There is little to stimulate the brain and much to induce sleep.

To work properly the brain needs constant arousal or stimulation from continuous sensory input. Hallucinations which can cause accidents have been noticed in pilots, astronauts and long-distance truck drivers. They may occur because the monotony of the work keeps the brain from being sufficiently stimulated.

STRESS AND NEUROTIC BEHAVIOR.

Chronic fatigue can and often does show itself in neurotic reactions. This has been documented in pilots and flight attendants who, because of the stress of heavy work loads and repeated body cycle-shifts over several days, cannot recover from acute or transient fatigue.

Acute fatigue occurs between a pair of sleep cycles. After getting a normal sleep and with proper nutrition this fatigue can be completely eliminated. But for the crew member, especially, this normal sleep period seldom occurs. Over a period of days or weeks chronic or cumulative fatigue appears and with it neurotic symptoms.

Some pilots suffer from psychoneuroses, which are defined as a slight loss of contact with reality--"getting angry over nothing". Such psychoneuroses commonly show up during the first five years following training and between ages 40 and 50.[J]   It's been estimated that 55% of pilot loss-of-license is due to psychoneuroses. *The PIA Air Safety Magazine* concluded that mental disease is the second most common cause of premature career termination of pilots.

Flight attendants are also affected, with intolerance to fatigue resulting in neurotic depressions and neuroses resulting in a gradual loss of professional motivation. This was especially true after flying for five years.[K]

STRESS AND INFECTION

People who fly often blame their numerous bouts with infectious illnesses like colds and flu on the fact that their exposure to disease-producing microorganisms is so high. While such exposure is real, we must remember that stress lowers the body's ability to fight infection because it affects the immune system--specifically the thymus gland and lymphatic system, which are weakened under stress.

Also, when we are trying to resist any particular agent, our resistance to other agents or stressors is lessened. It's like making the adjustment to the one problem is all we can handle at one time so we don't adjust to another problem. It is possible that for the traveler so much energy is used by the body to rephase its circadian cycles and counter the other stressors of flight that there isn't enough energy left to fight disease-causing microbes as well.

NATURE'S SELF-DESTRUCT SYSTEM

Distress, negative stress, can be devastating. Once the body reaches Stage Three of exhaustion it begins to self-destruct. With immunity down, microbes can take over and kill the body. The adrenal hormone cortisol is released to induce catabolism, the opposite of metabolism. Now, instead of changing food into energy and living tissue, it causes the body to break down essential body tissue for energy. Mental fatigue sets in and we cease to care to survive.

SOME ADAPT TO STRESS BETTER THAN OTHERS

None of us reacts to stress exactly the same. State of mind, anticipation, familiarization, and training [L] can alter the effects of stress. Having others around us reduces the effects of stress.

How well we tolerate stress depends upon how hard the body has to work to adapt to it and how many energy reserves we have. Some people have very low resistance to stress, reacting to it more quickly and becoming fatigued more easily. They succumb to lesser degrees of stress.

On the other hand some people can produce enough energy to cope while at the same time quickly rebuilding energy reserves. Dr. Selye believes that each of us is born with a certain amount of adaptive energy and vitality which is gradually reduced by stress. True physiological aging isn't determined by how long we live but by the total amount of drain on this supply.

With so many variables it is very difficult to predict how much stress is required to produce fatigue or collapse in any one individual. Our capacity to adapt to exceptional stresses is tremendous and amazing.

Dr. Selye emphasizes that what matters is not so much what happens to us but how we take it. It's our ability to cope with the demands made by events in our lives rather than the quality or intensity of those events that counts. The stressor agent is not so important as our preparedness to meet it. [M]

As frequent jet travelers it is up to us to be prepared to meet the stresses of air travel. This means understanding what stresses we face, how they affect our bodies, and how to make our bodies strong against them. This means eating food that will build the body and supply energy. This means getting good exercise. This means supplementing nutrients when needed. This means learning stress-reduction techiniques.

It means being kind to our bodies.

NOTES FOR THE PROFESSIONAL

A.   We don't know what the initial messenger or trigger is, but somehow a signal of stress reaches the nervous system which sends an alarm to the endocrine glands such as the pituitary and adrenal glands. These glands then produce adaptive hormones to help counter the stress.

Such hormones are either anti-inflammatory glucorticoids like ACTH, cortisone and cortisol, which inhibit defense reactions so that they don't become too excessive and exaggerated, or they are pro-inflammatory mineralcorticoids like ATH and aldosterone, which stimulate defensive reactions. Together these hormones help the body co-exist with a disease-causing organism, either by making the body less sensitive to it or by encapsulating the organism with a barricade of inflammatory tissue.

B.   This estimate comes from unpublished data from the 1966/67 National Health Interview Survey by H.E.W.

Dr. S.E. Roberts, in his book Exhaustion: Causes and Treatment, calls hypoglycemia the most common disease in the United States. "I would estimate that at least 50% of the work in this country is done by people who are extremely tired or exhausted--and don't know it. Often they do not mention fatigue or exhaustion as a chief complaint. They have accepted it as a part of life."

The subject of hypoglycemia and its seriousness is controversial in medical circles. Some doctors claim that fewer than 1% of the population suffer from it. Yet files from the Adrenal Metabolic Research Society of Hypoglycemia Foundation show that the average undiagnosed sufferer of hypoglycemia had visited 20 physicians and 4 psychiatrists before discovering, by word of mouth, pure chance or reading that they might have low blood sugar. They had been going to physicians who didn't believe that hypglycemia was widespread, and that what did exist they considered noncritical and faddist.

C.   Since orthodox medicine has been slow to acknowledge the seriousness of this condition it has also failed to adequately study the problem. As such, many vary in the way they interpret test results. One should find a physician who specializes in treatment and detection of hypoglycemia just as one would go to a heart specialist for detection and treatment of possible heart condition. (See Appendix)

D.   United Airlines doctors C.R. Harper and G.J. Kidera tested 175 of their pilots and found that 44, or 25%, had hypoglycemia by their criteria.

With such statistics in an airline that does little truly long-distance flying, one wonders what statistics would be found within an overseas carrier. While they have done no studies, Pan American Airways, in their industry magazine *Crosscheck* (May, 1978) points to the sinking spells experienced by crews as being caused by lack of sleep and hypoglycemia. A Georgetown University study investigating problem health areas common to flight attendants inquired into hypoglycemia. Results are not available as of this writing.

Flight Operations Magazine reports on five glaring errors made by an experienced pilot that led to a Boeing 727 accident because of mental confusion caused by abnormally low blood sugar. The brain operates primarily from glucose, sugar. When there isn't enough reaching the brain alertness, efficiency and emotional responses fluctuate abnormally. In this case the pilot was unable to perform psychomotor functions. During the preceding 13 hours he had eaten only a sandwich the night before and a cup of coffee the morning of the accident. Investigators concluded that both flight crews and management should be aware of the importance of maintaining adquate blood sugar levels through regular, well-balanced food intake.

E.   *Cresscheck,* a magazine for pilots of Pan American, recommended countering in-flight low blood sugar with light exercise, drinking fruit juice and eating protein rich snacks, while avoiding smoking, soft drinks and excessive amounts of coffee. United Airline doctors Harper and Kidera warned that all refined glucose (white sugar) products should be avoided as well. They suggested small protein snacks between meals at four-hour intervals, as well as unsweetened fruit.

F.   Catlett and Kidera found diabetes accounts for 9.7% of all medical groundings. They concluded that the effects of continued biological stress are cumulative and we will progressively lose our ability to metabolize carbohydrates normally.

G.   Additional stressors on flight crews include time-pressure stress, repeated lack of good sleep, and, especially for the flight attendants, often too many psycho-sensory task demands, inadequate compensation or recognition, challenge and interest in the work.

H.   More research is needed to determine the long-term effects of vibration, but we do know that vibration is an important, potential long-term stressor.

I.   In *The Hidden Dimension* (Doubleday, 1966) E.T. Hall discusses the problem of proxemics. "We are surrounded by a series of expanding and contracting space bubbles which are extensions of sensory experience: touch, smell, feeling and seeing. They link you with the world and protect you from it. Too much pressure on these vital zones of interactions throws your life out of kilter. Such overcrowding triggers the adrenal glands to release certain hormones into the blood stream to mobilize energy reserves and put the whole organism on alert. If this continues indefinitely, as in overcrowding, it seriously upsets the body chemistry and eventually brings shock."

J.   The first period may occur because of the newness of the work and travel bringing additional stress. The later may be due to outside changes in the pilots life, such as the life-transitional period he finds himself in between forty and fifty when he is reevaluating his life goals and values. Or it may occur because the pilot is tiring after dealing with jet stress for several years. His reserves give out. He reaches Stage Three of exhaustion.

K.   Pathology noted that stewardesses complained of nonspecific symptoms normally associated with intolerance to time-zone changes, including emotional instability. A French study traced 50 to 60% of the neuroses and neurotic depressions experienced by stewardesses studied to intolerance to fatigue and to sentimental conflicts. *

L.   Pilots are highly trained professionals. Their training diminishes to some extent the negative effects of stress as far as their ability to perform their jobs is concerned.

M.   Even Louis Pasteur agreed with this. On his death

---

* Understanding stress as we do, one must ask which comes first, the stress or the emotional conflicts.

bed he admitted that it is the condition of the body, not the microbe, that determines whether we get ill. Referring to the body's own balance or equilibrium as the "soil", he said, "The microbe is nothing; the soil is everything."

Chapter Five

Health and Disease and Their Relations to Jet Stress

ARE WE HEALTHY?

It's one thing to talk about doing all we can to make and keep our bodies healthy, and it's another thing to understand what this involves. Most of us consider ourselves healthy until some major degernative disease "strikes" us from out of nowhere. Even some doctors think this way. They are trained for and handle best "crisis" medicine, but they know little about disease prevention. Still, when we think about it, it is logical that disease doesn't just suddenly appear, but must develop. There is an area between total health and total disease, where we aren't as healthy as we could be, or as sick as we could become.

Health has been called the zest for living, the ability to wake up refreshed and eager to begin the day, the feeling of natural well-being without chronic reliance on cigarettes, alcohol and stimulants. Health is vitality. A healthy body radiates vigor, feels buoyant, moves easily and well. The body is alert, the mind is sharp and the spirit is strong. Nobel Laureate, world-reknown researcher and discoverer of vitamin C, Dr. Albert Szent-Gyorgyi describes full health as the condition in which we feel best and show the greatest resistance to disease. The World Health Organization defines health as physical, mental and social well-being, not merely the absence of disease and infirmity.

Health is the absence of symptoms. "We breath, eat, use muscles, without our attention being drawn to it. Health is deliciously expressionless, for as soon as we begin to talk about signs and symptoms order is lost and disorder takes place."*

The Chinese view health as a balance of forces of positive and negative, male and female, active and passive, which they call Yin and Yang. A   Man is thoroughly a part of nature, in unity with nature, neither more or less important than any other part. As such he is subject to the balanced forces of good and bad in nature. We become ill when the Yin and the Yang are not in balance in our body.

Those of us living in highly industrialized societies have lost sight of our true natures, of where we fit in the natural scheme of things. We are far removed from that time when we were close to nature, when our lives were obviously and totally involved in the cycles of nature, the movement of the seasons, the growth of crops. Medical writer Gary Null described our dilemna, "That we are less and less able, in modern, scientifically-oriented society, to interpret our physical needs by such basic awareness, is one of the problems of modern life. It is a mistake on the part of modern, urban, civilized people to believe that technology has so separated us from our animal state that the laws of nature no longer apply to us."**

We are a part of nature and subject to its laws. Health or lack of it doesn't just happen but is the natural result of a se-

* *Heart of Homeopathy*

** *Fasting, Biofeedback and Meditation*

quence of happenings. What we do or don't do, therefore, has a direct influence on our health. We are responsible for our health, and our sickness.

Health is continuum, a result of cause and effect. Once we are no longer sick, we may still be unhealthy. We can get over scurvy in the body but still have a vitamin C deficiency. The only change is that for the time being the problem is not terminal. Death isn't imminent. But we are not healthy.

Many of us live in this "grey area" where we don't feel great but we aren't really ill. There is a subtle incubation period with illness that lasts anywhere from several days, as in infectious disease, to several months and years as in degenerative diseases like cancer, arthritis, stroke, heart disease and diabetes. During this time the symptoms we feel are vague and seem unrelated. * It's too soon for a doctor to detect disease. B At this point he may resort to labeling the symptoms emotional or psychosomatic.

Whether or not we get sick depends upon our susceptibility and our ability to resist. When resistance is down we start to get sick.

Genetics

Many things determine if we will be ill and what form that illness will take. Genetics is one of those determinants. What we inherit can predispose us to certain health characteristics, both good and bad. Our inherited biochemical nature can predetermine what type of health problem we are likely to develop. *

But genetics isn't an excuse for one's state of health.

---

* Such symptoms are called subclinical.

While they do dramatically influence our health, it is up to each of us to make the best of what we inherited. We are responsible for our health. We are not helpless. What we do to our bodies has a direct affect on our health. The body will respond to the good we do for it and to the bad. It responds to every stimulus we give it. Nature works by very exacting rules and when we disregard them we pay a penalty. Disease, says naturopathic doctor Hector de la Fuente, "is a penalty--the result of a failure to obey the laws of the physical and spritual universe."

Thoughts and Emotions

Our emotions and thoughts can affect our health. A habit, a thought pattern or a philosophy that doesn't work for us can make us ill. Recent studies have linked particular personality traits with certain degenerative diseases like cancer and arthritis. *The Well Body Book* explains, "When the mind holds ideas such as worry, fear, anger, jealousy or hate, your body manifests these feelings as muscle tension, decreased blood flow and abnormal hormonal secretions. Eventually these states of consiousness result in disease. In this way people can literally create their own disease."

By the same token we can create a healthy body with thoughts and feelings. What we do with our minds and bodies will determine how healthy or how sick we are. Medicine cannot save someone who has decided con-sciously or unconsciously, that he will not be saved or that he wants to be sick. but we have all heard of the "miracle cure" of the person who was determined to get well. Our

---

* The biochemist can observe subtle, biochemical abberations before a disease or illness appears.

minds are an important aspect of our health.

Electrical and Vibrational Harmony

Our bodies are electrical in nature. The flow of electrical energy throughout the body must be balanced and harmonious for us to be healthy.

In the nucleus of all known, living cells there is an electrically-oscillating, twisted filament. This filament can receive and transmit radiations. A sick person has something distinctly wrong with this vibrational pattern, and it can be seen in the electrical aura surrounding his body. Georges Lakhovshy, A French Engineer, described disease as the lack of vibrational equilibrium of the cells.

When we understand this concept it is easy to see how a disruption of our normal body rhythms can alter these vibration frequencies and patterns, lowering our resistance to disease. Many diseases have disturbed circadian rhythms.* Psychotics show circadian changes in the amplitude of vibrations.

When this electrical flow of energy, which some call the "life force" or the "vital force", is moving freely and harmoniously throughout the body, the body can heal itself.* *

Influences of the Earth and the Universe

Doctors are beginning to believe that the daily and

---

* *Long-Term Air Crew Effectiveness*

* *   Some believe this energy flow follows acupuncture meridians and the body's governing vessels, which go from the head, through the middle of the body to the genitals.

seasonal rhythms of the earth may affect our bodies much
more than we have thought. They have discovered a "summer hormone" which occurs in measurable amounts only
during the summer. It influences the diet and the amount of
fat on our body. During the summer months the body requires less fat to hold in body heat. (Imagine what happens
when we fly from Anchorage to Guam and back to Fair-
banks, Alaska in four days.)

Scientists are also studying the influence of magnetic
fields on animal behavior. Inside the living cell are sensitive,
magnetic fields which seem to interact with one another.
Some believe that all living things know where they are in
time and space by the interaction of their cells with the electromagnetic fields and cosmic ray activity in the environment. If this is true, one can speculate that rapid adjustment
of the body's circadian cycles would not completely solve
the problem of "jet lag". The body would still have to get
itself in harmony with the new electromagnetic fields surrounding it.

It is even possible that our heart beat is related to universal rhythms.

Weather can affect our health. Dr. Stephen Rosen,
himself very weather-sensitive, says health is very much
influenced by both temperature and weather. Entire familes
of drugs can change their potency and side effects as a
direct consequence of the weather outside, especially
temperature conditions. He states that over 80% of some
120 separate studies have shown a positive association be -
tween illness or death--and weather. *

While many American physicians are amused, skeptical
or indifferent to this consideration, it is a commonly accepted fact in Germany, Hungary, Rumania and
Yugoslavia. Their doctors use unlisted numbers to find out

which ailments their patients are likely to suffer the next day or two as a consequence of forthcoming or expected weather events.

Our bodies are closely interrelated to the entire universe around us. We can create all the civilization we want but this basic fact will not alter. As we begin to recognize this in the Western World, we have developed a new interest in the study and understanding of Oriental philosophies and medicine.

Many ideas once considered odd and absurd are being supported and accepted by scientists. The body aura is an example. At one time people claiming that we have an aura surrounding the body were considered oddballs. Today we not only acknowledge its existence but we know that it is produced by the nerve network of the body producing a magnetic field that extends out from the body, and that it expresses the overall condition of the body. This is recorded by a special photographic technique called Kirilian photography.

THE BIOELECTRICAL AND BIOCHEMICAL NATURES OF OUR BODIES

As we have discussed, the bioelectrical aspect of our bodies is very important for health. When this electrical energy is hampered or prevented or altered we may become ill.

While this concept of our bodies is just now gaining a foothold in Western thought, naturopathic doctors and natural healers have been telling us for years that the proper

* *Weathering: How Our Atmosphere Conditions Your Body, Your Mind, Your Moods and Your Health; Deep Weather.*

electrical balance within the body is a prerequisite for health. Dr. John Christopher, nationally-known authority on herbs and natural healing, explains "Another essential item in building up the health of each patient. . . is the release of static electricity in the body by removing the shoes and stockings or socks and shuffling the feet through the lawn and grass 10 or 15 minutes a day.

"The hair acts as an antenna, pulling electrical energy from the atmosphere. As this electrical force comes in through the top of the head it distributes so many amps and/or ohms to each organ, cell and gland; then the rest of the electricity is supposed to pass out of the body again into the earth through the feet. But we wear rubber or synthetic-soled shoes and stockings so that electricity cannot be grounded properly. It collects as static electricity in the body." *

Another naturopathic physician who specializes in a deep massage similar to Japanese shiatsu claims he receives enough negative energy from his sick patients to make him sick. After working on patients he absorbs what he calls "bad electrical energy". He begins to hurt in different parts of his body. If he can go outside and walk barefoot on the grass for a short time the pain subsides.

While such descriptions are given in simplistic, unscientific terms, before we smile smugly and all knowingly let's remember that such energy transfer is readily shown with Kirilian photography.

Our bodies are not only bioelectrical in nature but biochemical as well. The chemical processes occurring within the body are very complex. Numerous factors must be present for a long chain of chemical events to occur in order to produce an end product needed by the body. If

---

*   Christopher's 3-Day Cleansing Program

one of these factors is missing or in short supply or overabundance the chemical reaction and its final result will not be the same.

One predisposed genetically to a disease such as arthritis, for instance, probably has some factor or factors within his body that cause the body to be unable to produce or use the chemical product(s) needed to utilize calcium properly. The end result is that calcium deposits itself in the joints rather than incorporating itself into bones and other places nature meant it to go.

This problem-factor can vary from one arthritic to another. Suppose there are 20 chemical changes that must take place involving 50 different substances. One arthritic sufferer may be missing a substance that he needs at the 15th chemical reaction, and without this substance the wrong chemical product is produced at this stage. Consequently, the remaining 5 chemical reactions are also altered. The end result is a deposit of calicum in the joints. Another person may be missing a substance need in the very first chemical stage. He will also develop calcium deposits in the joints.

What we see is that what will reverse the condition in the one patient will not reverse it in the other. While the problem is the same--a biochemical abnormality exists, it is this abnormality itself that varies. Arthritis is simply a descriptive term of the end result rather than a explanation of the cause of the problem. The problem is extremely individual and is the reason for the center and basic guiding principle of orthomolecular medicine: biochemical individuality.

THE BODY IN HARMONY

We are a complexly-interrelated community of organs and systems, with one organ or system dependent upon the other, contributing to the other, compensating for the other, trying to meet the constant demands of internal and external stress, trying to maintain homeostasis--consistancy with the body.

When the organs, systems, mind, emotions and spirit in each of us are functioning at optimum synergism--working together perfectly--we will enjoy total health, a state of wholism. With this harmony we can resist disease.

But when a disturbance occurs in this harmony, as occurs when our circadian rhythms are changed, resistance is lowered. Environmental influences like germs, pollution and stress of flying are less easily ignored. Eventually the body tires and physical symptoms of illness surface. The intrinsic cause of disease lies within us, not in the externals of germs and environment.

WE ARE RESPONSIBLE FOR OUR HEALTH

Medicine doesn't cure us. It may help us, but we are the cause and cure of any illness. If we want to be healthy we must, first and foremost, desire to be so. "Nothing is so curable as an incurable disease," says oriental teacher Kushi Michio Kushi, "and nothing is so incurable as the patient himself. It's difficult to get a patient to give up the ways that made him ill."

"People give little attention to their health until they are sick," says Julius Deintenfass. "Then they call a doctor and believe this ends their responsibility. Instead they should assume individual responsibility in caring for their health, following their doctor's recommendations by avoiding accidents, by positive mental attitude, by proper eating, rest and exercise."*

Infectious diseases were routed from developed nations by the beginning of this century, writes British professor and doctor Thomas McKeown.** Now we have a new set of factors that determine health. "Among such influences, those which the individual determines by his own behavior (smoking, eating, exercise and the like) are now more important for his health than medical care.

"It is assumed that we are ill and made well, but it is nearer the truth to say that we are well and are made ill.

"The public believes that health depends primarily on intervention by the doctor and that the essential requirement for health is the early discovery of disease. This concept should be replaced by recognition that disease often cannot be treated effectively, and that health is determined predominately by the way of life individuals choose to follow."***

READING OUR BODY'S LANGUAGE

We are responsible for our own health. To take this responsibility we must learn to be aware of what our bodies tell us. We can't always rely on laboratory tests, as many have learned the hard way. C

It takes a special alertness, a conscious effort to learn our body's language--to understand its signals and signs that tell

---

*   *What You Should Know About Health and Exercise*

**   *Human Nature*

***   *Prevention Magazine, 1979*

us what is going on inside. Yoga instructor Richard Hit-
tlemen teaches, "Know thyself. . . which weight you are
functioning at your best, exactly how foods you are eating
affect you, what value various sports and exercise routines
hold for you.*

We need to learn to recognize even minor signals. Dr.
Michael Samuels warns that small details accumulate with
each one sapping just a little bit of energy. The sum total is
lots of energy expended.**

Often these signals are so much an accepted part of our
lives we don't give them a second thought. A headache
after eating chocolate could indicate an allergy to chocolate.
Stomach uneasiness or general body uneasiness after a
meal could mean we need more digestive enzymes in the
stomach. Extreme loginess or sleepiness after a piece of pie
could indicate a blood sugar problem, sudden irritability to
one of the chemicals added to the meat for coloring or
preserving. Constant headaches are not health. Constant
backaches are not health. Constant fatigue is not health.
The body is trying to tell us something.

The point is that the body tells us what it likes and
dislikes. Until we learn it well, though, we can be fooled,
since at times the very thing it seems to crave the most, is
what it least should have. This occurs when the body no
longer can distinguish what is beneficial and what is harmful," explains Dr. John Diamond. "In fact, the body now actually chooses that which is destructive over that which is
therapeutic."***

This often happens with an allergy-addiction, where the
allergy to some substance builds up a physical dependency

* Yoga

** The Well Body Book

*** *Behavioral Kinesiology*

to the point that we become, unknowingly, addicted to that substance, which may be as innocuous as corn, or wheat, or milk. It takes some time for these allergic symptoms to appear. The body reacts to the allergen the same way it does to other forms of stress. After the initial reaction to it, the body appears to accomodate to the stress until it can no longer handle that particular stressor or allergen. It gets too exhausted to cover up the effects of the allergen and we suddenly discover that we have "developed an allergy". In reality, that allergy has been there for quite some time, but the body was coping. This may take years to occur but in the end we are not unlike the alcoholic. Even though the body craves alcohol, he knows it is bad for the body. Still he feels better after taking a drink. A food or chemical allergy can react the same way.

If we are willing to learn our body's language it will tell us what we need to know. This is difficult. It is much easier to play the child and put our health and lives into the hands of the Father-God-Doctor. Then we can eat and live the way that gives us the most immediate pleasure, and when this produces sickness we simply run to the doctor for a pill, and everything is okay.

Except that it's not okay. Chronic, disabling diseases like multiple sclerosis, arthritis and cancer are on the increase in spite of popular opinion to the contrary. Often the best an allopathic doctor, however sincere, can do is name our problem. If a medicine is given it often produces side effects and allergies, which means it is toxic to the body and the body is trying to get rid of it. Sometimes these side-effects and allergies are worse than the original problem while at the same time the original illness may not be helped at all.

The result is that every year the people of this nation become sicker and sicker. The San Francisco Chronicle (Sept 26, 1978) reported no significant decline in the incidence of major killer diseases for the last 25 years even with all our expensive machinery and wonder drugs. Fifty years after the discovery of insulin diabetes is increasing relentlessly. We now have upwards of 12 million diabetics in the United States. The Arthritis Foundation reports arthritis has increased 32% in the past 7 years, with 1 out of every 7 Americans suffering with it. One of every 2 persons over 65 have it in some form.

A Duke University study shows that a newborn baby in the United States has less chance of reaching 65 than infants from most of the world's developed nations. The life expectancy of a 45-year-old man has increased only 4 years since 1900. Dr. Hollis S. Ingraham reported in Public Health and Fitness that it is "general knowledge that length of life in the United States lagged seriously behind that of many other nations in the 25 years after World War II." The diagnosis of cancer is a diagnosis of death, which is why it is so feared.* Heart disease is not uncommon today in children, nor is cancer, the leading killer of children under 15 years of age, the 4th leading cause of death for children between birth and age 20.

ALLOPATHIC MEDICINE

I remember a delightful man in the small town where I grew up. He ran a store and suffered some sort of strange illness of the lungs that he got as a child working in the marble mines of Italy. Hardly anyone in town had heard of this terrible disease. He died, choking with emphysema. Now,

---

* The diagnosis of cancer is not the diagnosis of death to those who seek metabolic cancer therapy from a physician who believes in the trophoblast theory of cancer. Unfortunately few Amercians are aware of this alternative and so, for them, it is truly a diagnosis of death.

thirty years later, emphysema is a household word and is reaching epidemic proportions.

Allopathic medicine, which we in the United States have preferred, has not been terribly successful; From 45 to 65 the American male has survived less well than in any other comparable area of the world. After age 65 his life expectancy has been about average, but well below the best."

It seems time to question the methods and results we are getting with allopathic medicine and look for alternative approaches to health care.

THE MODERN ALTERNATIVE

The orthomolecular physician offers an alternative approach. Coming from the ranks of traditional, orthodox medicine, he was trained in and practiced allopathic medicine--"crisis" medicine as some call it. Frustrated with discouraging results he began to look beyond established orthodoxy in his reading, study, research and clinical practice. He examined age-old alternative health methods like acupuncture and acupressure, iridology, herbology, naturopathy and homoeopathy. With his strong medical and scientific background he demanded scientific explanations for their claims and apparent cures. He demanded results.

He studied healing philosophies of other cultures. In the process he discovered certain basic ideas underlying all avenues and beliefs: that each of us is biochemically unique, that health means maintaining harmony in the body, which is bioelectrical and biochemical in nature, that any medicine should be non-invasive—not harmful to the body— except in immediate life and death crises, that medicein is used only to revitalize the body's own healing forces and it is the patient who heals himself.

He studied body chemistry, he studied diet, he envision-
ed the body as a whole, unified organism where each part
was interdependent upon the other parts. He realized that
atherosclerosis was not cured by cutting out a few arteries or
scrapping them clean of fatty plaques. Whatever caused
those deposits to build up is in the body and more will grow
in other arteries.* By the same token cutting off an infected
foot is not assurance infection has been removed from the
body. If the body is not strong enough to get rid of the infection on its own it can continue to spread. Cutting out an of-
fending cancer tumor from the stomach won't remove the
cause of cancer, only the tumor, an end result. Whatever
allowed the cancer to develop is still in the body.

Along the way these physicians also rediscovered proven, medical techniques that had lain quietly by the wayside
because orthodoxy didn't have time for them, or because
they were popular therapy, or because there was little
economic benefit from them for the supporting medical
arms such as drug companies, who therefore didn't spend
money to promote them.

Chelation therapy**is an example. Twenty-five years ago
chelation therapy was already in common use for removing
lead and mercury from the blood. Then they discovered it
also removed unwanted calcium, an integral part of those
plaques that can cut off blood circulation in the arteries.
Thus it was useful for many forms of cardio-vascular

---

* This was demonstrated by one of the heart-transplant patients who died a few years
after his operation, not from the body rejecting the new heart but from a heart attack. The
new heart had been thoroughly examined prior to implant in the patient and found to be
completely free of any atherosclerotic plaques. Yet within 2 years his body filled those
arteries with enough fatty plaques that they finally cut off blood flow to the heart muscle.
He died from a heart attack.

** Chelation therapy is discussed in detail in Chapter Nine

disease, kidney stones, strokes, emphysema, heavy metal poisoning and osteroarthritis.

Chelation occurs constantly in nature and is as old and natural as life itself, yet orthodoxy frowns upon its use for other than treatment of lead or mercury poisoning, for which it is the treatment of choice. They try to prevent its use for the other diseases even though a growing body of evidence shows that the process of atherosclerosis, for example, is almost completely preventable and is substantially reversible when chelation is used along with other modalities like diet and exercise.*

With the effectiveness of chelation therapy proving itself daily, entrenched orthodoxy ridicules its use and suggests instead bypass surgery, which is merely a temporary, palliative measure that treats symptoms but cannot reverse or cure the disease. There is no evidence that it prevents death from heart attack or that it prolongs life. It is however, very lucrative.

By-pass surgery was adopted for wide clinical use before it was well understood and the "proof" to support its value comes from questionable sources and at best is biased. In fact it appears that the operation itself can cause significant damage to the heart and actually accelerate the progression of coronary heart disease. It can surgically induce a heart attack, grafts can become occluded (closed-off) within one year of surgery and it often speeds up the disease in the arteries receiving the grafts.* *

---

* There is evidence that atherosclerosis may be related to stress since stress causes an increase of low density lipoproteins and decrease of high density lipo-proteins in the blood, a condition that is favorable for plaque formation.

* * When a cardiac surgeon was asked why by-pass surgery was used without controlled studies and why all hospitals can use it even when they fall short of the guidelines, he answered, "Well, you could say that we sacrifice people and some people die, but people are dying off like flies anyway. They're dying of heart attacks by the millions. Any you could say that there are too many people anyway." (ByPass Surgery)

I offer this example to show that orthodoxy not only does not have all the answers but actively discourages, through professional and legal pressures, alternatives to their favored techniques.

The concept of orthomolecular medicine was developed by Dr. Humphrey Osmond and Dr. Abram Hoffer, psychiatrists with brilliant credentials in biochemistry and psychiatry, when they theorized that schizophrenia resulted from a malfunction of the adrenal glands, which would secrete a toxic adrenochrome which in turn produces the schizophrenic symptoms. Careful attention to diet and nutritional supplementation, with an emphasis on niacin and vitamin C brought amazing results. This supported their theory that our thoughts, emotions and actions are affected by the physical condition of the body, and vice versa. If the right chemicals aren't available, the nervous system can't function properly. Once the chemical imbalance is corrected, physical and emotional symptoms disappear.

It was Nobel Laureate Dr. Linus Pauling who coined the term "orthomolecular", which means "right molecule". The object is to get the best molecular, biochemical environment in the body so it can function properly. This includes making sure that we have all the natural substances the body needs, in the right proportion. Often this means treatment with vitamins, mineral, enzyme and glandular supplements. The patient is expected to understand and fully participate in his treatment. He has access to his medical files and he and his family are educated regarding treatment.

From the concept of orthomolecular medicine the framework of wholistic medicine emerged. Some people hear this term and immediately shut-off their minds, afraid they might get involved in some counter-culture fad.

Actually the concept is very simple and basic. It is really

two concepts. First, the whole spectrum of health care is considered. Alternative methods like botanical medicine, acupuncture, and homoeopathy have proven their worth in restoring health, even without double-blind laboratory studies, over many centuries. Rather than reject such methods as "medical myths" open-minded doctors have put their scientific discipline and clinical know-how to work to test their validity, at times finding that these scoffed-at treatments have a scientific basis as well as a clinically-healing effect.

The late Dr. Ray Wixom, a clinical ecologist, told me that a copper bracelet would cure arthritis in 3% of the sufferers. He explained to show how the body would utilize the copper from the bracelet to replace a substance the body needed. "In 97% of the arthritics the copper bracelet won't do a thing. But if you are in that 3% you won't suffer from arthritis, I just don't laugh at any old-wive's tales. If it works, it works."

The wholistic approach is concerned with the whole body rather than just the part that seems diseased. This is logical since the body works as a whole, integrated unit, and when one part isn't functioning properly other parts will not do as well as they should either. So we consider all aspects--the physical, the chemical, the mental and the emotional.

Wholistic medicine requires patient participation. No doctor nor any approach can hand us health gratis. We have to be responsible and active in our health program. We have to want it, work for it, be open and willing, and broadminded. We have to understand what is happening. "The key to wholistic healing," says Dr. William McGarey, director of the A.R.E. clinic in Phoenix, Arizona, "is that medicine exists for the patient. Traditional medicine has gotten away from the consideration of the individual as a whole human being. It's too mechanistic, too scientific and too disease-oriented."*

We are beginning to see a new breed of doctor who uses a wholistic approach to health as a viable alternative to allopathic medicine. But such changes take time. Orthodoxy is notoriously slow to make changes, especially in medicine.

For one thing doctors wish to be cautious, and so they should be. As one observer remarked, "The doctor has a person's life in his hands, so he is right to proceed with caution. It is a question of degree. He must not proceed so cautiously that thousands of people die each day because he is unwilling to embrace the speculative future."**

Yet many people die because allopathic medicine has no answers yet is unwilling to embrace that speculative future. Caution is only one reason this occurs. The other reason is that established orthodoxy, in whatever field, has a tendency to believe it has a corner on knowledge, so anything or anyone who disagrees must be wrong. Dr. Selye stressed this point, "Had I known more I would certainly have been stopped by the biggest of all block to improvement: the certainty of being right."***

Such changes are slow to come and often take generations. Max Planck of the famous German Max Planck Institute commented, "A new scientific truth does not triumph by convincing its opponents and making them see the light. But, rather, because its opponents eventually die and a

---

*   Wholistic Medicine Treats the Whole Person

**   Let's Live, Aug, 1978

***   Stress of Life

new generation grows up that is familiar with it."

Change is in the air. A wholistic approach to health, with physician and patient working together, is the future of medicine. It can be the best direction to take in overcoming stress--especially jet stress.

NOTES FOR THE PROFESSIONAL

A.   This concept of physiological homeostasis and adaptive self-organization is essentially the same as those of modern cybernetics, which studies the feedback mechanisms within the body. For example, the sympathetic nervous system can be considered Yang operating in balance with the parasympathetic system. considered Yin-- the active with the passive.

The basic principles of immunology, according to Dr. Philiop M. Toyama in his article in the *North Carolina Medical Journal* (May, 1972) can be stated by using terminology as antigen (Yin) and antibody (Yang).

B.   Dr. Selye calls this grey period the time of "just being sick". There are very few signs and symptoms that are actually characteristic of any one disease. Instead most symptoms seem to be common to many, perhaps all, diseases.

C.   In a study 17 laboratories tested 91 patients with 20 tests per patient. Fifty per cent of the results were incorrect.

Chapter Six

Resisting Jet Stress With Food

WHAT WE EAT IS IMPORTANT

A healthy body is a must for combating jet stress. Few of us have that. Most of us are so used to not feeling well that we don't know what it is to feel really good.

If the body is to be healthy we have to be sure it gets all the materials it needs to do its work--to produce energy for us, to remove toxic by-products of energy production, and to regenerate or rebuild itself. Unlike those little air ferns sold in variety stores, it must be fed what it needs for life.

Almost as important is that the body isn't fed what it doesn't want or can't use. When we give it something it doesn't want or can't use it tries to get rid of whatever it is. In the process precious energy is used to detoxify the body which could be used for life-producing functions.

This means that what we eat is extremely important. We are realizing that most illness derives from faulty diet, either directly or indirectly, including such childhood disabilities as autism, and drug and alcohol abuse.[A] When the body gets food it can't digest and assimilate, chemical waste products result--toxins, acids and deposits. These cause congestion and stress within the body. While the body is busy defending itself from this there isn't as much time and/or energy to adequately fight off disease and generate new tissue.

By the same token, when it doesn't get the nutrients it needs it can't produce the energy and substances needed to resist disease and rebuild itself.

This seems so obvious, yet every fourth person in the United States suffers from one or more degenerative diseases, which are usually attributable to poor diet.* The early beginnings of arteriosclerosis have been documented in over 60% of American men of age 21. [B] The U.S. Department of Agriculture has calculated that better nutrition could reduce diabetes by 50%, heart disease by 20%, obesity by 80%, alcoholism by 33% and intestinal cancer by 20%. Nutritionally-oriented doctors would find such estimates very conservative.

"During this century, the composition of the average diet in the United States has changed radically," reports the Senate's Select Committee on Nutrition and Human Needs. "Complex carbohydrates--fruits, vegetables and grain products--which were the mainstay of the diet, now play a minority role. At the same time fat and sugar consumption have risen to the point where these two dietary elements comprise at least 60% of total caloric intake, and increase of 20% since the early 1900's.

"These and other changes in the diet. . . may be as profoundly damaging to the nation's health as the widespread contagious diseases of the early part of the century." Too much fat, too much sugar, and too much salt may be prime factors in the 10 leading causes of death, including cancer, in the United States. They conclude, "The eating patterns of this century represent as critical a public concern as any now before us."**

* Other factors are lack of consistent exercise and a stressful life.

** Dietary Goals for the United States

The amount of fat we Americans are consuming is increasing greatly--much of it coming from fast-food chain hamburgers where fat content averages 30%. In 1960 per capita consumption of beef, a principal source of dietary fat, was 85.1 pounds per year. In 1976 it was 128.5 pounds. We ate 50 million hamburgers that year.

Americans are eating almost 125 pounds of sugar per capita per year* and the same amount of white flour. "This is a completely incredible nutritional folly," remarks Dr. Paavo Airola, well-known international authority on health and nutrition, "nothing less than an act of unintentional national suicide.

"An excess of sugar and refined carbohydrates in our diet is not only responsible for most of our hypoglycemia epidemic but also a major contributing factor in an epidemic growth of most of our other degenerative diseases such as diabetes, heart disease, tooth decay, periodontal disease, osteoporosis and even cancer."**

Diet is a serious business. It's time we stopped making fun of so-called "food faddists" and began to look at the serious state of our health. We can't console ourselves with fairy tales about our great American Diet with the mistaken belief that we are living longer than our ancestors who ate a more natural diet. A 60-year-old man today can expect to live only about a year longer than could a 60-year-old man in 1779.***

---

* That's 1 teaspoon of sugar ever half hour, 24 hours a day for every American.

** *Hypoglycemia, A Better Approach*

*** Dr. John Bjorksten, *The Relevant Scientist*, 1971

NATURAL AND RAW FOODS ARE PREFERABLE

The average American is eating too much sugar, too much fat, too much salt and too many refined carbohydrates. The food is nearly always cooked, often overcooked and too-often deep-fat fried.

The best food is food in its natural form. That means that nothing has been added and nothing has been removed. It isn't refined. It contains no additives.

Refining removes many nutrients. What it replaces under the guise of enrichment are artifical and fewer. Jane Kinderlehrer describes "enriched" succinctly. "If someone stole your wallet with $200 in it, your favorite snapshots, credit cards and driver's license, and returned your emptied wallet, license and 20ᶜ for car fare to you, would you consider yourself enriched?"*

Processed, refined foods are what we call "junk foods"--sneak thieves of essential micronutrients stolen from other foods we eat. Given our present state of technology we can't process a food into a product as nutritious as the original product. In the first place the processing damages some of the nutrients and in the second place we haven't been able to identify all the nutrients that are in the natural product so we can't replace them.

This was shown by a biochemist who took a natural bran product, carefully removed all the known nutrients and then fed the supposedly worthless residue to a group of laboratory rats along with their regular diet. The rats thrived, compared to the control group not given the "worthless" supplement.

Dr. Stan Malstrom explains another reason we can't duplicate nature's food in the laboratory. "In whole foods

* *Confessions of a Sneaky Organic Cook*

there is much life energy that we know little or nothing about. For example, man can create sea water which chemically is exactly identical to ocean water, yet in which ocean fish cannot live. Add sea water and the fish flourish. We have much yet to learn."*

Chemical Additives

Every year the American adult consumes, in addition to the 115-plus pounds of sugar, 15 pounds of salt, 8.4 pounds of corn syrup (sugar) and 4.2 pounds of dextrose (sugar), as much as 10 pounds of over 2000 different chemicals. In most cases the safety of these chemicals has not been proven while some are known to be carcinogenic, some mutagenic, and some interfere with body enzymes, thus hindering normal metabolic processes.

No one can say honestly that these additives are safe. Some speak of a "threshold" of exposure below which there is allegedly no risk. This is the basis for FDA regulations allowing their usage. But Dr. Samuel S. Epstein, environmental toxicologist at Case Western Reserve Medical School feels, "There is no threshold. Lower concentration of carcinogenic chemicals simply means lower incidence of cancer."**

Even if it is proven some day that chemical additives are safe in certain, minute amounts we are not getting minute amounts of these chemicals. Nearly all supermarket and restaurant foods contain them. Ten pounds of 2000 chemicals constitute more than a "minute" quantity.

* *Own Your Own Body*

** *Nutrition Journal*

Fake Foods

Refined foods include more than just natural foods that have been processed. Some may be the product of a chemists lab. Food technologists can start from scratch with their chemicals and give us a totally fake food. Raw materials for imitation chocolate and imitation cherries, tomato paste extender and imitation raisins come from plants, animals and petroleum products. A medicine chest of additives is needed to hold them together so they look real.

Synthetic milk, for instance, is based on sodium caseinate, bolstered with vegetable fat, emulsifiers, buffers, protein stabilizers, body agents, sweeteners, flavorings, colorings and preservatives. *

The raisin in a cookie might actually be granules of sugar, corn syrup (sugar), vegetable oil and fats along with natural or artificial raisin flavors. The cherry in your donut might be sodium alginate solution, suitably colored and flavored, which was dumped into a bath of calcium salt to form the cherry "skin".

Start reading the ingredients on packages of the food in the supermarket. You'll be surprised how much "food" is devoid of food.

Should we finally discover that all these chemicals are perfectly safe we are still faced with the fact that we are eating something devoid of nutrition in place of nutritious food. Food manufacturers are interested in making the product look, act and taste "right". Little concern is given to its nutritive quality.

I say "taste right" because our taste buds have become so accustomed to the taste of these highly-processed and fake foods that natural foods often taste strange. Once I offered a

* *The Progressive,* Madison, Wisconsin

friend a garden-fresh, organically-grown ripe, red tomato from my own garden. She took one bite, made a face and complained that it tasted funny. What she was experiencing was the full, sweet natural taste of a tomato. What she was expecting was a woody, tasteless, gassed, hard, unripe supermarket tomato.

John and Karen Hess comment in their book, *The Taste of America*, "Good food in America is little more than a memory, a hope. Americans have been mouthwashed by generations of bad food and brainwashed by generations of bad advice about food." They call this the "death of the palate".

Fortunately taste buds can change. Once we get reaccustomed to natural, whole foods the typically normal American "white food" fare is bland to tasteless, except for the flavor of the chemicals.

Raw is Better.

To get the most out of the food we eat it should be raw as often as possible, with a few exceptions. Dr. Stan Malstrom recommends we eat at least 75 to 90% of our food raw. Dr. Paavo Airola prefers up to 80%, warning that some foods are better eaten cooked. Members of the cabbage family, rhubarb, spinach and asparagus, which contain oxalic acid that inhibits certain important enzymes in our bodies, should be cooked. Carrots have more food value when cooked. So do grains, which should either be cooked, preferably steamed, or sprouted in order to break down the phytin they contain. Phytin binds the minerals in the food, preventing the body from using them. But all seeds, nuts, fruits and most vegetables can be eaten in their natural, raw states.

An added benefit from raw foods lies in their purifying properties. They tend to act as antidotes against poisonous additives and pollution that we inadvertently absorb. Apples, apricots, cauliflower, carrot juice, beet and turnip tops, grapefruit, lemons and oranges, peaches, raspberries, blackberries and blueberries are supposed to have such purifying properties.

Raw lemons, we are told, are especially good since they stimulate and rebuild the liver. The liver is the chemical factory of the body, and one of its jobs is to get rid of unwanted chemical substances in the body. Dr. Airola reminds us that a toxic, malfunctioning, overworked, tired liver almost always is a cause of disorders in sugar metabolism like hypoglycemia. Perhaps, then, it would be a good food for the traveler.

CARBOHYDRATES ARE BEST
(IF THEY ARE UNREFINED AND COMPLEX)

Far and away the majority of experts, including many aerospace doctors queried, recommend eating primarily lots of complex, natural carbohydrates. This means fruits and juices, vegetables, grains, seeds and nuts. Since they are composed of very, very large molecules the body takes some time to break them down into simple sugars. As a result they trickle slowly into the blood stream, preventing the sudden rise in blood sugar that occurs when we eat refined carbohydrates. White flour and white sugar products contain simple sugars consisting of very small molecules that pour like a torrent into the blood stream. As a result the body has difficulty responding adequately and properly. Blood sugar levels rise dramatically, as do levels of cholesterol and fats. On the other hand natural carbohydrates help maintain normal insulin and fat levels in a proper balance.

Dr. Bill Gray, M.D., a specialist in biological medicine, nutrition and homoeopathy, describes what happens. "Normally carbohydrate molecules from natural carbohydrate-rich foods are slowly broken down from their long chains into small molecules, and ultimately absorbed slowly in the small intestine.

"The process of refining a carbohydrate breaks them into small molecules; the subsequent flood of glucose into the bloodstream causes a tremendous reaction of the pancreas, adrenals, liver and possibly of other organs, to restore the blood sugar to normal. After continued exposure to this reaction the reaction itself becomes abnormal, resulting in the symptoms of hypoglycemia."*

Another reason that the air traveler should eat natural carbohydrate foods is to help counter hypoxia due to altitude, carbon monoxide or strenuous work. According to Hansen and Claybaugh, researchers at the Tripler Army Medical Center, Hawaii, "The individual metabolizing primarily carbohydrates has the need for 8% less oxygen uptake through the lungs than if he is metabolizing fat.

'With limited oxygen available, such as at high elevations, or with reduced oxygen transport capabilities, such as with strenuous work, or with lung or heart disease, these few percentage differences may be biologically significant.

"This is an additional advantage in (using) carbohydrate for fuel. We suggest that in air travel of patients with impaired oxygen transport, one should consider carbohydrate feeding."*

---

* *Hypoglycemia, A Better Approach*

* *Aviation, Space & Environmental Medicine,* Sept 1975.

Grains in their natural, unrefined state are the best form of carbohydrate available, according to Dr. Airola. They are superb, potent health-building foods with a nutritonal value unsurpassed by any other food. Eaten with seeds and nuts, grains should be one of our prime foods, he believes.

Grains contain all the important nutrients, in a perfect combination and balance, that are essential for human growth, sustaining of health and prevention of disease. They are the best natural source of unsaturated fatty acids and of lecithin, important in combating heart disease. Their vitamin content is unsurpassed, expecially in vitamin E and the antistress B-complex vitamins.

Grains are gold mines of minerals and trace elements. They also contain pacifarins, which act like antibiotics, and auxonesm, which can help the body produce vitamins and prevent premature aging by helping cells rejuvenate. Finally, they add bulk and roughage (or fiber) to the diet.

Travelers suffering with jet stress would be especially interested in brown rice, millet and buckwheat. These contain molybdenum which helps proper metabolism of carbohydrates. As we have seen stress can hinder proper carbohydrate metabolism. They are also high in minerals magnesium, zinc, potassium, chromium and manganese which promote normal sugar metabolism.

Seeds and nuts have been recommended by flight surgeons and many flight crews snack on them throughout the flight. The best nuts are almonds, hazelnuts and peanuts (really a legume), with almonds being the least likely to go rancid. Flax seeds, sesame seeds and nuts are complete, high-quality proteins.

These should be eaten raw and fresh. Raw seeds and nuts do have the disadvantage of vulnerability towards rancidity and this should be watched for. Rancidity in the body creates "free radicals"--fragments of a molecule that tear away from its source and try to join other normal molecules. This can seriously damage the molecule causing it to mutate, changing its genetic code to become a different cell, or it can cause a chain reaction and destroy the molecule. Then cells die, enzymes fail to function, energy is reduced and the body's ability to renew itself and resist and recover from stress is diminished. *

Luckily we can almost completely suppress free radicals with antioxidants like vitamin D and B-15, selenium and ginseng.

Sunflower seeds are especially susceptible to rancidity. A good rule of thumb in assuring your seeds aren't rancid is to check their color. If sunflower seeds are not medium grey, or if they are whole or partly yellow, white, black or brown they are rancid.

Sesame seeds also need to be carefully purchased and used. Ninety-nine percent of the time they are found in their unhulled state, and this is not preferred. They contain the same oxalate that spinach, rhubarb and kohl products have, only it is ten times greater. Since they grow in hot climates and are picked by hand they can be covered with bacteria, which washing doesn't remove. There is one company that strips off the hull mechanically without chemical processors and corrosive chemicals. These are the best.

We get the most out of seeds when they are ground in a small nut grinder and eaten immediately, added to sauces or cereals or salted and sprinkled on top rice, or added to beverages.

Vegetables are best eaten raw, with the exceptions of the ones mentioned earlier. The best way to cook a vegetable is to steam it or quickly saute it Chinese-style. High heat and water can remove many nutrients so the less used of either,

---

* Free radicals have been assoicated with the aging process.

the better.*

The avocado is an especially good vegetable for anyone suffering with hypoglycemic symptoms since it contains a special kind of sugar which actually suppresses insulin. It also contains complete nutrition, consisting of protein, fats, carbohydrates, vitamins and minerals in excellent proportions.

Raw fruit is an excellent food. The best are strawberries, pineapple, sour apples, cherries, papaya, peaches, grapefruit, lemons and limes--fruits which are not excessively sweet. They may be juiced or eaten whole.

Eggs and dairy products are also excellent. Soured milk, especially, is good since it is partially predigested, making it easy for the body to assimilate. The milk sugar has been converted into beneficial lactic acid, a benefit for the hypoglycemic. These cultured milk products, including kefir, yogurt, cottage cheese and buttermilk, have nearly identical nutritional value, while they all improve the flora of the intestines. This encourages healthier digestive and eliminative tracts.

Milk is best when it is raw. High-quality, unpasteurized, uncontaminated milk from certified dairies is safe, despite the dairy lobbyists who try to scare us into believing otherwise. Once milk is heated during pasteurization the calcium and protein are chemically altered so that the body cannot use them as readily. Arthritis has been created in experimental animals by feeding them pasteurized cow milk, and reversed with raw goats milk. Supermarket processed milk can be loaded with toxic and dangerous drugs, hormones, chemicals and residues of pesticides, herbicides and detergents.

---

*   For more information on cooking techniques you may wish to read my book, *The Beginner's Natural Food Guide and Cookbook* which helps you make the transition into using natural foods.

Dr. Carl Pfeiffer, in *Zinc and Other Micronutrients*, considers milk the best source of a balanced solution of calcium, magnesium and phosphorus. He recommends every adult drink one glass a day. Since milk is a common allergen, one should be alert to any allergic reaction to the milk which would indicate he shouldn't drink it.

VEGETABLES vs. MEAT

So far we have suggested a primarily vegetarian diet. This is the usual recommendation of up-to-date nutritional experts.

There are many justifications for this position. Meat is high in fat and may therefore contribute to heart disease and cancer. Dr. Gio Bori, director of the National Cancer Institute observed. "Colon cancer has been shown to correlate highly with consumption of meat, even though it is not clear whether the meat itself or its fat content is the real correlating factor."[*]

Colon cancer may also derive from undigested meat that remains too long in the intestinal tract. Toxic by-products form as it lies in the colon slowly decomposing. The resulting putrefaction pours toxic substances into the body and irritates colon lining.

It seems our intestinal tracts are longer than they should be for meat-eating animals. Comparative anatomy shows that carnivore have short intestinal tracts and strong digestive juices. this allows rapid digestion of the meat with the byproducts quickly passing out of the body. Vegetarians, on the other hand, have long intestines, measuring up to 12 time the length of the spine. That is

[*] *Self-Help Update*, Jan/Mar, 1979

what man has, along with short, comparatively weak jaws, short, canine teeth, and clawless hands. Dr. W.S. Collens of Maimonides Hospital, Brooklyn, reported at a recent medical conference, "Examination of dental structure of modern man reveals that he possesses all the features of a strictly herbivore animal."

Man seems to fare well on vegetables. Dr. Owen S. Parret described what happened in Denmark when the entire country went on a vegetarian diet during World War II. After a year of no meat a world record was established for lowered death rate: 34% among the males and nearly as much among the females. There was also a marked decrease in illness. The next year, when the normal meat diet was resumed, the death rate returned to prewar level.

Dr. Irving Fisher of Yale University put meateaters and vegetarians through a series of endurance tests. The vegetarians outperformed their carnivorous counterparts.

On the other hand it is easier to obtain high-quality protein from animals and fish. And, according to Dr. William Kelley, some of us require meat to remain healthy. Once a strong advocate of the vegtarian diet for everyone, he discovered people have different body metabolisms, which he classified into ten types ranging from those who need a fair quantity of meat to those who shouldn't eat meat at all. He devised a computerized test to help the individual determine his metabolic type. *

PROTEIN, SUGAR, SALT AND FAT: HOW MUCH AND WHAT KIND

Protein

We can get all the protein we need from plant sources. According to the Pritikin Longevity Center if we eat enough calories of unprocessed food to sustain life we are not likely to be deficient in amino acids. The Max Plank Institute in Germany, the most respected nutrition research center in the world, finds vegetable proteins not only equal to but actually superior in biological value to animal protein. In other words they are used more efficiently by the body. This means that the protein in potato is biologically superior to that in meat, eggs and milk. Further, protein, eaten raw, as is easily done with vegetable protein, but difficult with animal protein, has an even higher biological value. We have to each twice as much cooked protein to get the same protein value we would get from raw protein.

Protein is manufactured by the body from amino acids. We make all these amino acids in the body except for 8 of them which are called Essential Amino Acids. These Essential Amino Acids must be obtained from the food we eat. They must also be eaten together, at the same time, all of them-in order for the body to be able to make protein from them.

Foods that contain all eight Essential Amino Acids are considered "Complete protein" foods. These include soybeans, peanuts, almonds, buckwheat, sunflower seeds, pumpkin seeds, potatoes, avocados and all green, leafy vegetables, according to the Plank Institute. Dr. Paavo Airola points out that the protein in alfalfa, parsley and potatoes is comparable to the protein in milk. "It is virtually impossible," says Dr. Airola, 'not to get enough protein in your diet provided you have enough to eat of natural, unrefined foods."*

---

* It is not likely that we are cast forever into a particular type. Body chemistry can change.

* *Hypoglycemia, A Better Approach*

Not all plant foods contain all the Essential Amino Acids. Others are very low in some of them. This is not a problem since we can eat those that are complimentary to one another. One low in a particular Essential Amino Acid would be eaten with one high in that substance. For example corn and beans or beans and rice provide a complete set of Essential Amino Acids when eaten together. They work synergistically with one another so that the combination becomes greater than the parts. *

If such combining is too time-consuming or otherwise impossible, a full protein complement can be assured by including seeds, nuts, milk products, eggs and/or sprouts with each meal.

How Much Protein?

Regardless of the source, be it animal or vegetable, we may consume more protein than we need or can use profitably. Recommendations for the daily amount of protein needed range from 20 to 60 grams. Finnish, American, Swedish, Japanese and German studies show that protein intake between 25 and 35 grams a day is enough to sustain good health. The Food and Nutrition Board of the National Academy of Science, collaborating with the World Health Organization, has lowered its daily recommendation from 120 grams to .4 grams daily per pound of adult body weight when the protein comes from an animal source. This is 66 grams for a 165-pound man and 52 grams for a 128-pound woman.

According to Dr. Paavo Airola the body's metabolism has

---

* These combinations are described in detail in *Diet for a Small Planet* by Frances Moore Lappe.

evolved to handle only 20 to 25 grams per day. He warns that a diet containing 60, 80 or 120 grams puts a great stress on the system. Extra energy is needed to excrete the nitrogen by-products that are created. This contributes to fatigue.

The toxic by-products that are not eliminated can cause a wide variety of symptoms which are themselves harmful to health. These toxic residues, including uric acid, urea, ammonia and toxic purines, accumulate in tissues, creating a biochemical imbalance and over-acidity in the body. They chemically interfere with muscle and nerve function, reducing strength and endurance. Some remain in the intestine to putrefy there causing constipation and self-poisoning (autotoxemia).

The result is a chemical environment ripe for disease. Some suggest that colon cancer, so widespread today, may be related to this putrifaction. Excess protein is associated with mental disorders and premature senility because of biochemical inbalances produced in the tissues, overacidity, intestinal putrefaction, constipation and degeneration of the vital organs.

Too much meat protein tends to cause severe deficiencies of vitamin B-3 and B-6, which are needed for metabolizing protein. Since these vitamins are not found in meat they must be taken from other foods or the body's stores. Because meat is very high in phosphorus meat protein can produce a magnesium deficiency. Over 90 grams daily of animal protein tends to withdraw calcium from bones--a situation that could lead to osteoporosis.

Excess protein is not stored as protein. What the body cannot use as protein is changed into sugar and burned as energy or it is deposited in the body as fat.

There is no clear-cut consensus on exactly how much protein is best. Americans eat about 100 grams daily, which is more than we probably need. During times of stress the body needs more protein.*

The Senate Select Committee on Nutrition made these diet suggestions for Americans: reduce sugar, fat and table salt. Them be sure to include food that contains enough fiber.

Sugar

Refined sugar has been blamed for contributing to nearly every physical problem we experience today, including tooth decay, ulcer symptoms, indigestion, T.B., scurvy, mental illness, diabetes and heart disease as well as cancer.

Dr. John Yudkin, Professor of Nutrition at Queen Elizabeth College, University of London, finds sugar the culprit in heart disease, elevated triglyceride levels associated with cardiovascular disease, diabetes and other forms of carbohydrate intolerance, ulcers, and some forms of indigestion.

Sugar produces higher than normal levels of insulin, uric acid (involved in gout) and cortisol, the adrenal hormone associated with catabolism--the process that breaks down lean tissue for the body to use as energy.

The national epidemic of hypoglycemia may come from eating so much sugar. So believe Drs. Cheraskin and Ringsdorf, leading orthomolecular physicians, who explain why this could be so. The brain and nervous system are more sensitive to chemical reactions than our other organs and tissues. Refined sugar enters the blood stream so quickly that brain and nervous tissues are overwhelmed. Since

* However, the pilot and flight attendant should consider avoiding meals with lots of animal protein during flight when they must stay alert, since animal protein contains fair amounts of the amino acid L-tryptophan, which induces sleepiness.

the brain mostly uses glucose for energy and the glucose it receives varies so drastically and quickly when we eat refined sugar, we may find we aren't as alert, can't learn as well, and are easily irritated. Emotional disturbances are the first symptoms of the body not being able to handle the stress of sugar dependency.

Dr. Abram Hoffer correlates sugar consumption not only with heart disease but with peptic ulcer and ulcerative colitis, not uncommon complaints of flying personnel. These are related to a certain type of saccharine disease with relative hypoglycemia playing an important part. [C] He also points out that sugar is addictive. It can produce addiction as severe as any drug addiction, with the only difference between heroin addiction and sugar addiction being that sugar doesn't need injection, is readily consumable because of its availability, and isn't considered a social evil. But the strength of sugar addiction and the withdrawal symptoms are as severe as those accompanying withdrawal from drugs. A sugar addict could be called a "sugarholic".

If you decide to cut down on your sugar consumption by eliminating sugar products you have only put a foot in the door. We eat lots of sugar and most of it is hidden. Our purchase of refined sugar has dropped from about 50 pounds in 1900 to 25 pounds per person per year in 1971. But the use of hidden sugar accounts for more than two-thirds of all refined sugar consumed in the United States.

Sugar is in nearly every food we buy in the supermarket, including salt, processed meats, frozen and canned vegetables, crackers, mayonaise and ketchup. [D] The largest single industry using refined sugar is the beverage soft drink industry--nearly 23 pounds per person per year. [E]

To avoid eating a lot of sugar we have to read labels, realizing that oftimes a food will be touted as containing no sugar when in fact the only sugar it doesn't have in it is sucrose--common white table sugar. It may still have corn syrup, sugar, fructose, sorbitol, corn sweeteners, glucose, dextrose, sucrose, dextrin or maltose. These are sugar-- plain, refined, simple sugar. Brown sugar is nothing more than refined, white sugar crystals sprayed with molasses syrup, sometimes with food coloring added. Raw sugar is banned in this country so the so-called raw or raw-like sugars listed on the label are still refined, simple sugar.

The informed consumer realizes what he is reading on the label, and also knows that when sugar is listed first, second. or third there's a lot of sugar in that food.

There are those who argue that sugar is sugar, that the body needs sugar and will convert what we eat into sugar anyway, so there is nothing wrong with eating white table sugar. It's true that carbohydrates will eventually break down into simple sugars like glucose and fructose in the body. So will some protein. But because these are complex foods, both in bulk and structure, this breakdown takes some time to occur. Sugar doesn't suddenly and dramatically hit the blood stream, traumatizing the body. In addition the nutrients the body needs to metabolize these complex foods are already present in the foods themselves.

On the other hand refined sucrose, a combination of glucose and fructose that we commonly call white table sugar, is rapidly hydrolyzed, absorbed, shunted into the liver and converted into triglycerides. These triglycerides are released into the blood and stored as fat deposits. The result is that the body has received a shock by the too-rapid absorption of sugar into the blood, and blood fat levels rise, a situation linked to artery disease. *

---

* The cholesterol plaques we worry about plugging up our arteries also contain these triglycerides.

What's more, since table sugar is "pure" it doesn't carry with it the nutrients needed for its metabolism in the body. It must rob what it needs from stores of nutrients already in the body or from other food that is eaten. Thus the body doesn't get the new supply of nutrients either. While sugar is stealing these important nutrients it adds nothing to the body in return.

Because of this, eating large quantities of sugar can lead to malnutrition. It becomes a diluting agent, displacing other nutrients far more essential than sugar. Dietary Goals warns, "The most immediate problem cited by nutritionists is the danger of displacing complex carbohydrates which are high in micro-nutrients, with sugar, which is essentially an energy source, offering little other nutritional value. This not only increases the potential for depriving the body of essential micronutrients but . . . sugar calories may actually increase the body's need for certain vitamins."

A vicious cycle can develop. Vitamin inadequacy often makes us crave sugar. Experiments done with children discovered that those on a properly designed diet chose less candy than those on a deficient diet.

Glucose is an essential body sugar, but it is not essential as a pure substance in food. It is safe in its complex form, bound up in natural food. It is safe when it is slowly released in the body from some form of natural carbohydrate, which also carries the required nutrients for its own metabolism. As *Harvard Medical School Health Newsletter* points out, "blood sugar" can be obtained from almost any source--including fruits and vegetables. We don't need it for so-called quick energy unless we have been on prolonged fasting. Body stores of sugar, glycogen, can be quickly converted into blood sugar to meet any sudden demand.

What sugar we do use should be in its most natural form. Maple syrup, molasses, sorghum and honey are acceptable in moderate amounts. Fructose, while less toxic than glucose or sucrose, is still a simple sugar that is quickly broken down in the body into glucose, requiring insulin from the pancreas. Like other pure sugars it lacks the normal quota of vitamins, minerals and enzymes needed for the body to use it.

Elimination of refined sugar from our diets is not easy because so much is hidden. Prepared foods, including restaurant food, are full of it. What can the traveler do? The best he can do is avoid the obvious sugar-foods, the non-obvious when possible, and avoid all sugar at home by preparing the food without sugar.

Salt

While it is true we need salt, most of us consume up to 20 times as much as we need. This excessive amount of salt in our diets can contribute to kidney and heart disease, high blood pressure, hair loss and skin disorders. It may also help induce hypoglycemia by causing potassium to be lost from the blood, leading to a drop in blood sugar. The blood sugar drop triggers the onset of stress and much potassium is lost into the urine while sodium and water stay in the body. *

Like sugar, a lot of the salt we eat is hidden. Salt is used in food processing to peel, sort and float the food. It is used to prevent discoloration. Because it is so cheap it is used to cover the lack of flavor in food. Sodium nitrates are found in many processed foods where it is used as a preservative to mask odors and inhibit molds and bacteria. Baking

---

*   Dr. Airola recommends countering this by taking potassium chloride tablets which quickly raises the blood sugar level. Anyone prone to blackouts might find this useful, he suggests.

powder, soda and M.S.G. or Accent contain salt. Canning the food decreases the potassium in the food while greatly increasing the sodium. A cup of fresh green beans, cooked without salt, has 12 mg of sodium compared to 2,312 mg. in the canned variety.

Supermarket salt has been so highly processed that it is "pure", devoid of the natural trace minerals it originally contained. The salt crystal has become extremely small. This a thigh molecular bond. This is why it does not dissolve readily when sprinkled over food, and why it leaves us feeling thirsty afterwards. The same amount of natural sea salt will dissolve easily when sprinkled over cooked food and will not leave us thirsty.

Of course all salt is sea salt since inland salt was left from the seas that once covered the earth. Some minerals have been leached out of land salt over the years. In any case it is better not to use salt on food. We can get nearly all we need from restaurant foods. What salt we do add should be a sea salt or granulated kelp, or a mixture of the two. Herbs can substitute for salt by adding flavors rather than saltiness.

Fats

The average American diet is 40% fat--too much by nearly any nutritional standard. We eat the equivalent in fat of more than a cup of shortening each day. Such an excessive amount of fat in the diet has been linked to cardiovascular disease, multiple sclerosis and diabetes. [F]

Experts disagree on how much fat is optimal for us. Orthodox nutritionists recommend that 25 to 30% of our total calories should be fat. Pritikin's Longevity Center place their patients on a 10% fat diet. This latter may be too low.

It is a question of whether we are eating to correct some

body malfunctions of to maintain a healthy body, explains Dr. Paavo Airola, who believes the best level is 20% fat. What we would or would not eat on a therapeutic, healing diet may differ from what we need to maintain a healthy body once that physical problem has been corrected. Once a condition has been remedied, dietary requirements should change to assure full maintainence of health.

Other doctors agree with Dr. Airola, among them Dr. Gary Gordon, President of the American College of Medical Preventics. He believe that the 10% fat intake is too low for many once their blood fat levels have dropped. On a maintenance diet most of us need more fat to fulfill the body's normal dietary needs for essential fatty acids. Otherwise health problems related to an abnormally deficient diet of dietary fat may develop within 6 months to a year. Too little fat can produce exzema and other skin disorders. It can also contribute to a deficiency of the fat-soluble vitamins A and E, which require fat for their utilization in the body.

There is general agreement that we can satisfy our body's need for fat by eating raw fruits, vegetables and grains. At the very least we should try to avoid deep-fat-fried foods and fatty meats.

Cholesterol--Good or Bad?

Many people gave up eating eggs fearing they would cause cholesterol build-up in the body. Today our egg consumption is one-half what it was in 1945, yet we see no comparable decline in heart disease. In a large group of doctors on whom very detailed health records were kept, 50% avoided eggs completely. They maintained dangerously high cholesterol levels. When all were encouraged to eat eggs during the next year cholesterol levels fell. In another study people fed a mono-diet of 18 eggs daily showed a dramatic lowering of blood cholesterol.

Dr. Kurt Donsbach, of the International Institute of Natural Health Science, calls eggs one of the finest foods which will not effect blood cholesterol or blood vessel disease except to lower the cholesterol and make vessels more resistant to disease. The quantity of cholesterol in an egg, says Donsbach, is but a fraction of that manufactured every day by the body. In addition it contains lecithin, which emulsifies cholesterol much as dishwashing detergent emulsifies grease from our dirty food plates.

Many doctors are concluding that there is no general relationship between the cholesterol in the blood and the fatty foods we eat. Dr. Donsbach points out that the studies done associating diet cholesterol with blood cholesterol levels used vegetarian rabbits who have no mechanism for handling cholesterol. When these studies were done on dogs there was no effect noted on blood cholesterol.

Cholesterol is not some terrible enemy lurking around in our bodies waiting for a chance to cause a heart attack or a stroke. It is essential to our health. Found in high concentrations in the liver, intestines, brain, adrenal glands, bile and the protective sheathes around nerve fibers, it is needed by the body to synthesize Vitamin D-3, sex hormones and the steroid hormones used in combating stress.

Cholesterol is so important to the body that the body makes it in the liver and intestines. If we don't eat enough of it the body will manufacture the difference--often in excess of what it needs. Dr. Abram Hoffer, orthomolecular psychiatrist, believes it is foolish and a silly waste of body energy to require the body to metabolize its own cholesterol when we could eat the amount we need and leave that energy for other, more important functions.

Cholesterol in our blood doesn't only come from eating fat. Refined white sugar and white flour can cause our bodies to make cholesterol. Eighty percent of the cholesterol in the blood is synthesized within the body from acetate radicals found in carbohydrates, proteins and fats. Refined carbohydrates furnish large amounts of these acetate radicals. Simple sugars like table sugar, honey and syrup, which consist of one, two or very few molecules, are changed into fats in the body. This increases the levels of triglyceride fats and cholesterol in the blood stream. "Simple carbohydrates raise blood fats," warns Dr. Pritikin, "while complex carbohydrates do not; they make them go down."*

We have come to realize that how much fat we eat is not the only consideration for keeping levels of fat low in the blood stream. These levels also depend on internal metabolism and on other foods we eat as well as on exercise. Fat levels increase where we don't have enough nutrients. A diet rich in sugar must eventually cause such a deficiency, not only of most nutrients but also of fiber. This lack of dietary fiber will elevate blood fats. On the other hand eating whole grains and vegetables and fruits will supply not only nutrients but sufficient fiber. Vitamin C and vitamin B-3 (niacin) help to regulate cholesterol levels.

Rather than eliminate eggs from our breakfast we might fare better eliminating sugar and refined foods from all three meals.

UNSATURATED FATS vs SATURATED FATS

Contrary to popular opinion, unsaturated fats are no bet-

---

*   *Liver Longer Now*

ter than saturated fats, and are possibly worse, warns the Longevity Center. Saturated means that the fat molecule has just about all the hydrogen atoms it can absorb. Unsaturated means there is still room on the molecule for more hydrogen.

In an experiment on young pigs Dr. Fred A. Kummerow, professor of food chemistry at the University of Illinois, found that polyunsaturated fatty acids that were altered during the hydrogenation process, as occurs when corn oil is made into margarine, were more likely to cause fatty degeneration of the arteries than butter, eggs or beef fat. [G]

These polyunsaturates may increase blood pressure, deplete the body of Vitamin E, and cause premature aging. Since they tend to oxidize easily they use up supplies of anti-oxidant Vitamin E. At the same time they create "free radicals", which play havoc with the molecular structure of cells, altering the structure of the cell and oftimes killing them. This free radical activity has been blamed for premature aging.

Polyunsaturates may contribute to cancer and atherosclerosis as well. At a Los Angeles V.A. hospital patients fed a high, polyunsaturated diet developed 60% more cancers than the control group. Monkeys fed a diet heavily laden with peanut oil, and unsaturated fat, developed severe atherosclerosis--a fatty degeneration and thickening of artery walls. [*]

Peanut oil is a low-density lipoprotein. A lipoprotein is a lipid--an organic substance insoluble in water but soluble in alcohol, ether, chloroform and other fat solvents. Lipids are found in the blood stream and carry cholesterol. It is very likely that the real culprit in heart and cardiovascular disease is not the cholesterol itself but rather the type of lipoprotein

---

[*] Reported by Dr. Robert W. Wissler, University of Chicago.

that carries it.

There are two types of lipoproteins: low-density (LDL) and high density (HDL). The low-density kind tends to deposit its cholesterol load on the artery walls while the high-density ones appear to pick up excess cholesterol and carry it to the liver where 95% is excreted from the body.

It's obvious that we want very few low-density lipoproteins and many high-density ones in our bodies. Complex carbohydrate foods provide high-density lipoproteins while refined foods produce low-density lipoproteins. Small amounts of alcohol, losing weight, not smoking, eating fish, and aerobic exercise such as running seem to increase HDL and decrease LDL. [H]

Stress itself can raise the level of fats in our blood. To cope with all this the traveler can eat whole, natural, unprocessed foods, avoid coffee, smoking and heavy drinking, be careful to get enough fiber in his food and maintain sufficient levels of antistress vitamin C, B-3 (niacin) and lecithin. Ginseng may also be helpful. [I]

Our bodies need both saturated and unsaturated fats. The best form of saturated fat is natural butter. Unsaturated oils should be raw, high-quality, unrefined, unheated, unprocessed and fresh; The only two oils that can be truly cold-pressed where no heat is used at all are olive oil and sesame oil. There is no legal definition for describing the method of extracting oil or refining it, which makes labeling misleading. "Cold-pressed" in trade terms means the seeds are heated to 200 degrees Farenheit before they are presed to extract oil.

The blander, less-flavorful oils are probably the most refined, while stronger, heartier, dark-colored oils are probably the least refined. These latter still contain the natural Vitamins A and E, natural lecithin and other food factors put into them by Mother Nature, which gives them their characteristic dark color.

Oils shouldn't be heated, but eaten raw on salads. They should never be used in breads and baked goods. Butter is better for sauteeing or light frying. "A limited amount of butter is preferable to products made from hydrogenated refined vegetable oil,*" warns Dr. E Cheraskin in his book *Psychodietetics*. "Hydrogentated fats encourage a cholesterol problem by disturbing cholesterol metabolism."

A serious problem with fats is their tendency to become rancid. This occurs when they are exposed to heat, light and oxygen. That's why we avoid oils processed with heat, kept unrefrigerated and in clear bottles. The chemical changes occuring with rancidity create a number of decomposition products. These products contribute to liver enlargement, depression of growth, irritation of the digestive tract, diarrhea, cancer and death in laboratory animals. It may also lead to premature aging, as mentioned earlier. When oil "flows more slowly or is getting dark it should be discarded," cautions Dr. Stephen Change, food scientist at Rutgers University. "The same is true if it forms a persistent fine foam during frying."** J

It isn't far-fetched to assume that the deep-fat fried foods so popular in America may be cooked in oils that are becoming, or are rancid. It would be smart to avoid these foods. Oils we use in our own cooking should be stored in dark bottles or metal cans away from light and should be refrigerated. As further protection we can take extra Vitamin E to counter rancidity.

* Margarine is an hydrogenated, refined vegetable oil.

** *Aviation Medical Bulletin*, Feb. 1978

DIETARY FIBER

Dietary fiber, or roughage as Grandmother called it, are those parts of the plant or foodstuffs we eat which our digestive system cannot break down. It can be cellulose, hemicellulose, legnin, or pectin, depending on what plant it occurs in. For instance bran is mostly cellulose while apples and grapes are mostly pectin. (Stringy, tough meat does not contain fiber.)

The lack of fiber in the refined, American diet slows down the time it takes for food to move through our bowels. This is called the bowel transit time. On the other hand a high-fiber diet makes stools bulkier and softer so they pass through the intestines more quickly and easily. In a person living in primitive conditions this may take only 24 to 36 hours but in the average American the bowel transit time is from 48 to 62 hours. With such long transit times bowel tissue is exposed to more toxins and cancer-causing substances produced in the intestines to help break down the food there. [K]

Because many Americans don't get enough of this fiber in their diets many are constipated. Constipation is also one of the side-effects of travel. Stress itself can cause constipation. So can faulty nutrition, lack of enough exercise, dehydration, over-refined foods, vitamin and mineral deficiencies (in particular the B-Complex vitamins, inositol and Vitamin K), liver dysfunction, too much animal protein in the diet which putrifies in the intestines, specific food allergies, habitual failure to answer calls of nature, and habitual use of laxatives.

Taking laxatives introduces a harsh chemical to the colon that irritates the intestinal cells while they get the intestinal "conveyor belt" speeded up again. But they ignore the problem of why the cells are acting to cause constipation. The cause has not been remedied.

In place of chemical laxatives many use bran, the most effective edible form of fiber we can get. One ounce of miller's bran, part of the wheat kernel which is removed to make white flour, is equal to two and a half pounds of salad. Usually 1 tablesoon of bran daily will prevent constipation.

Sometimes all we need to counter constipation is plenty of exercise. If exercise, a high-fiber diet and bran still don't do the job we can add yogurt, licorice tea, soaked prunes and figs, B-Complex vitamins*, the brewers yeast, whey powder and psyllium of flax seeds. L

In his excellent books, *All You Ever Wanted to Know About Fiber* and the *Save Your Life Diet* Dr. David Reuben warns that our modern diet is far too deficient in natural fibers, but adding whole grains with fresh fruits and vegetables to our daily meals will produce natural, regular elimination. Both the F.D.A. and *Aviation Medical Bulletin* recommended this as well, suggesting we increase fiber intake with whole bran breads, cereals and fresh fruits and vegetables.

WHY HAVEN'T YOU HEARD THIS BEFORE?

By now you can see the benefits of eating foods that are natural rather than refined. But why hasn't your doctor told you this? Why do doctors continue to insist that the Average American Diet is nutritious and sufficient in itself for good health?

The answer is that most doctors simply don't know any better. They were trained in crisis medicine. They were taught to counteract symptoms of illness with drugs and

---

* The Longevity Center Uses pantothenic acid (vitamin B-5) especially.

surgery. They were not taught preventive medicine to any degree and they were not taught nutrition at all.

In addition they find it hard to imagine that diet can be so important because the medical schools would certainly have taught them about it if it were. Doctors aren't charlatans. They are interested in patients' well-being. They assume the medical schools are too. * If the schools don't teach nutrition then nutrition must be unrelated to health. It's a sad commentary that "the average physician knows a little more about nutrition than the average secretary--unless the secretary has a weight problem. Then she probably knows more than the average physician."* *

The study of nutrition is in its infancy. There is a lot that is unknown and a lot that is based on speculation-some valid, some not. "Even fitness people don't talk about diet," says Dr. Tim Smith of the Total Health Clinic sportsmedicine center in Oakland, California, "because they don't know much about it."

Another problem is conflict of interest. A study compiled by Dr. Michael Jacobson and Mary Bohm at the Center for Science in the Public Interest concluded "eminent nutritionists have traded their independence for food industry's favors." This conflict of interest is rampant among leading "academic authorities on nutrition--nutrition and food science professors at Harvard, the University of Wisconsin, Iowa and Massachussetts and other prominent universities work hand-in-hand with food and chemcal companies. They sit on the Board of Directors, act as consultants, testify at Congressional Hearings on behalf of industry, receive in-

---

* Medical schools are largely founded by drug and chemcial companies who have a vested interest in medical techniques that require the use of as many of their chemical products as possible.

* * Reported by Dr. Jean Mayer in the *Medical Tribune* (Jane 19, 1970).

dividual research grants, and serve as 'university representatives' on Federal advisory committees."* * *

One such example is Dr. Frederic Stare, head of the Department of Nutrition of Harvard School of Public Health. Also director of Continental Can Company, he has consulted or testified at government hearings for Kellogg, Nabisco, the cereal Institute, the Sugar Association, Carnation Milk, and Pharmaceutical Manufacturers Association, promoting, among other things, sugar. Dr. Stare believes that sugar is not only healthy but that we don't eat enough of it. Such statements are in direct conflict with studies and conclusions issuing from Harvard Medical School.

WHAT ARE WE GOING TO EAT ?

As much as possible we should eat pure, natural whole foods, mostly uncooked. "A good diet," describes L. Jean Bogertin in her classic Nutrition and Physical Fitness, is "based on meat, milk, fish, poultry and eggs, whole grain cereals, legumes and nuts, leafy green vegetables and other vegetables and fruits." While the American Medical Joggers Association does not endorse the use of any specific foods, spokesman Dr. Thomas Bassler advises, "Avoiding highly-refined foods is recommended: sucrose, starches, saturated fats and distilled alcholol. otherwise a normal, well-balanced diet containing fresh fruit, raw vegetables and not too much meat is best."* *

The cardinal rule of Dr. E Cheraskin, well-known for his pioneering work in nutrition and co-author of

---

* *A Report to the Consumer* (Newsletter)

* * *The Complete Book of Running*

Psychodietetics, is "Avoid as much as possible those foods which have been refined or processed and that contain food additives and chemical pollutants. Foods that increase the likelihood of disease should be avoided, including sugar, white flour, hydrogenated fat, food preservatives and the many artificial flavoring and coloring agents."

Airline doctors and aerospace physicians have given the same advice. The recommendations become repetitive. *Crosscheck*, * a Pan American magazine for pilots, suggests they eat no refined carbohydrates, inlcuding sugar and all refined starches. * * Instead they suggest protein-rich meals eaten every 4 hours, especially when on flight duty, with fruit or protein snacks for pick-me-ups at odd duty times. Coffee and soft drinks should be eliminated in favor of low-fat milk or fruit juice.

Simply stated, it's "if many made it, don't eat it", * * * or more to the point, "Eat only those foods that spoil, rot or decay,-- but eat them before they do." * * * *

Knowing what we should eat is one thing. It's quite another to make the change. "Changes in food consumption are extremely slow in coming about," comments Graham T. Molitor, former head of General Mills Washington D.C. office and now in private practice. "It had taken about 50 years, for example, to make the switch from butter to margarine in many families. * * * * * The tragic thing is that the biggest inducement to altering one's diet is the fear that comes after a serious illness, and by that time it is

* May, 1978

* * See footnote page 120

* * * Dr. Abram Hoffer

* * * * Elmer V. McCollum, professor emeritus, John Hopkins University

* * * * * Will it take another 50 years to switch back to butter now that the truth about cholesterol and hydrogenated polyunsaturates is known?

often too late for diet to make much difference."*

I, for one, prefer to make the changes at the risk of being labeled a food faddist by the uninformed rather than risking a serous illness by default.

A WORD ABOUT COFFEE.

We drink a lot of coffee. Two and one half billions of pounds of coffee are consumed yearly in the United States. This high coffee consumption may explain, in part, our high incidence of heart disease. Paul reported in 1962 that frequency of heart disease was positively and significantly related to the amount of coffee consumed in the 2,000 Western Electric employees he studied. Work by Samuel Bellet showed that caffeine increases the free fatty acid levels of the blood, making it easier to cause fibrillations in the hearts of experimental dogs. This increase in fatty acids in the blood stream, which can lead to atherosclerosis, diabetes and heart disease, caused Dr. Pritikin to conclude that "coffee, and in particular the caffeine in coffee, appears to increase the incidence of heart disease."*

Caffeine may be carcinogenic. In studies by Huhlman, the caffeine caused chromatid breakage in human cells, the same as the breakage caused by exposure to radiation. "There is a strong likelihood that caffeine may prove to be one of the most dangerous mutagens in man."**

Caffeine not only masks fatigue but has a direct effect on glucose response curves, making us appear "more diabetic"

*   Are You Eating Right?

**   *Liver Longer Now*

***   *Cancer Research*

after drinking coffee than before. It will also drastically lower blood sugar levels in the hypoglycemic. Dr. E.M. Abrahamson tells of patients whose hypoglycemia was controlled by proper diet but who had violent blood sugar reactions when they took as little as one cup of coffee.

The caffeine in coffee is a powerful drug, acting upon the central nervous system as a stimulant, stimulating all portions of the brain, breathing, and heart muscle. Its effect upon blood pressure is unpredictable. Says Dr. Samuels in the *Well Body Book*, "If you are taking caffeine in any amount you are taking a drug which affects your entire body as potently as many powerful precription drugs, and the effects of it are not under your conscious control."

Coffee is addictive. Dr. E Cheraskin warns that heavy coffee drinkers experience the 3 distinct signs of addiction: intolerance for the drug, withdrawal symptoms when it is removed, and a craving after deprivation. Withdrawal symptoms include headache, irritability, nervousness, restlessness, and inability to work effectively. Drinking a cup of coffee promptly relieves these withdrawal symptoms.

We don't have to drink excessive amounts of coffee to develop anxiety symptoms. One to 3 cups can produce an emotional reaction: even one cup contains 90 million grams of caffeine. At least 25% of Americans over the age of 17 drink 6 or more cups each day. Enough coffee was sold in 1970 to provide the nation with 180 billion doses of caffeine. Caffeine, nicotine, alcohol and other legal drugs, cause more damage to the mind and body than all the psychoactive drugs combined, warns psychiatrist Dr. E. Cheraskin.

Coffee isn't the only source of caffeine. Tea, cola, chocolate, nonprescription headache and cold medicines and over-the-counter stimulants contain caffeine. Instant coffee can have as little as 66 mg per cup while cocoa can have up to 50 mg and cola 15 to 30 mg. Dr. Wiley, one-time head of what is today the FDA, warned about caffeine in cola drinks in his book, *History of a Crime*, "The effect of drinking caffeine on an empty stomach and in a free state is far more dangerous than drinking an equal quantity wrapped up with tannic acid in tea and coffee."

It's not always possible to eat and drink what is best for us, and sometimes we want to "treat" ourselves. If we hope to cope with the stress of jet travel we have to do the best we can as often as we can. This means eating unrefined foods and avoiding drugs as much as possible.

Still the demands on the body from jet stress can be so great that we could not consume the calories of food needed to cope. When that happens we need to consider supplementing the diet with concentrated nutrients.

NOTES FOR THE PROFESSIONAL

A.   Dr. Allan Cott, New York Psychiatrist, believes that improper diet is the major factor in hyperactivity and schizophrenia. Dr. Emmanuel Cheraskin, a pioneer in orthomolecular psychiatry, notes that 10% of all school-age children have emotional difficulties that require psychiatric treatment. These emotional ailments hospitalize as many victims as all other illnesses combined. The prime culprit, according to Dr. Cheraskin, is diet.

B.   These findings came from autopsies of Korean and Vietman war casualties--our fighting men who should be in prime health. Dr. Gary Gordon, founder and president of the American College of Medical Preventics, attributes this high incidence of cardiovascular disease to the high fat, Typical American Diet, which is often 3 times as high in fat as that of poorer countries. This, combined with little physical activity and high environmental pollution, which builds up residues in the body of heavy metals like lead, mercury and cadmium, impairs the cell's ability to deal with the fat that is eaten.

Dr. Richard E. Welch believes that the one million Americans who die every year from cardiovascular diseae do so because of the high-calorie diet with its serious deficiencies, along with lack of consistent exercise and a stressful life.

C.   The usual rules for avoiding heart disease include exercise, relaxation, a low fat diet and no smoking. There is a group of people off the coast of West Africa who, due to their isolation and history, follow these rules. Since no cars are allowed they get lots of exercise, by tradition, few smoke, the diet is not excessive in fat, and for the most part they lead relaxed lives. Yet they suffer from the same pandemic of heart disease as other western countries. Since 1900 their sugar consumption has increased to the English level of 120 pounds per person per year.

Dr. Hoffer also cites studies where 16 to 25% of all cases of peptic ulcers come from hypoglycemia. He suggests that this occurs because sugar inhibits the digestion of protein in the stomach. Sugar and protein together in the stomach produce a rapid acid fermentation, causing putrefaction which produces a variety of ptomaines and leucomaines. To make things worse, with all this bacterial decomposition, the protein cannot be used nutritionally as it should.

D.   *Consumer Reports* lists Heinz tomato ketchup as 29% sugar, Wishbone Russian dressing 30% sugar, Coffeemate is 65.4% sugar, and Ritz crackers 11.8% sugar. The government's *Dietary Goals for Americans* reports that Shake "N Bake is 50.9% sugar, Hamburger Helper is 23% sugar and Skippy Peanut butter 9.2% sugar.

E.   Soft drink consumption doubled between 1960 and 1975. We are drinking 221 16-ounce cans per person every year.

F.   Dr. Roy Swank, professor eneritus at the University of Orgeon Medical School, connects a high fat intake with multiple sclerosis. A recognized expert in M.S. treatment, Dr. Swank highly recommends a very low intake of fat in his book, *The Multiple Sclerosis Diet Book: A Low Fat Diet for the Treatment of M.S. and Stroke.* His research has shown that there is no exception to the rule that areas where M.S. is prevalent are areas of high fat intake and vice versa. His diet is centered around fresh vegetables, fruits, whole grains and whole grain products.

Dr. Pritikin of the well-known Longevity Center in Santa Monica, California points out that diabetes occurs when blood fat levels are too high. It's cure and prevention correspond to a reduction in blood fat levels that come with eating a low fat/high complex-carbohydrate diet.

G.   After eight months the groups fed hydrogenated fat containing 50% altered or "trans" fatty acids had a higher plasma level of lipids (fats) and cholesterol and a much greater incidence of atheromatous lesions in the aorta.

H.   The Framington Heart Study suggests that jogging will decrease the saturated fats while increasing the high-density lipoproteins in the body. The director of this study announced that Harvard alumni tested showed that the ones who don't jog have a 85% higher death rate and heart attack rate than those who do.

Thomas Cureton observed in *The Physiological Effects of Exercise Programs on Adults* (1969) after analyzing 10 studies at the University of Illinois, that exercise reduces cholesterol in the blood when it is vigorous enough, long enough and of an aerobic type.

I.   Dr. A. P. Golikov, Russian scientists, found that eleuthero-ginseng, sold in the United States as Siberian ginseng, reduced cholesterol levels and caused favorable shifts in protein and lipid metabolism.

J.   Dr. Stephen Change, Rutgers University food scientist, conducted a 15-year study on rancidity and found that fats and oils used in frying for a long time underwent changes in composition. The longer and more often they were kept at high heat and exposed to oxygen, the more dangerous they became.

K. In his study of primitives Dr. Denis Burkitt, reknown medical researcher who discovered and after who Burkitt's lymphoma was named, concluded that their rapid bowel transit time provided protection against all types of cancer.

L. Flax seeds have extraordinary nutritional value, containing great amounts of the highest quality essential fatty acids. They are highly mucilaginous and therefore are soothing to the entire intestinal tract, particularly the terminal portion, the colon. Dr. Paavo Airola says flax seeds can prevent and/or remedy constipation.

Chapter Seven

Special Nutrition For Reducing Jet Stress

FOOD ISN'T ENOUGH

Sometimes food isn't adequate for supplying us with all the nutrients we need. When we are flying our bodies face so many challenges that it would be very difficult to consume enough nutritious calories to supply it with everything it needs. Still, if we want to be healthy we must guarantee every cell that it will get the chemicals it needs to grow, repair itself and reproduce. If any single chemical is missing the body will know and won't be able to work as well as it could. Even a mild deficiency can increase our susceptibility to infection and injury, slow down our mental processes and tend to cause depression. Total nutrient sufficiency is very necessary. It is the guiding code of orthomolecular nutrition: each individual taking the optimum level of each nutrient.

Even when we aren't flying we aren't likely to get all the nutrients we need from the food we eat. There are many reasons for this. For one thing the farming techniques and the soils used to grow our foodstuffs often prevent the plants from getting the minerals they need for themselves, let alone for us. Deficient soils prevent the plants from forming amino acids in the proper quantity and quality. Department of Agriculture yearbooks show that our wheat was 30% protein in 1939, but today is only around 8 to 9% protein.

Also, processing destroys a multitude of nutrients by removing all those parts of the food that might decay or not be temptations for bugs. This, of course, means that the very life of the food is removed, as when the germ of our grains is removed, because it is that life-giving part of food where we find the nutrition. What isn't missing because of these factors is often lost through techniques used in the processing and in our home-cooking: peeling, too much heat, and soaking and boiling food in water. These will contribute to the demise of beneficial nutrients. Nobody eats perfect food.

Besides all this, we are daily bombarded with pollutants both in the food and in the air, which the body must try to remove or render harmless. This takes extra nutrition. So does illness, consumption of drugs and medicines, and, needless to say, stress. Under stress our body's requirements increase manyfold. Other factors include life in a big city, lack of nutritional education, and personal laziness.

The result is that many of us must supplement our diets with concentrated nutrients in the form of vitamins, minerals and whole food supplements. As Doctors Ringsdorf and Cheraskin note, "No one can or will eat optimally 100%. Thus, an excess of essential nutrients is desireable as a hedge against malnutrition from primary or secondary dietary deficiencies."* Dr. Samuels, in the *Well Body Book*, writes that if we eat mostly processed foods there is a high probability that we are deficient in vitamins A and E, the B-Complex and protein. Dr. Tim Smith of the

---

* *Psychodietetics*

Total Health Care Clinic in Oakland, California says, "I think people would see, almost immediately, no matter what their diet, an amazing difference if they would just take vitamins."

Supplements won't make up for eating poorly. The science of nutrition and its technology today isn't advanced enough to be able to provide us with all the nutrients the body needs in supplemental form. Many chemical factors are still undiscovered. No chemical nutrient works by itself. They work in clusters and in combination with any number of other chemicals. We don't know all these cluster combinations.

There is still a tremendous amount to learn. That is why whenever possible, physicians prefer to use concentrates from natural food sources like yeast, molasses and wheat germ, kelp or dessiccated glandular tissues, which offer their nutrients in the company of other trace substances that naturally accompany them. These "fellow travelers" seem to vastly increase the effectiveness of essential nutrients.

An Individual Matter.

We also have the problem of biochemical individuality. No one of us needs the same amounts of every chemical and some of us may not be just deficient but may, because of heredity or life situations, be actually vitamin-dependent. These people can't function properly without certain nutrients in such an immense quantity that they could never eat enough food to get them all. Needs also vary according to age, type of work we do and the amount of stress we encounter. Smoking and pregnancy also change our needs.

Dr. Abram Hoffer in his book *Orthomolecular Nutrition* writes that clinical nutrition today must be built around 2 main concepts: the individuality and variability of human beings, and the orchestra-like function of nutrients acting in harmony. We have to be concerned with genetics, the psychosocial environment, and the biophysical environment. This means that requirements for nutrients may vary by a factor of 1000 from person to person and from time to time for the same person.

Many nutritional experts feel that Americans of all classes are suffering from deficiencies of many kinds. Surveys are bearing this out. One shows that approximately 30% of the American population is deficient in calcium. Experts realized in the mid-70's that while the Recommended Daily Allowance (RDA) for zinc is 15mg. most Americans consume only 8 to 11 mg. Their absence results in sepcific disease. They cannot be made by the body.

Minerals are simple, inorganic chemicals like lead, zinc, copper, calcium and potassium. Like vitamins, if they are absent specific deficiency symptoms will appear. They act in concert with vitamins, and any cell deficient in a single nutrient will not be able to perform at its best level. Dr. William Strain describes how minerals work, like vitamins, in clusters "like a giant spider web; if one branch of the web is pulled, the whole web of trace elements becomes distorted."* Because of this it's wise to take slightly more than we seem to need.

How can we ever know just what we need? Unfortunately diagnostic techniques are still not entirely accurate, and there are few practicing doctors who are familiar with the latest advances in nutritional therapy to apply these techniques. There are a variety of tests, including a blood test to determine levels of potassium and zinc, among others, and

* *Zinc and Other Micronutrients*

a hair analysis test to determine other elements present or lacking such as magnesium, a deficiency which is not easily discerned in the blood because as much as half the magnesium stored in the bones may be released into the blood before a decrease in blood serum levels will occur. The doctor can also test with a technique called applied kinesiology. Then he will make determinations from these tests, using the very latest information available in the field. Often he will refer to computerized data. Needs might be based on symptoms. The supplementation program would thus be individually determined.

When there is no professional available to determine just what we need we may have to resort to lesser alternatives. *The Dictionary of Food Supplements* recommends the use of a multiple vitamin-mineral supplement as a base, with the addition of specific nutrients including yeast, wheat germ, molasses, kelp, lecithin and other multiple-nutrient foods. These foods provide all the nutrients the body needs in combinations nature intended.

Dr. Cheraskin advises that one look for nutritional supplement combinations which provides all the essential vitamins and minerals plus many so-called nonessential elements. He warns that many commercial brands use starch or sugar as fillers or coatings, preservatives, and color dyes. These should be avoided especially if we have hidden or known allergy to any of these substances. Oftimes a patient thinks he is allergic to a vitamin when in fact the allergy is to the additive.

Supplements may also contain copper which, while it is needed in the body in very minute quantities, we normally get all we need and often we have too much because of the widespread use of copper water pipes. It's better to avoid a supplement that contains copper. [A]

Natural food stores carry many good brands of food supplements and the personnel of these stores are usually
knowlegeable and will be able to help you understand what
you are looking at and buying. Some companies package
their products in month supplies, providing two individual
packets of supplements per day. These contain not only the
known vitamins and minerals but many of the whole food
concentrates in an attempt to provide these "clusters" of
nutrients that nature would normally provide. These are
very handy for the traveler. However, these may not be sufficient in themselves for the individual who has serious
health problems or who is under the amount of stress
associated with jet travel.

It is always best to find a nutritionally-oriented doctor to
find out what is best for you. The final determination, of
course, of just what and how much one takes is up to that
individual since it is through self-experimentations under
the guidelines of the doctor that will finally tell what optimum requirements are.

WHAT IS THE MARGIN OF SAFETY WITH FOOD SUPPLEMENTS?

What about overdosing? Unlike drugs, vitamins and food
supplements are essential to the body's normal functioning.
They are intended to be in the body, to nourish it, to provide missing nutrients and to sustain health. Drugs aren't intended to do this.

"Regarding vitamins, in general there needs to be comparatively little concern, partly because of the small
amounts involved, "says Dr. Robert J. Williams, discoverer
of pantothenic acid (B-5) and Director of the Clayton Foundation Biochemical Institute at the University of Texas,

where more vitamins and their variants have been discovered than in any other lab in the world. "In many cases they can be ingested at levels 1,000 or more times the ordinary levels with no harm. Each vitamin must be considered, however, as a separate problem."*

A discussion of vitamin toxicity must specify the exact vitamin, the toxic dose and the duration of treatment, advises Dr. Abram Hoffer. Without such specificity generalization about vitamins being toxic are meaningless. Every chemical that is used in quantities larger than the body can dispose of, is toxic. If too much vitamin is present the cells extract what they need and leave the rest in the blood, from which it is readily removed for future use by cells or as waste for elimination.

Huge quantities of vitamins could be dangerous only in the same way that drinking too much water is dangerous. You get rid of what you don't need.

The margin of safety is tremendous according to Doctors Cheraskin and Ringsdorf. The few studies to date which seem to support the idea that vitamins A and D could be potentially toxic used fantastically large quantities to demonstrate an ill effect. "You'd have to sit down and plan your own demise to take a damaging dosage of these nutrients," they report in their book, *Psychodietetics*.

Dr. Williams addressed this vitamin A controversy in testimony before a Subcommittee on Public Health and Environment (U.S. House of Representatives, Oct 1973). "Considerable attention has been paid to vitamin A in this connection because there is evidence that at very high levels of intake it can be harmful. The threat of vitamin A toxicity has been exaggerated. So far a I know there has never been a human death ascribed to the ingestion of vitamin A,

* *Dictionary of Food Supplements*

whereas in the case of a 'safe' drug like aspirin, 200 deaths per year have been ascribed to its use. Vitamin A is a natural organic constituent of our bodies and such substances are not dangerous like drugs which are completely foreign to our bodies."*

A therapeutic index exists to measure toxic doses of substances. If the substance is low on the index it is toxic, but if it is high it is non-toxic. The index shows insulin to be low and therefore a dangerous drug. Vitamins, on the other hand, have more favorable indices than chemical tranquilizers and antidepressants.

Also, the sheer bulk of a substance like vitamins make it relatively safe. No man could swallow 100 grams of vitamin in tablet form without vomiting. There is no record of anyone committing suicide with vitamins.

Dr. Abram Hoffer recommends we use slightly more vitamins than we need to make sure we get all we require. The danger of overdose imbalance is rare when the usual, megadose orthomolecular quantities are used. More often the probem is not enough of the substance rather than too much.

Minerals, however, don't allow for the same spread of safety. Even so it is better to have slightly more than we need since the cell can exclude much of what it can't use and the body can eliminate more. The rule of thumb, says Dr. Hoffer, is that mineral which the body can readily excrete, like zinc, can be considered relatively safe even in quantity.

General guidelines on the amount of mineral nutrient adults need in given in Dr. Hoffer's book, *Orthomolecular Nutrition*. A simpler approach is using a product called Mineral 72, which comes from an ancient inland

* *Dictionary of Food Supplements*

sea bed near Las Vegas, Nevada. It contains 72 different minerals. Better yet are prescribed minerals with dosage based on hair analysis tests and blood tests.

Supplements work best in the body when taken with meals or just before, so that all the essential nutrients are present at the same time in the digestive tract. Vitamin B-6 is best taken before meals and vitamin E and iron should be taken separately, allowing 12 hours in between, if we use synthetic rather than natural forms.

IS NATURAL BETTER THAN SYNTHETIC?

The question of whether to use synthetic or natural vitamins is another present-day controversy. As in so many areas of nutrition there are no sure, lab-tested answers.

Except for whole food supplements like dessiccated liver, raw glandulars and food yeast, there really are no natural supplements. Most so-called natural supplements on the market are primarily synthetic with some natural product added. Since nature doesn't concentrate nutrients,the sheer quantity of natural vitamins we would have to take for megadose levels would be staggering.

Believers in 100% natural vitamins claim they are so effective in that natural state that very low potencies do the same that high-potency synthetics will. Dr. John Diamond, developer of the field of behavioral kinesiology and a psychiatrist, finds the lower-potency, more natural substances more likely to be beneficial than the high-potency, synthetic types.

The problem with synthetic vitamins is that technology still cannot duplicate nature's food assortments in labs and food factories to synthesize a complete, balanced assortment of the 40 or more nutrients that our bodies may need.

Some of these nutrients aren't known. In many cases synthetic products tend to omit these collateral nutrients because we simply don't know what they are.

Obviously this is an area ripe for investigation. Until basic studies are made and specific guidelines formulated it's best to eat a variety of foods, supplemented by whole food supplements and vitamins and minerals made from the most natural substances and containing the fewest fillers, preservatives and colorings.

While we want to take a full spectrum of nutrients, there are some that are more valuable for the traveler than others. We might need greater amounts of these.

VITAMINS

Vitamin A

Vitamin A can help counter the damaging effects of stress. [B]   It seems to prevent the adrenal gland from enlarging, which normally occurs under stress. At the same time the thymus gland shrinks in reponse to stress. This lowers our immunity to disease. Vitamin A can protect us against general infection. Taken in dosages of 28,000 I.U. to 75,000 I.U. per day it has fought off infection and allergic symptoms. It helps maintain the mucous membranes of the mouth and the respiratory system and urinary tract. Resistance to colds is improved with its use.

Vitamin A also detoxifies certain, poisonous chemicals, as discovered by Japanese researchers. This means that it might help counter the effects of ozone exposure, both by detoxifying it and by supplying the membranes of the respiratory system and most especially the lungs with needed nutrients.

Vitamin A deficiency shows itself in dry skin. The flaky, dry skin we often experience in flying may be due not only to dehydration but to a slight lack of enough vitamin A.

We have heard that vitamin A can be toxic. Since it is not excreted every day but stored in the body such toxicity is possible but highly unlikely. Cases of vitamin A toxicity are extremely rare and involve flagrant violation of common sense, like taking up to 500,000 units daily for a month. This possible danger has been highly exaggerated.

Vitamin E

Vitamin E helps to combat stress and to detoxify the body. As an antioxidant it prevents vitamin A from oxidizing and counters oxidation of other fats in the body. It is known to preserve the health of our lungs. It combats air pollution of carbon dioxide and carbon monoxide and ozone, as well as the effects of hypoxia, by allowing us to use more effectively what oxygen we do inhale. This decreases breathing difficulties we might otherwise have, which means less fatigue.

It also seems to reduce blood clots. Dr. Gary Gordon, President of the American College of Medical Preventics, recommends that anyone flying should take a minimum of 800 I.U. (International Units) daily to maintain normal adhesiveness of blood platelets and thus prevent the common problem of a blood clot forming in a vein of the leg during prolonged sitting and during takeoffs.

Since the various tocopherols that make up vitamin E have differing function, a mixed-tocopherol product is often best.

Vitamin B-Complex

All the parts of the B-vitamin complex have not been identified, but it is generally considered an antistress vitamin --sort of a "nerve food". Vitamin B-1 helps in the metabolism of carbohydrates and fats, which is important under stress, expecially for the hypoglycemic and diabetic. Vitamin B-2 decreases the craving for sugar and helps maintain the mucous membranes of the respiratory tract, important where air dryness and ozone gas occur. Vitamin B-3, niacin, will greatly benefit the hypoglycemic and diabetic also. Because of its effect on carbohydrate and sugar metabolism it is often used successfully in drug and alcohol abuse rehabilitation as well as being one of the main substances given for emotional problems like schizophrenia, which is often associated with blood sugar problems. Niacin is also important for the proper functioning of our nervous system. It keeps the gastro-intestinal tract, another target area in the body under stress, working well. Vitamin B-6 is especially helpful to the hypoglycemic. Pantothenic acid, B-5, helps us produce the important adrenal hormones used to combat stress--glucocorticoids and mineral corticoids.

One faction of the B-complex that is controversial in the United States at the present time, while being well-accepted in many other countries, is vitamin B-15, or pangamic acid. This may not be a vitamin at all since it has not been proven an essential dietary requirement whose absence would lead to deficiency disease. But it appears to be a very important nutrient, nonetheless, regardless of its label. It was first isolated by E.T. Krebs, developer of vitamin B-17, the controversial laetrile used in cancer therapy. The Soviets experimented with it on 1000 patients and in animal tests before they introduced it into their pharmacies in the mid-60's. They were so excited about it that one doctor predicted it would become as common as table salt. Unfortunately it will be some time before it will become so common in the United States because it is still relatively expensive. Manufacturers and retailers are constantly battling with government agencies and regulations to keep it on the market.

Since this substance is found in nature where other B-complex vitamins are found, Dr. Krebs named it B-15. Like vitamin E, it will oxygenate body tissues by increasing the supply of oxygen in the blood, as well as influencing how much oxygen the body tissue can absorb. Russian scientists report it is highly effective in improving oxygen metabolism and is supposedly the only substance available that can REVERSE emphysema. It also detoxifies pollutants in the blood that would otherwise consume oxygen. We can see how it could help combat not only hypoxia but fatigue.

Also like vitamin E, vitamin B-15 is an anti-oxidant. It also aids in protein metabolism while at the same time normalizing metabolism of fats and sugar. [C] It is believed to relieve symptoms of cardiovascular conditions, normalize cholesterol levels in the blood, and keep the blood vessels free of other fatty deposits.

Reportedly Russian athletes eat B-15 like candy. It has been rumored that Mohammed Ali uses it. Experiments on swimming rats and human rowers show it causes less build up of lactic acid, which is the cause of muscle fatigue. It provides a second wind by retaining muscle glycogen, thus reserving energy, reports Dr. Richard Passwater. "If I get tired during the day," explains Dr. Robert Atkins in his book *Dr. Atkins Super Energy Diet* "I take 3 B-15's and I'm no longer tired." [D]

Since vitamin B complex is water soluble it is unlikely we could overdose on it. What we don't use is excreted in the urine, leaving the urine a rich yellow. There are different suggestions for how much we'd want to take while we are traveling. E The easiest advice to follow comes from Dr. Tim Smith, head of a sportsmedicine clinic and himself a long-distance runner. "As far as I'm concerned, vitamins B and C are indispensible in stressful times, especially vitamin B. The need for it can increase ten-fold. People just don't understand this.

"I use a "biotest" for dosage. If the urine remains a rich, chrome yellow I have enough. If it isn't, I need more. That way I know I'm ahead of the game.

"The only time I got sick in a stressful time,* I hadn't taken the vitamins. But I have gone through situations where I know I should have had some breakdown, but it hasn't occured, and I credit this to the use of the vitamins." His recommendation is to maintain high levels of vitamins C and B in our bodies at all times.

MINERALS ARE AS IMPORTANT AS VITAMINS

Zinc

Zinc is perhaps one of the most important minerals for us. yet many Americans consume only marginally adequate levels of zinc, at best. F   This may be true because zinc is often lacking in our food because there wasn't enough of it in the growing soil for the plant to absorb and pass on to us. What the raw food does manage to absorb can be destroyed during the processing of food when the fiber is removed, with the remainder being lost into the cooking water.

---

*   Dr. Smith runs double marathons--52 mile races.

It could be that the reason we eat foods so full of salt and sugar is because we've lost our sense of taste and smell due to zinc deficiency. We require the salt and the sugar to make the food "taste like anything".

Besides loss of taste and smell, lack of zinc can cause night blindness, cataracts, canker sores, acne, boils and excessive body odor. If wounds take a long time to heal a zinc deficiency should be considered. What we often call iron deficiency anemia may really be a deficiency of zinc and vitamin B-6 rather than lack of iron.

Zinc can help protect our bodies against pollutants in our environment like lead and cadmium. It speeds up healing in general and stomach ulcers in particular, it improves flexibility of rheumatoid arthritics and reduces swollen prostate glands. It is important for healthy skin, nails and hair. *

Oysters, wheat germ and bran have the highest zinc content. There's lots of zinc in red meats, sea foods and herring. Grains, nuts, seeds and legumes are nearly equally as high as good sources of zinc.

We needn't worry about getting too much zinc. It is very difficult to overdose on zinc. If anything,we probably don't have enough.

Iodine

Iodine is important for the areas of the body that have mucous membranes like the nose and lungs. It plays a critical role in the lymphatic system, which determines our immunity to disease. Both of these are important to the flying traveler.G   It can also relieve certain charley horses or

---

* White spots under the fingernails can be an indication of zinc deficiency.

cramping in the leg muscles.

Kelp is a good source of natural iodine.

Potassium

Cramping of the leg muscle may occur not only from lack of enough iodine but lack of enough potassium. Such cramping is a clear warning of potassium deficiency which can precede a cramp in the heart, setting off a fatal fibrillation of the heart muscle.

Previously we discussed how stress from flying may cause us to lose potassium, with the result that we feel and look bloated because we retain sodium. Diuretics taken to remove this excess fluid further depletes our potassium reserves. Flight personnel, especially, should be aware of this.

We can replenish the potassium lost by eating and drinking fruit, fruit juices and vegetables. Morton's Salt-Substitute can also restore potassium. [H]

Body pollution by "heavy metals"

Some minerals are not easily excreted from the body. They can build up to toxic quantities which are harmful to us. These include lead, mercury, copper and cadmium. Toxic levels of these heavy metals are associated with several physcial problems.

To lower these toxic levels, it isn't always necessary to decrease exposure to the metals. Sometimes we are deficient in one or more of the "good" minerals like potassium, calcium or zinc. When the deficiency is taken care of, so are the toxic levels or heavy metals. For instance, copper levels in the body can be reduced with supplements of zinc, manganese and molybdenum, which decrese the body's ability to absorb copper.

In other cases heavy metals can be eliminated from the body using chelation therapy* and/or the use of other minerals like selenium or whole food supplements. Selenium is an antagonist to mercury poisoning, arsenic, silver, copper and cadmium toxicity.[1]   Brewer's or nutritional yeast, garlic, liver and eggs can reduce these pollutants. Sodium alginate, a natural substance in brown seaweed, is reputed to neutralize lead in foods, air, water the body tissues, while chelating other heavy metals out of the body such as Strontium 90, which occurs from nuclear fallout. In fact ½ teaspoon or 3 to 5 tablets daily of sodium alginate reportedly prevents absorption of Strontium 90.

Calcium is an excellent natural chelating material. It binds itself to metals like lead and carries them out of the body. It has been especially successful combined with Vitamin C and B-complex vitamins. Calcium is found in bone meal and dolomite.[J]

Since the traveler needs to keep his body in the best shape possible, and since traveling itself requires extra nutrients, the person who travels benefits by being aware of these mineral pollutants and how to avoid and/or get rid of them.

WHOLE FOOD SUPPLEMENTS--NATURE'S OWN

Whole food supplements are nature's way of supplementing our foods with concentrated nutrients combined just the right way. Bone meal, dolomite, food or brewer's yeast,

---

* More on chelation therapy in Chapter Nine

kelp, blackstrap molasses, dessicated liver and wheat germ are whole food supplements.

Brewer's yeast or food yeast (also called nutritional yeast) is the dehydrated by-product of the beer-brewing process. It is up to 50% high-quality protein. It is the best source of the B-vitamin complex which is essential for good carbohydrate digestion and utilization. The best antistress food known, it contains vitamins B-1, B-6, B-12 and pantothenic acid. Yeast is an unmatched source of trace minerals selenium, iron, zinc and chromium.*

Yeast contains a substance called the "glucose tolerance factor" which helps the body maintain the delicate balance between low and high blood sugar. With enough chromium in the diet, which yeast provides, the bacteria in the intestines manufacture this G.T.F.[K] "If you suspect you have impaired glucose tolerance like diabetes or hypoglycemia," suggests Dr. Carl Pfeiffer of the Brain Bio Center, "brewer's yeast tablets, 6 each morning and night, are an indispensible supplement to the diet."

This makes yeast an imporant addition to the diet of the traveler who may suffer temporary or permanent hypoglycemia because of the stress of flying and travel.

Bone meal and dolomite, a finely-pulverized, natural limestone, are good sources of magnesium, calcium, potassium and phosphorus, properly balanced with one another. Supplementation could be two 300 mg. tablets morning and night, especially if we use bone meal, and especially if we are hypoglycemic or on a high-protein diet which "pulls" calcium from the body. It may also help us sleep better.

Wheat germ and dessicated liver tissue have anti-fatigue

---

* Chromium is specially involved in sugar metabolism, providing healing factors for the hypogycemic.

nutrients that can't be found anywhere else. These anti-fatigue nutrients are so effective that Drs. Cheraskin and Ringsdorf report when they were added to the diet of animals who are strenuously exercised their endurance was prolonged 300% or more. [L]

Garlic is another anti-fatigue food.* It also fights bacterial infection and detoxifies the body. [M]

Kelp, or seaweed, is a super food loaded with minerals and trace elements and rich in high-quality protein, with a well-balanced potassium-sodium content. It can have more vitamin C than oranges. Vitamins A, B, K, B-12 and D are in kelp as well. Kelp contains essential iodine, and since it is in its natural state is not likely to have any toxic effects on us.

Blackstrap molasses is the residue from sugar processing. It is rich in calcium, iron, potassium and the B-complex vitamins, especially B-1, B-2 and B-3 (niacin).

While they are not nutritional supplements per se, digestive enzymes may be very important to the traveler. Most of us over the age of 30 have lost a substantial amount of the necessary digestive juices in the body to digest fats and proteins adequately and properly. Nearly a third of the American population (some estimates are as high as 75%) don't secrete enough hydrochloric acid to digest their food properly. [N] Eventually this indigestion can lead to malnutrition.

Digestants are available in natural food stores. Usually they contain a combination of papain from papaya, pepsin and hydrochloric aicd. One tablet taken with a meal is usually sufficient.

---

* More on garlic in Chapter Nine.

VITAMIN C: THE CRITICAL ANTISTRESS VITAMIN

I have left the discussion of supplemental vitamin C, or ascorbates, until last, because it is so crucial to our well-being.

Ascorbic acid, the most common form of vitamin C and the one we are most familiar with, comes from a carbohydrate similar to the sugar glucose. It is made from glucose by plants and in the liver of nearly all animals except man, guinea pigs and monkeys. We are unable to make our own ascorbic acid, which leaves us in a chronic state of subclinical scurvy.* Dr. Irwin Stone, world-reknown researcher of ascorbates, warns that every one of us who doesn't take enough supplemental ascorbate suffers from this genetic disease, which he calls hypoascorbemia.○

Hypoascorbemia is relatively symptom-free because what symptoms we experience are usually attributed to the problems that result from not having enough. For example when we have a cold we blame the symptoms on the cold rather than a lack of this nutrient. Hypoascorbemia is diagnosed by clinical or chemical testing or by long-term observation.

How much vitamin C or ascorbate each of us needs is varied and variable. Orthodox medicine has frowned upon the large doses recommended by vitamin C enthusiasts, including scientists researching the ascorbates for the past 50 years. They think of scurvy as a simple dietary disturbance that is corrected with diet alone.

Researchers Irwin Stone and Albert Szent-Gyorgi believe the problem is much more serious than a simple lack of enough ascorbic acid in our foods. They envision each of us

---

* Sublcinical means that the disease or symptoms are beginning but they are not obvious.

with an inherited liver enzymes disease that must be corrected. Correction requires large dosages at therapeutic (healing) levels. They suggest we attempt to duplicate what other animals synthesize routinely in their bodies to meet their needs, just as we would do if we were able.[P]

To duplicate this natural phenomena they recommend we take from 10 to 20 grams (that's 10,000 to 20,000 milligrams) daily, especially when we're under stress of any kind.

Stress increases our need of ascorbates drastically. In general it's better to be safe than sorry. Toxicity is not a problem.[Q]   Dr. Irwin Stone recommends we supersaturate the body with ascorbates to be sure it is reaching all the cells. Flight crews under stress of flying should take ascorbates in amount that will produce "bowel tolerance". A selftest developed by Dr. Robert Cathcart,[R]   it means we take ascorbic acid until we almost have diahrrea, and then we back down a little. This makes the body the indicator of how much it needs at any one time.

The body has numerous uses for ascorbates

Ascorbates speed up the enzyme processes within our bodies which is important for nutrition, digestion and biochemical utilization of fats, proteins and carbohydrates.

They are essential for our nervous system, expecially the brain. They help blood coagulate properly and aid in the metabolism of several amino acids (proteins). They are used to fight mental and medical stress and to combat drug addiction.

Ascorbates can neutralize the harmful effects of poisons that we find in the body, whether organic or inorganic. They neutralize toxins from animals and bacteria and have been used in treating tetanus, botulism and snakebites. [S] They detoxify the body of heavy metals like mercury, arsenic, lead, chromium and gold. They prevent the conversion of nitrites into toxic and cancer-causing nitrosamines in the stomach.

Ascorbates can make drugs work better while minimizing their side effects. [T]   They counter effects of radiation, ozone and carbon monoxide poisoning. [U]   Cadmium poisoning has also been reduced with ascorbates. [V]

Ascorbates given in megadose quantities have killed a wide-spectrum of viruses with no toxic side effects. They also kill bacteria by controlling and maintaining the white blood cells which devour and ingest invading bacteria. That is why ascorbates have been useful in "curing" colds and bladder infections. [W]

Ascorbates are related to the health of our heart and arteries. "There is a definite relationship between vitamin C and heart disease," writes biochemist Richard Passwater in his article "Awesome Ascorbates". Vitamin C is the third most significant major deficiency appearing with heart disease. [*] Within 6 to 12 hours after a heart attack the vitamin C level of the blood drops sharply to levels typical of people suffering from scurvy. The injured heart makes withdrawals of ascorbate from the blood to rebuild and repair its tissues.

Without enough vitamin C certain chemical compounds in the linings of our arteries is lost. This causes roughness and irregularities where cholesterol and other blood fats and minerals lodge, which can build themselves into plaques that block circulation of blood through the arteries. With enough ascorbic acid, especially when it is combined with

---

[*]   The first is vitamin E and the second is the trace element selenium.

calcium, these plaques break down through a chelation process. *

Ascorbates are crucial to the body's ability to make and maintain collagen, a protein-like substance that is the structural cement of the body, holding tissues and organs together and supporting them. * * With insufficient or poor quality collagen in our early or middle years we may find ourselves suffering when we are old from arthritis and joint diseases, broken hips, heart and vascular disease that ends in deathly strokes or a stroke that leaves us senile and incapacitated.

Collagen is also connected with the aging process. Free radicals from oxidation make us age more quickly. Vitamin C helps anti-oxidant vitamins E and B-15 prevent this oxidation of collagen, thus reducing the number of free radicals in our bodies. "Optimum amounts of vitamin C would be important in any attempt to slow the aging process," writes A.L. Tappel, in *Geriatric* (1968).

With enough ascorbic acid in the body we handle carbohydrate foods better. Under stress we tend to become intolerant to carbohydrates, which leads to hypoglycemia or diabetes. We are finding that during low blood sugar attacks ascorbic acid will raise the blood sugar levels, and if used long enough will prevent the attacks of low blood sugar altogether. [X] The diabetic on insulin often finds that he can control his high blood sugar level with less insulin if he uses ascorbic acid as well. [Y]

Ascorbates are important for the health of the eye. Cataracts, the leading cause of blindness in the United

* Results have been seen in clinical medicine rather than research.

* * In people suffering from scurvy this collagen becomes watery and the victim becomes literally "unglued".

States, have been alleviated with much success using 1
gram of ascorbate daily. The second leading cause of blindness is glaucoma, caused by high pressure within the eye
ball which destroys nerve cells. Large doses of ascorbic acid
or sodium ascorbate have reduced this eye pressure.*
Diabetes, the third cause of blindness, can be affected by
the use of ascorbates as we discussed previously.

Ascorbates and Stress

Of special interest to the traveler exposed to jet stress is
the use of ascorbates as an anti-stressor. Under stress we
secrete more hormones from the adrenal glands. This
causes a depletion of of ascorbic acid from the glands.
Ascorbate levels can drop from 500mg/100mg to
300mg/100mg in 30 minutes after we encounter a stressful
situation.

Since we can't produce more vitamin C other tissues in
the body are robbed of their stores of ascorbates to replace
what is lost from the adrenals. When the ascorbate is gone
from those tissues as well the blood has no way of getting
more ascorbate so the adrenals stop producing these essential stress-fighting hormones. Vitamin C is so important as a
anti-stress substance that Dr. Irwin Stone, who has researched ascorbates for the past 50 years, calls it an an-
tistressor rather than a vitamin. [Z]

A personal example of vitamin C combatting stress
comes from Dr. Tim Smith, long-distance runner and head
of a sports-medicine clinic. "The only time I have run a
marathon race of 50 to 60 miles that my legs, knees and
muscles didn't hurt was when I took 1 gram (1,000 mg) of

* More research is needed.

C with a drink every 3 to 4 miles. The next day it was as if I had not run at all. It was like someone had waved a magic wand."

Why is there a controversy over vitamin C?

Why, if ascorbates can do all these important things for us, has orthodox medicine ridiculed its use? Dr. Pauling believes it is because the use of large doses of ascorbate challenges myths that have dominated health science for decades. One myth is that vitamin C is simply a food nutrient, required in minute quantities to prevent scurvy, and that short of scurvy there is no such thing as vitamin C deficiency. Such thinking fails to acknowledge that deficiencies occur in degrees and classifies, by definition, ascorbates as a vitamin, failing to recognize that they are, in fact, essential chemicals needed in very large amounts in the body for optimum health.

This "vitamin mental block" has produced a prejudice in many of the tests using ascorbates for disease. The result is conflicting and inconclusive results. By thinking of ascorbates as a vitamin which is only needed in minute quantities scientists fail to apply the common principle of pharmacology for treatment of illness--adjust the dosage levels to get the effect desired. Therapeutic, healing dosages were not given. Instead very low, vitamin-level amounts were used. Miracles were expected with only trace amount of ascorbate. Even a miracle drug given in trace amounts rather than therapeutic doses would be ineffective.

Explains Dr. Stone, "What is needed is dosage at medication level. No one would expect to relieve kidney colic with a 5-grain aspirin tablet. By the same logic we cannot destroy the virus organism with doses of 10 to 200 milligrams of ascorbate. When we administer sulfa or mold-derived drugs we usually get 48 to 72 hour cures when dosage meets needs. So it is laying no claim to miracle working when we give sufficiently large quantities of ascorbate that can clear up virus infections within a similar time."

Thus far we have discussed using food and food supplements to help us build and maintain a strong, healthy body to combat jet stress.

There is one more critical ingredient for health--exercise. Exercise is so crucial for overall health that well-known nutritionist Dr. Paavo Airola warns that if we had to choose between good food or exercise, exercise must come first for a modicum of health.

NOTES FOR THE PROFESSIONAL TRAVELER

A.   In his book Psychodietetics Dr. Cheraskin explains how to read the labels of food supplements. Other reference books on supplements include *Orthomolecular Nutrition* by Dr. Abram Hoffer and Morton Walker, and *Zinc and Other Micronutrients* by Dr. Carl C. Pfeiffer.

B.   Writing in *Infectious Diseases* (Sept 1975) Dr. Eli Seifter reported on the protective value of vitamin A against general infection. After testing animals injected with pox virus he concluded that vitamin A may be useful for immunizing both man and livestock against viral disease. He believes it counters stress by preventing the adrenal gland from enlarging.

C.   Because of its effect on sugar metabolism, Vitamin B-15 has been used effectively in the treatment of alcoholics. Dr. I.V. Strelchuk of the Central Research Institute of Forensic Psychiatry in Moscow reports that B-15 neutralizes the craving for liquor in alcoholics. After 30 days of pangamate Russian drunks can't stand the sight of vodka. It also protected against cirrhosis of the liver and hangovers.

D.   Therapeutic dosages of B-15 are usually 10 to 150 milligrams (mg) daily for 3 to 4 weeks. As a diet supplement Russians use 50 mg. while Americans typically use up to 150 mg, which is generally 3 tablets.

B-15 is commonly available in health product stores. Some airline company stores carry it.

E.   Dr. Gary Gordon recommends we take at least 250 to 300 mg. of B-5, pantothenic acid, while we are traveling, along with 5 to 10 grams of vitamin C.

An overdose of vitamin B-3, niacin, or niacinamide (which doesn't cause flushing), can make us vomit. Drs. Cherasin and Ringsdorf use this as a dosage test, giving B-3 until the patient vomits, and then backing down by 1 gram. It is very unlikely any of us would use enough B-3 to vomit. These doctors are using it therapeutically in unusually high dosages given under carefully monitored situations for specific healing purposes.

F.   Federal Proceedings (March, 1976) reported that a group of adolescent girls studied showed that they were receiving only ⅓ the RDA of zinc. The Journal of the American Dietetic Association reported a study of school girs and college women who where getting less than ⅔ the RDA. They also reported a study of persons who averaged 69 years of age. They were getting only 2/3 of the RDA, which, remember, is very low to begin with. The Journal of Gerontology (1977) reports that subjects with an average age of 75 were also getting only ⅔ the RDA.

G.   Women are warned that iodine deficiency can produce a situation where she can become infected with that dread, vaginal itch, trichomons, but with enough iodine this infection is impossible. Sticky thick and ordorous secretions in the mouth and vagina can be changed to clear, limpid fluid without odor, at the same time encouraging a high degree of lubrication, when enough iodine is present.

H.   Dr. Pfeiffer suggests that some sudden deaths in runners could be due to insufficiency of potassium' He advises drinking a glass of orange or grape juice before exercising. Dr. Tim Smith of the Total Health Care Center, Oakland, California, concurs with Dr. Pfeiffer. He makes it a habit to consume large quantities of juice before he runs. Pilots and flight attendants might benefit by doing the same during flight.

I.   Selenium is an antioxidant like vitamin E, and helps vitamin E work better. It is found in meat, sea foods, cereal and human milk. Supplements of selenium in addition to what we eat can amount to 50 to 150 micrograms (mcg) a day.

J.   Offical estimates put 30% of Americans at deficiency levels of calcium. Dr. Charles McGee, M.D., recommends calcium supplements of from 1200 to 1500 mg. daily.

K.   Scientists are developing a synthesized form of Glucose Tolerance Factor (GTF) to use in treatment of diabetes and other carbohydrate diseases. It is used along with insulin to maintain the delicate balance between high and low blood sugar. In its pure form G.F.T. is completely nontoxic when given by mouth or intravenously to mice and rats. The F.D.A. is testing its use for humans.

Yeast needs to be complimented with calcium in the form of one calcium tablet of bone meal, calcium lactate, dolomite or calcium magnesium so the high phosphorus content of the yeast is porperly balanced. Powdered calcium lactate can be added to the yeast itself. It is easiest to buy the yeast already balanced with the calcium.

Since yeast is high in protein it is best eaten between meals or on an empty stomach, to be sure there is enough hydrochloric acid in the stomach for complete digestion of the yeast. An alternative is to take a digestive enzyme tablet along with the yeast.

While some love the taste of yeast, many cannot stand it.

Those who love it usually add it to shakes or to fruit juice. It's tastiest added to a cup of hot water and seasoned with Spike, an all-purpose seasoning found in natural food stores. This makes it taste like chicken soup and is palatable to nearly everyone.

In the beginning only ¼ teaspoon at a time should be taken. It interacts with bacteria in the intestines, tending to produce gas. Gradually we can take more. A "flush" sometimes occurs after drinking the yeast, which is normal. It's the niacin, B-3, factor working the way nature intended.

L.   The anti-fatigue nutrient in wheat germ was recently identified as a vegetable called octacosanol.

M.   Recommended dosage while flying is 2 capsules four times a day, with meals and at bedtime.

N.   Symptoms associated with not having enough hydrochloric acid for digestion include a sore mouth, rawness, burning with rawness, burning with dryness, cracks or sores at the corners of the lips, a burning sensation in the stomach, feeling full long after eating (especially meat) and noticeable gas in the stomach.

Most Americans, about 3 out of every 4, suffer from not having enough digestive juices in the stomach rather than too many, including many who think of themselves as ulcer-prone. Symptoms of underacidity and overacidity are the same. When digestants are taken by people who think they are overacid, 75% lose their distress with the first bite of food. Of course, if you are truly hyperacid you wouldn't include digestive enzymes in your health program.

It's been suggested that if we take enough of these digestive enzymes we can reduce the ill effects of so-called "bad-water" when we travel. Dr. Gordon explains that of-times what we are really dealing with is not "bad" food or "bad" water but food and water that have a bacterial population different from what we're used to. Europeans traveling in the United States often feel sick from our food and water as we sometimes do in their coutries. Dr. Gordon recommends 2 or 3 tablets with meals to prevent gastroenteritis. The extra enzymes and extra acid sterilize whatever bacteria are present.

O.   There a five steps involved in converting glucose into ascorbic acid. We lack one of four enzymes, called gulano lactone oxidae (GLO), which we need to complete the fifth and last step of this conversion.

Dr. Stone in his book *The Healing Factor* explains, "Chronic or biochemical scurvy is a disease that practically everyone suffers from and its individual severity depends upon the amount of one's daily intake of ascorbic acid. It is a condition where the normal biochemical processes of the body are not functioning at optimal levels because of the lack of sufficient ascorbic acid."

P.   A goat the size of an adult human normally pro-duces 13,000 mg. (13 grams) of ascorbate a day, and more if it is under stress. A mouse, based on an equivalent 70 kilo man, produces 19.3 grams daily, and this amount is quadrupled under stress.

Yet the RDA for man is only 45 milligrams, 300 to 400 times less than the mouse normally produces. The National Research Council of the National Academy of Sciences recommended monkeys be supplemented with 3,830 mg. (nearly 4 grams) every day. Yet they feel man, as large as he is, needs only 60 milligrams daily.

Q.   Dr. Irwin Stone calls ascorbate the "least toxic substance that we know of." It has been administered intravenously in huge doses without registering any serious side-effect.

R.   Dr. Robert Cathcart has treated nearly 7,000 patients in the past 10 years with intravenous "drips" of ascorbates for colds, flu and viral infections, hepatitus, mononucleosis and pneumonia. Results have been uniformly good with no bad side effects. "It doesn't in itself cure but it helps meet the stress," he explains. "You get well quickly. And as you do you find that you can tolerate less and less ascorbic acid until you go back to a maintenance dosage when you're well."

S.   Dr. Frederick L. Klenner has been using metascorbic therapy clinically for the past 30 years. When he found his two dogs near death from poisoning and a third one already dead he injected 8 grams of ascorbate solution into the two dogs. They recovered quickly. (The solution was a combination ascorbate of potassium, sodium, magnesium and manganese.)

T.   Dr. Libby in Los Angeles uses 60 grams of ascorbate to detoxify heroin addicts with almost immediate success. The addict gets no high and no withdrawal. He simply stops using the drug.

U.   Guinea pigs given an equivalent of 9 grams of ascorbate per day were exposed to carbon monoxide and more than twice the fatal dose of radiation. Those whose bodies were saturated with the ascorbate survived.

In 1958 Mittler reported that a single injection of ascorbic acid into mice before exposing them for three hours to air containing very high levels of ozone at 8 to 25 ppm provided a higher rate of survival than amoung the untreated mice.

V.   Cadmium poisoning is a serious air pollution problem. Two thousand tons are lost into the air every year, with much of it finding its way into the food chain through soil. High cadmium levels are linked to high blood pressure and seem to depress the body's ability to produce antibodies to fight infection and disease.

The National Bulletin (Sept, 1976) reported that Environmental Protection Agency investigators found "ascorbic acid added to the cadmium-containing diet significantly alleviated or prevented almost all aspects of cadmium toxicity."

W.   The virus is the simplest, most primitive form of infecting agent--a sort of transitional substance between living and nonliving matter. As it gains a foothold in the body and becomes active the body produces antibodies against the virus. When this happens in animals the liver begins to manufacture more ascorbic acid. Since man can't do this he must take very large doses of ascorbate--sometimes up to 30 to 50 grams intravenously as soon as possible. Says Dr. Stone, "It kills every virus we ever tried and we have tried every virus in the book."

It has been known for a long time that relatively low levels of ascorbate will inhibit the growth of bacteria. Slightly higher amounts will kill them. It controls and maintains the white blood cells which devour and ingest invading bacteria. The number of white blood cells present is directly related to how much ascorbic acid is in the blood. Ascorbic acid has inactivated diphtheria, tetanus, dysentery, staphylococcus, anaerobic toxins, T.B., typhoid fever, typhus and Rocky

Mountain Spotted Fever.

Dr. Stone treats his colds by taking 2 grams (2,000 mg) of powdered ascorbate dissolved in water when the first symptoms of a cold appear. He repeats this every 20 to 30 minutes until he reaches bowel tolerance. Bowel tolerance levels are maintained until the cold is gone. If the cold has already taken hold before treatment begins it will be milder and won't last as long.

Urinary infections are not uncommon among flight attendants. Dr. Stone advises taking 2 grams of ascorbate every 2 hours. This should continuously bathe the complete genitourinary tract in a fluid that will kill bacteria and viruses while detoxifying and healing any wounds. If an antibiotic or other medicine is used for the infection ascorbic acid makes it work better.

X.   Guinea pigs depleted of ascorbic acid showed an intolerance for glucose. Under stress they were less able to tolerate sugar, in direct proportion to how long they were deprived of ascorbate. This was rapidly reversed when they were given ascorbate.

Y.   Pfleger and School have shown that ascorbic acid can so improve the action of insulin that the diabetic could control his sugar tolerance with a lower level of insulin. A student working with Dr. Linus Pauling substituted ascorbate for insulin and found that 1 gram of ascorbate equaled 2 units of insulin.

Z.   Reviewing the first 20 years of research on ascorbic acid, including over 242 references, Pirani determines that "during protracted stimulation of the adrenal cortex the administration of ascorbic acid is indicated." (Healing Factor)

Chapter Eight

Exercise--A Must For Reducing Jet Stress

When jet stress really has you down the last thing you want to do is exercise. You're just too tired, you feel, to waste energy exercising. You need to save all you have just to cope with life.

I remember trying to ski in my days of flying. Before my skis were on I would have a headache and be sick to my stomach from the altitude. My boots shot darts of pain up my legs when I tried to walk in them. Even the weight of the skis and boots pulling down on my legs while I was riding on the chair lift was painful and exhausting.

That has changed for me and it can for you, too. It must, if you are going to be able to handle the stress of flying.

THE BODY IS MEANT TO BE ACTIVE

Why exercise?

Because it's the logical thing to do.

Biologically we are muscular creatures. We are made for physicial activity. When we succumb to the physically-lazy ease and comfort of modern living, warn Drs. Samuel M. Fox and John L. Boyer, cardiologists and members of the President's Council on Physical Fitness and Sports, we pay a price. Every part of mind and body becomes less efficient.*

Our muscles are elastic, capable of contracting and stretching many times the size of their relaxed length. Such supple, elastic, good-working muscles hold the organs of the body firmly, supporting them and gently massaging them as we move around.

An unused muscle becomes less elastic, less able to stretch. Because they have less blood flowing to them the cells of the muscle are more prone to infection. They take longer to ward off disease or heal. When we increase the exercise a muscle gets, slowly, over a period of several days or weeks we stimulate growth of capillaries in that area. This brings nourishment and energy to those muscles and neighboring organs.

HEALTH AND EXERCISE CAN'T BE SEPARATED

Health and exercise are inseparable mates. "Regular physical activity is associated with a better state of well-being, enhanced quality of living, and apparently reduced morbitiy and mortality from ischemic heart disease," according to the National Workshop on Exercise.**

Exercise can give us more strength, endurance and coordination--important to us all, but especially so to the pilot. It can improve our appearance, posture and mental outlook. It can eliminate chronic tiredness, tension and minor body pains that accompany jet travel.

*   "Physical Activity and Coronary Heart Disease"

**   The Complete Book of Running

Exercise can protect the heart by minimizing the effects of atherosclerosis. It can prevent degenerative disease while reversing those already present. It can reduce the severity of degenerative diseases.

Those who are physically active adapt better to stress. They have less nerve and muscular tension. They don't fatigue so easily. They also age later, tend not to be obese, have lower blood pressure, are stronger and more flexible, and show a greater breathing capacity.

On the other hand lack of exercise can produce disease. Called hypokinetic diseases by doctors Hans Kraus and Wilhelm Raab, directors of cardiovascular research at the University of Vermont, such diseases include coronary heart attack, diabetes and ulcers. Since they are the result of inactivity they are more frequent in the sedentary person. [A]

EXERCISE AND HEART ATTACKS, STROKES, WEIGHT CONTROL, AGING AND TENSION

Heart Attacks and Strokes

I should think anyone under a lot of stress would want to exercise as a preventive against developing heart problems. The second cause of death during the past decade for pilot was cardiovascular disease, with the 45 to 60-year old group leading the statistics. While airline medical directors quote statistics that show that heart attacks are not more prevalent among pilots than among the public in general, the fact that death from heart disease is the number one killer in this nation leaves little to reassure the traveler dependent on that pilot to get him to his destination safely. *

"Lack of exercise is the major cause of coronary heart disease," claims Dr. Raab in the *Physical Fitness Journal.* The right kind of exercise will reduce the risk. While it won't invariably prevent heart attack, it will make its occurence much less likely. If there is an attack it will probably be less severe, and you are more likely to survive. [B]

How does exercise do this? Generally it makes the heart muscle more efficient. The coronary arteries that supply blood, oxygen and nutrients to the heart muscle seem to grow larger, while those that are blocked develop bypasses. Heartbeat slows, more blood is pumped with each contraction of the heart, and the working muscles remove more oxygen from the blood during exercise for use by the heart. [C]

At the same time exercise lowers blood levels of cholesterol and triglycerides which constitute the dangerous plaques in the arteries that doctors believe cause a blockage leading to the heart attack or stroke. It also increases the proportion of desirable high-density lipoproteins (HDL) * * in the blood while decreasing the undesirable low-density lipoproteins (LDL). [D]

"There is no disagreement among (heart and research scientists) that the nation's number one killer, heart disease, could be sharply reduced if the individual followed a sane program of non-smoking, exercise, diet and avoiding stress," states Dr. James Crane, a medical examiner for the FAA and originator of the term "jet lag". He advises a vigorous, constant, daily exercise program. "Perspiration

---

* We are likely to see a change in these statistics as the long-term effects of jet stress finally take their toll on pilots who have been flying jet aircraft for twenty years or more. A major international carrier has recently had one man die in his bathroom of a coronary the day he finished his check-out as a captain and completed 2 medical examinations. He was 39. Another died in a Tokyo lobby during a layover. Still another died during landing into Los Angeles.

* * Lipoproteins were discussed in Chapter Six.

should replace smoke as the odor of the day."

Exercise and Weight Control, Aging and Tension

Jet stress is hard enough on us without adding the extra burden of too many pounds of fat on the body. Exercise can help us reach and maintain our normal weight. Physical inactivity is the single most important reason so many of us in modern, western societies are overweight, declares Dr. Jean Mayer in *Overweight: Causes, Cost and Control.*

The older the body is the more trouble it has handling stress. Many of the physical changes we associate with aging can be arrested and sometimes reversed by exercise.[E] Continued exercise of the cardio-vascular and neuromuscular systems postpones the gradual dimunation of neuromuscular function that we usually experience as we get older. With exercise we keep better simple reaction time, choice reaction times and movement times. Exercise can do a lot to reverse the long-term effects of smoking, drinking and overeating.

Exercise can help to relieve tension that makes us nervous and unable to sleep when we're under stress. Dr. deVries and Gene M. Adams report exercise reduces tension more than the tranquilizer meprobate (Miltown) in dosages of 400 mg. * While leaving no side effects like the drug leaves. According to the President's Council on Physical Fitness, exercise can eliminate chronic tiredness, tension and minor body pains.

ARE YOU PHYSICALLY FIT?

"Physical fitness really implies more than the ability to do

---

* *American Journal of Physical Medicine*

a day's work without running out of gas or surviving the emergency of snow shoveling or grass cutting," explains Richard Keelor, Director of Program Development for the President's Council on Physical Fitness and Sports. "It is also a state of well-being that breeds confidence, poise, posture, physical ability and an exhilarating feeling of buoyance."

It's never too late to become physically fit. Sedentary old people who start training become as fit as long-time athletes. People over 60 derive benefits from exercise so mild that it would have little effect on younger people. Even walking produces measurable results.

As one doctor capsulized it, "Most of us don't wear out, we rust out."*

AEROBIC EXERCISE FOR PHYSICAL FITNESS

The first step is to choose a good exercise program that will build endurance and efficiency of the heart, lungs and muscles. That means forgetting about non-endurance exercise like golf, tennis doubles and softball, volleyball and casual swimming (except for recreation). G   The American Medical Association's Committee on Exercise and Physcial Fitness report that such effortless exercises "do not provide any hidden benefits or values. Their most serious shortcoming is that most of them do little to improve fitness of the heart and lungs, which are most in need of exercise today."*

Exercise that will build physical fitness must be intense and endurance exercise. Such exercises are aerobic, like

---

*   *Complete Book of Running*

running, swimming, cycling, rowing, rope skipping, vigorous skiing and skating, soccer, handball, hockey and basketball (when it requires sustained running.)[H]   These require endurance, thereby benefiting the heart and lungs while strengthening muscles, ligaments and tendons. They also influence cortisol processes associated with stress, improving the body's regulation of anabolism and catabolism.

Which aerobic exercise is best? Dr. Tim Smith of the Total Health Sports Medicine Clinic in Oakland, California says variety is the best. "Run today, bike tomorrow, swim the next day." This would take the stress off the same muscle groups that would be used over and over if we repeat the same exercise. Such overstrengthening of a certain muscle group to the exclusion of others is called overbalancing. When key stress points take a constant beating sports injuries can occur. Varying the exercises can prevent the same muscles from being stressed day after day.

Unfortunately we are creatures of habit and repetition. Usually we find one exercise we prefer over the others and slip into that one. It's difficult to keep variety in an exercise program.

WALKING, JOGGING AND RUNNING

Of all the aerobic exercises Dr. Smith prefers running, which he calls "unequivocably the best". For one thing we can't make excuses for not running. No equipment is needed and it can be done anywhere in any weather for no cost. Cycling requires a bike. Swimming requires a pool and swim suit. Exercises like basketball, handball and hockey require sustained running, but also require sufficient skill before we can develop endurance with them. We also have to take time out to serve the ball. This reduces the sustained quality of the exercise.

In his sports medicine clinic Dr. Smith says no one except the long-distance cycler has scored consistently higher than runners in cardio-vascular output. Cardio-vascular output is determined by how fast after vigorous exercise the heart and pulse return to normal rates and levels.

The most fit are cyclers, runners and swimmers. "when put on an exercise treadmill and monitored with an EKG machine, all the other usual sports like tennis, racquet ball, squash, tai chi, karate, football and soccer don't measure up."

The fault is not with the exercise per se. To be effective any aerobic exercise must be done often enough, hard enough and long enough that the body definitely has to adjust its circulation and respiration. Some of the above exercises are too intermittent to do this satisfactorily.

Vigorous walking can give us the same benefits as running but it must be vigorous, not just strolling. Sedentary men between the ages of 40 and 56 were tested after doing vigorous walking. They showed changes occuring similar to those found with running. Vigorous walking can raise the heart rate as high as running. There is less incidence of leg and orthopedic problems and less discomfort during exercise than running.

Interval jogging offers variety while improving fitness. Here jogging is alternated with vigorous walking during the exercise session. This combination has been incorporated into the rehabilitation program of the Longevity Center at Santa Monica, California. Called "roving", the patient combines walking and running for a distance goal of so many miles (varies with the individual) for 4 to 5 times a week. Distance rather than time is important in this program. There is no strain or competition. Distance is increased when the individual is ready.

Roving is a variation of the interval jogging, but one must remember that it is designed for rehabilitation. Participants are no longer sick, but they are not healthy. For full aerobic results one would have to be sure the walking and running were vigorous enough.

There is no distinction between running and jogging. Some like to consider jogging anything that takes more than 8 minutes to go a mile. But some people have to work hard to go a mile that fast and others can run it easily. Most runners call all running just that--running.

Why does anyone run?

For one thing it's simple. Running can be done anywhere, requires practically no equipment and costs very little. It is one of the healthiest and one of the simplest exercises. It is as competitive or non-competitive as you want to make it.

There are other benefits. "You quit smoking in order to run long distances," says Dr. Ronald M. Lawrence, founder of the American Joggers' Medical Association and fellow of the American College of Sports Medicine. "Your consumption of alcohol drops for the same reason. You simply have more fun when drinking and smoking don't slow you down. Eating habits change because good nutrition is an integral part of aerobic exercise. You sleep better but require less sleep. Your sex life is enhanced. Anxieties decrease and you're better prepared to cope with stress. Work productivity improves."

If running helps relieve anxieties, helps us sleep better and reduces stress we can see the obvious benefits for the traveler. Its relaxing affect can approach what we feel with meditation, with the easy rhythm, repetitive movement and sound of the running in a quiet environment taking us into an altered state of consciousness, inducing alpha brain waves. Says James Fixx, author of *The Complete Book of Running*, "I have been through a transcendental meditation program and for a period of time meditated regularly. Running has much the same effect on me as T.M.' [1]

Fixx also views running as a way to revive a tired body. Stress on one system of the body helps to relax another, he explains. When we are tired, feeling washed out with all energy gone, running will make us feel better. He says, "We'll feel better as soon as we start, and by the end of half and hour we'll feel restored. It's a pleasant discovery."

Besides reducing the stress and tension which could help us sleep better while traveling, running has all the physiological advantages of other aerobic exercise. These advantages are obvious for the traveler, expecially where it counters the effect of hypoxia. The heart pumps more blood with each beat and so beats at a slower rate, still getting a good supply of oxygen into it. Blood pressure goes down. Our ability to use the available oxygen increases. The lungs process oxygen more capably. For a given amount of work the body is more efficient mechanically, using less oxygen per unit of work. This improves our endurance.

"Running," exclaims Dr. George A. Sheehan, cardiologist, runner, a leading spokesman of the running world, "is a physiologically perfect exercise."

Starting the running habit.

The most important move is that first step out the door onto the running path. You aren't likely to enjoy running right away or if you run only occasionally. Many runners don't begin to enjoy the sport until they have been at it for several weeks or even months. To feel profound changes you'll probably need to run 45 minutes to an hour at least 4 days a week, according to Fixx.

If you decide to take up running the first rule is to make it a habit. In the beginning you'll probably miss days, but as time goes on you'll hardly miss one. In the beginning plan not to run too far, but run at least 4 times a week. It is the repeated running that brings improvement.

Fatigue comes from running harder and farther than we can comfortably handle. The rule is: don't strain. We want gradual inprovement.

We can tell if we are going the right speed for us by the "talk test". If we can talk without using long sentences we are doing fine. If we have to stop for a breath after every couple of words then we are running a we are running a little too fast.

Running Style

The Complete Book of Running   gives some simple guidelines on running style. Keep the body straight with head up. Lean slightly forward. Don't exaggerate the arm motion. Run with elbows bent but not held tightly against the chest nor too high. The forearms should be roughly parallel to the ground. Hands should be relaxed and not held in fists. Rather than land on the ball of the foot which could hurt the Achillies tendon, land on the heels and roll forward, pushing off with the toes. The length of stride should be whatever is natural, with hips, knees and ankles relaxed. Try to run in a vertical plane, parallel to the direction of motion. Breathing should be natural with the mouth open wide.

How we run is a very individual thing. Style is as individual as our voice and fingerprints. Find a position that is most natural for you and think of gliding over the ground.

The warm-up

Running is a very uncomplicated exercise but it does require warm-up exercises each time before starting a run. These are primarily stretching and strengthening exercises because running will overdevelop the muscles along the back of the leg and thigh and the lower back, causing them to become short and inflexible. Their antagonists, the muscles on the front of the lower legs, thighs and abdomen will become relatively weak.

Dr. Sheehan suggests 6 exercises to warm-up with: 3 for stretching and 3 for strengthening. Each is done for a minute, alternating 10 seconds of exercise with 10 seconds of rest. For example, to stretch the calf muscles stand flat-footed about three feet from a support like a wall or tree or back of the car. Lean against it with your hands, keeping the knees locked, legs straight and heels on the ground. After 10 seconds relax for 10 seconds, then repeat the routine for 1 minute.

To stretch the upper thigh in the back of the leg called the hamstring, put a straight leg, knee-locked, on a stool or chair or car bumper, keeping the other leg also straight with the knee locked. Lower head to the knee of the extended leg until you can feel the muscle "pull". Do this for 1 minute, alternating 10 seconds of exercise with 10 seconds of rest.

The third stretching exercise is for the lower back as well as the hamstrings. For this lie on the floor, bringing straight legs up over the head, trying to touch the floor with the toes until you feel the "pull". Again alternate 10 seconds of exercise with 10 seconds of rest for a total of 1 minute.

An alternative for these stretching exercises can be found in yoga postures. With any such stretching exercises it's important to move slowly and smoothly, gently coaxing the muscles into stretching.

Strengthening exercises are for the shin muscles, thigh muscles in the front, and the abdomen. For the shin and thigh muscles sit on a table with legs hanging down and a 3 to 5 pound weight hanging on the toes. (An old can of paint is good.) To strengthen the shins flex the foot at the ankle at 6-second intervals. To strengthen the thigh straighten the leg, lock the knee and hold for 6-second intervals.

A sit-up with bent-knees will help strengthen the abdominal muscles. Lie on the floor with knees bent and feet close to the buttocks. Raise the body up to sitting position and lie back down. Do this up to sitting position and lie back down. Do this for up to 20 times, depending on your strength. (*Runner's World,* Dec 1975)

These warm-up exercises are important and can help prevent undue stiffness and fatigue as well as injuries. They also make running more comfortable. Less muscle tightness and leg cramping will occur.

The Cool-down

The cool-down at the end of a running session is as important as the warm-up at the beginning. We can't just stop running, hop into the car or sit by the roadside and relax unless we want sore muscles. Sore muscles occur when we fail to flush out metabolic waste products that build up during exercise.

Continuing to walk or move after running can help

remove these wastes from the muscles by helping to return blood to the heart. Blood in the veins returns to the heart by a squeezing action of the muscles around them which sort of "milk" the veins, shunting the blood to the heart.

After vigorous running the heart will continue to pump additional blood to the leg muscles for a short period of time. When we abruptly stop running this additional blood will pool in the lower part of the body. This can make us dizzy, even to the point of fainting. But walking until the pulse rate and breathing is back to normal will prevent this.

Once breathing and heart rate are normal at least 6 minutes of strengthening-stretching exercises should be done.

What to wear.

You can wear just about anything. One item you don't want to economize on is a good pair of running shoes. Running shoes are specially made for running, with special support to enhance the forward motion of running. Sneakers and basketball shoes are not as sturdy and give poor lateral support.

Choose a shoe that is comfortable for you. Don't just buy one that is on sale if it doesn't feel really good. Running shoes are extremely comfortable and whatever price you pay for a good, comfortable shoe will be worth it to you.

For the rest of the clothing, wear whatever is most comfortable for you. There are running shirts and shorts available that are light-weight and very comfortable. There are sweat-pants and jackets that are comfortable and handy in cold weather. Some people run in regular jeans and T-shirts.

Layering is a good idea, expecially if weather conditions

are unpredictable. Remember that you will get quite warm while running. During cool-down you can get chilled because the perspiration from running· is evaporating. Layering can allow enough flexibility to keep you comfortable most of the time.

In cold weather hats are vital. Up to 80% of body heat is lost through the head. The chest, abdomen and back should also be protected and kept warm. Cotton gloves or mittens are very welcome in cold weather. There are plastic-framed nose-mouth masks that look like surgical masks which contain replaceable foam-like mouthpieces to warm up cold air before it hits the lungs.

Where to run.

Run wherever it's convenient and pleasant for you. Some people prefer to plan runs from where they live or work so they are more likely to take that first step outdoors. Others prefer parks. It's smart to avoid smog, car pollution, traffic and hard surfaces like cement (as a precaution against developing back injuries or knee problems).

Don't trust car drivers. They may not see you because of other traffic, sunlight in their eyes, glare, or because they have been drinking.

RUNNING INJURIES

While running is excellent for cardio-vascular conditioning it may be harmful to some other parts of the body. Whether it is or not, and if it is to what extend it is harmful, is still in debate. If you are out of shape and begin a running program as though you were a teenager or a college athlete you risk injuries. If your back is weak you are more likely to develop back injuries unless you do back-strengthening exercises. If you don't warm up before exercising you risk injury.

Running, per se, doesn't cause back problems, believes orthopedic surgeon Dr. Bruce Robison. When runners experience back injuries it is usually becuase the injury was already there, lying dormant, and running reawakens it. On the other hand, he warns, there are people who simply don't have the body geometry to run. "Then we see knee, lower-leg, foot and ankle, hip, back and neck injuries that are the result of repetitive impact on those areas. However, this can be reduced or avoided with well-designed cushioned hard-surface shoes that have a firm arch support. "It is important to run on a soft surface, and conditioning is very important," warns Dr. Robison. [J]

Dr. Smith suggests that often we confuse concomittants with cause and effect. We are looking at concomittants."

Can running harm the heart? Actually running has been used successfully in cardiac rehabilitation programs. "It's impossible to damage a healthy heart with exercise, no matter how severe," claims Dr. Earnest Jokl of Kentucky, an authority on the physiology of exercise. "Unexpected fatal collapses during exercise do happen, but rarely."[*]

At present there is little scientific evidence to resolve the issue of sports injuries. [K]   The best we can do is avoid such injuries using common sense. If we are in condition, appreciate our limits, build improvement gradually, warm up and cool down, use good running shoes and run on soft surfaces we are less likely to develop injuries. Nutritional supplements of vitamins A, E, C, and B to counter stress, as well as potassium and magnesium to reduce muscle cramps

[*]   *Complete Book of Running*

may help. ** So may vitamin B-15 and the anti-fatigue supplements we mentioned earlier. A variety of aerobic exercises will reduce the amount of repeated stress on the same organs and muscle groups.

Running isn't for everyone. Author James Michener calls it "one of the world's dulliest pastimes." Actor Robert Morley doesn't believe running helps us live any longer. In an interview with Dick Cavatt he quipped, "It's just that running is such a bore that runners don't mind dying younger."

If you agree with these men and running isn't for you, and swimming, the best aerobic exercise of all, isn't feasible on a regular basis, you might consider using a minitrampoline or the Exer-Cor.

USING THE EXER-COR

The Exer-Cor* is the only exercise machine on the market today that allows us to exercise in an horizontal position. Hands rest on foam-cushioned forward pads and knees on rear pads. Arms move forward and back while knees move toward and away from the chest. The head turns from side to side, following the leading hand. This makes the hips rotate in relation to the shoulders and the spine bend gently from right to left.

Since the exercise is done in a horizontal position the stress of gravitational pull on the body is reduced. Normally our body organs hang down and press one upon the other as gravity pulls on them. This is relieved with the Exer-Cor. There is no sudden flexing or twisting. All four limbs are

---

*   "The Jogger's Nutrition Guide" (Let's Live, June 1979)

** Cost is around $250. See Appendix for sources.

guided in perfect, rhythmic, synchronized movement.

All major muscles of the body, including the back, neck, abdomen, thighs, buttocks and other spine supporting muscles are exercised at the same time. It gives us the aerobic benefits of running when we exercise hard enough to elevate the heart rate and sustain deep breathing.

One of only two machines ever endorsed by the world-famous Gonstead Chiropractic Clinic in Mt. Horeb, Wisconsin, it is highly recommended by Dr. Alex Clox of that clinic, "The Exer-Cor is useful to all patients. We recommend it to anyone interested in exercise."

THE MINITRAM ALTERNATIVE TO RUNNING

The "minitram" is a very small trampoline that a person can easily afford. It is lightweight and is small enough to be stored away in a corner or under a bed. There are many brands on the market. They all consist of a mat and frame that sits close to the floor, joined with alternating extension and compression springs to create a flow of energy when you jump upwards and gravity pulls you back down.

Physical fitness expert, Albert E. Carter explains how it works. "As you land, the inertia of your body traveling at 32 feet per second is added to your normal body weight. The combination of both your weight and the deceleration forces you into the mat, stretching the springs. Your cheeks sag. Your muscles tighten against the strain. Your internal organs move against each of their anchors. Every cell wall is stressed by the increased pressure. Every part of your body is exercised--your eyelids, nose, fingertips, toes.

"Your body slows, stops, and changes direction. Not a single cell is exempted from this added pressure of acceleration. Every cell has to change direction; every cell is exercised. Immediately the tension of the springs responds to the combined force of your weight and deceleration. You accelerate into space.

"The earth slows your upward momentum until the gravitational pull equals your upward thrust. At that moment your body becomes weightless. In that moment of weightlessness your muscles relax, your cells expand, and your body is rejuvenated by the unique feeling of floating."*

The minitram exercises 100% of all body tissue simultaneously, including tissue of the arteries, veins and internal organs, which are stretched and compressed in a positive way. It promotes both isotonic and isometric exercise. Isometric exercise occurs when the muslces are held at a fixed length. Isotonic exercise continually raises and lowers a load, alternately shortening and lenghtening the muscles.

Developers of the minitram claim it is 3 times as effective as jogging and greatly exceed and other exercise in value. It is designed to scientifically reduce muscle trauma and shock far below the tolerance levels that are comfortable to the human body during running. This, they feel, prevents the waste of energy and effort that is used in conventional exercise to combat the stress and shock of such exercise. Thus, exercise on the minitram is more effective for the amount of energy expended.

The minitram can be used for aerobic exercise. That means it's proper use can build lung capacity, thus increasing our ability to utilize oxygen. According to physician and author, Dr. H.R. Alsleben, "Even minimum effort and gentle use forces 100% isometric/isotonic exercise. It creates a natural demand for oxygen, our lungs respond and develop to supply it. It allows a saturation of oxygen to the max-

---

* *National Exchange,* Oct 1978.

imum tolerance of the person. Continual use and exposure promotes and sustains fantastic lung capacity and a peak in stamina."

Manufacturers recommend using a minitram* 2 or 3 10-minute periods every day, at your own pace. If you aim for top physical conditioning you would need to begin with 1 to 2 minutes doing 150 steps, counting every other step, per minute. Every 2 days this is increased by 1 minute until you have a 30 to 40 minute training program. Then you increase to 160 to 180 steps per minute.

YOGA--STRETCHING FOR RELAXATION

The yoga we are interested in for exercise is hatha yoga, meaning persistent, discipline activity for control and perfection of the body.

Yoga is a series of postures that we move into slowly. They are designed to alternately contract and stretch different sets of muscles. Between each posture all muscles are relaxed.

This sequence increases the flow of blood and lymphatic fluids to and from the tissues and organs. Such increased circulation ennervates glands, nerves, blood vessels and organs.

At the same time it is very relaxing. This isn't a contradiction. The contracting muscles release tension and blocked energy. Muscles relax. The mind relaxes. Muscle stiffness leaves. You feel more supple, flexible and graceful.

Yoga is a centuries-old exercise form considered a medical tool for preventing illness and healing the body by

---

*   Cost for a minitram runs around $100, depending on the brand. Check the appendix for sources.

millions of people over thousands of years. It is both isometric and isotonic exercise. Except for aerobic benefits it has all the qualities of exercise that experts say good exercise must have: horizontal, semi-horizontal, prone and supine positions; deep breathing; repeated moderate contractions of the muscles; gentle flexings of thighs, back, neck and arms; posture improvement through lying flat, standing straight and stretching tall; and relaxation.

While yoga is not an aerobic exercise it is easy to see how it might be helpful to the traveler whether he has been sitting for long hours on an airplane or doing hard physical labor throughout the flight. The improvement in circulation and release of tension could encourage sleep besides producing an over-all feeling of well-being.

I know a flight attendant for a major airline who faithfully attends yoga classes while she is home. When she returns from flight she rushes to the first available yoga class, off-times risking a speeding ticket in her attempt to get to class on time.

She feels yoga helps her recover more quickly from the flying. She feels less tired after yoga and believes it helps her body readjust to her home time zone. She feels she tolerates flying much better since she began doing yoga.

TAI CHI: "THE ONLY EXERCISE"

Like yoga, Tai Chi is a very old oriental exercise form. Tai Chi is done standing in essentially one spot while continuously and slowly moving the body in what looks like a strange, slow dance. One muscle group is tensed, then relaxed as the opposing group is tensed. It is from this concept of opposites that Tai Chi gets its name, refering to the Chinese concept of Yin and Yang--the opposites of the universe.

Tai Chi is similar to yoga in concept but movement is continual with Tai Chi without the relaxation between postures that is characteristic of yoga.

Andy Wong, Chinese acupuncturist and Tai Chi instructor, calls Tai Chi "the mightiest exercise, the only one". he explains that Tai chi improves circulation so basic for health, through its continuous motion, balance, concentration, effective breathing and agile movements.

When properly done the body shows no jerkiness. Movements are curved and the body remains in esentially the same horizontal plane. Movements from right to left are smooth and continuous so that all the muscle groups are properly and alternately exercised. "This accomplishes the opposite effects of Yin and Yang," explains Mr. Wong.

Like yoga, Tai Chi is not aeorbic. Still it might be a good exercise for the traveler since it requires so little space and no equipment. It could even be done on the airplane, though uninformed passengers might wonder at the strange actions of a pilot or flight attendant doing Tai Chi in the galley area.

Like yoga it may be able to relieve tense msucles, improve circulation, and relax the traveler so he can sleep better and adjust to his new surroundings more quickly.

AEROBIC DANCING: THE DISCO EXERCISE

Like running, aerobic dancing is gaining wide popularity. It is a fairly new exercise that combines aerobic exercises to raise the heart rate and keep it there with calisthenic-type movements. It's done to music.

Clothing consists of tennis shoes, shorts and a T-shirt and support hose. Unfortunately you have to find a class and sign up for a period of time, usually for 3 months. Costs run around $2.50 per session. You also have to be willing to attend regularly-scheduled classes which is not always possible for the professional traveler.

While it isn't an exercise you can do anyplace, anytime, it could still be a good alternative exercise while you are home. It's a well-rounded exercise program that combines many aspects of body conditioning.

And it's fun.

RACQUETBALL: A HYBRID SPORT

Racquetball is a hybrid of handball and tennis. It is a fairly new sport described as hot, intense and infuriating. Anyone, regardless of sex, age and skill level can enjoy it immediately while getting a good workout at the same time.

The game consists of hitting a rubber ball about half the size of a tennis ball onto the front wall, then watching while your opponent hits the ball. Then you try to hit it back to the front wall again before it bounces twice. A good player uses all four walls and the ceiling to return the ball. A point is scored when the opponent fails to return the ball to the front wall before it hits the floor twice.

Courts can be found at colleges or community centers and in private clubs whose dues range from $200 to $1000 annually.

You need a racquet, tennis shoes, shorts and a shirt. In the beginning of its popularity any old clothes were suitable to play in. This is changing and in some places racquetball players are becoming as designer conscious as tennis players.

There have been some injuries reported from racquetball, according to the *Physician and Sports Medicine* magazine.

As reported in *Aviation Medical Bulletin* (May 1979) injuries include getting hit with the ball while you watch the
opponent hit it, running into the wall while trying to make a
shot you should have conceded, getting hit with the racquet
through carelessness or overenthusiasm of your opponent,
and pulling muscles and spraining ankles because you
haven't warmed up properly before competing.

These injuries can be avoided, advise Drs. Clifton Rose
and James Morse who compiled the above list. Exercising
court etiquette, complying with court rules, wearing safety
goggles, learning how to play the game properly, avoiding
variations of the game, playing defensively, and warming-
up and stretching before competing can prevent injuries.

Racquetball can be a very good aerobic exercise. To be a
good aerobic exercise it must be continuously played. It
cannot be a stop-and-go game or the aerobic benefits are
lost.

It also isn't one you can do anytime, anywhere. Like
aerobic dancing racquetball can be a pleasant and effective
alternative and variation in an exercise program.

HOW MUCH EXERCISE?

How much exercise is enough? That depends on what
we want and how much time we are willing to devote to it.
There are no minimums because there are too many
variables like time restrictions, age, obesity and disease.
How hard we work, how often, and for how long are the
keys to how beneficial the exercise will be for us.

To get the benefits of better circulation and respiration
that aerobic exercise can bring we must exercise hard
enough and long enough to get the heart rate up to at least

a 70% intensity level and keep it there. Eighty per cent is better.

The following table from the *Physical Fitness Research Digest* (Jan 1977) shows what the average maximum heart rate is, by age.

% of Maximum Heart Rate	HEART RATE BY AGES					
	10	30	40	50	60	70
60	120	115	110	105	100	95
70	140	135	130	125	120	115
80	155	150	145	140	135	130
90	180	175	170	165	160	155

(If you are age 40, working at 80% of your maximum heart rate your heart beat should be 145 beats per minute durning exercise.)

How long and how often we exercise is equally important. While we are building fitness it's important to "overload", to extend our limits of performance often so we will improve. Once we're on a maintenance program we should exercise at least 3 days a week for 30-minute sessions. Forty-five minutes is even better.

Dr. Time Smith of the Total Health Center in Oakland, California, says, "When people say, 'How much?' what I hear them saying is 'How little can I get by with? What's the least I can do and still be healthy?' What do they mean by being healthy?"

"If we run a mile and a half 4 or 5 times a week, says Smith, running at a moderate pace, we'll stay in decent shape although we won't improve very much. Current thought is that we need 1 hour of aerobic exercise a day, 6 days a week, at 75 to 80% of our maximum heart rate, for 'immunity' from disease," reports Dr. Smith.

In the *Complete Book of Running* James Fixx suggests we do 20 to 30 minutes a day, 4 days a week, for good health. Dr. Hans Kugler outlines a nearly 100% efficient program in his book, *Dr. Kugler's Seven Keys to a Longer Life,* where he states that as a minimum vigorous exercise should be done at least 3 times a week for at least 30 minutes each time. *The Physical Fitness Research Digest* in its Jogging Series says some improvement will come with running only 2 days a week, but 4 days is better for improving working capacity, cardio-vascular fitness and body composition. L

CHECKING YOUR PHYSICAL FITNESS

Before deciding to begin an exercise program, especially one of aerobic exercise, you should consider seeing a doctor to have your physical fitness checked. This is important if you have been sedentary, are over 30, are obese, or suspect or know of any physical, biomechanical or metabolic handicap or disease.

A doctor may give you an EKG while you exercise on a treadmill to test for potential cardio-vascular problems. This exercise EKG, which cost around $100, takes the heart rate up to 90% of its maximum and monitors what happens. Seldom would we encounter stress that would be that great.

While the EKG isn't 100% accurate it is still a valuable test. Dr. Smith warns that the usual resting EKG is worthless, like buying a used car without road-testing it first. The exercise EKG is like the road test.

Another test that could be helpful in determining an exercise program is the thermogram which measures the blood flow and circulation of the body by recording the infra-red emission of heat from the body. Skin temperature is recorded photographically. This noninvasive, painless and harmless test helps in diagnosing the potential of stroke and hardening of the arteries.

A sports medicine clinic* can give pre-exercise physicals, using the results to develop an exercise prescription indicating where you are physically and what you can do to achieve a given state of health. An individualized exercise program can be set up that would give you the proper exercise, times and intensities.

If this is too official for you you may prefer to test your fitness yourself with Dr. Leroy Getchell's self-test. Dr. Getchell directs adult physical fitness classes at Ball State University and is a staff member of the Human Performance Lab, as well as author of *Physical Fitness: A Way of Life*. He feels that if we can walk for a mile or two and not feel discomfort or dizziness, and then alternately jog for 30 seconds and walk a minute and still not have any problem, we are probably okay.

Most people, according to Dr. Getchell, can start out with just a little activity and gradually build themselves up. If there's a problem they will have some indication like chest pains or dizziness. But they shouldn't feel fatigued an hour after a workout. If they do that's a sign that it was probably too vigorous for their condition and that they should modify the next day's workout by easing up.

If there is the slightest doubt he recommends getting an exercise EKG.

Another self-test is the Harvard Step Test. Devised by the

---

* Sports-medicine clinics are located all around the country. For one nearest you write: American Physical Therapy Association, Sports Medicine Section, c/o George J. Davies, 2036 Cowley Hall, Physical Therapy Dept., University of Wisconsin, LaCrosse, Wisconsin 54601

American Medical Association's Committee on Exercise
and Physical Fitness, it is described in detail in the *Complete
Book of Running*. Essentially it involves stepping up and
down on a bench for a few minutes, then checking how
quickly the heart recovers from that effort. While it is not
thorough like an examination would be it may give you an
indication of your level of fitness.

There are no 100% guarantees with any of these tests,
but the more we know the better we can plan our exercise
programs.

Whatever the program and exercise we choose we
should start slowly, maybe simply walking slowly in the
beginning, gradually increasing the pace as conditioning improves. From there we can try vigorous walking, then interval walking-jogging, and finally running. [M]

Some people can run right away. Even so emphasis
should be on endurance rather than speed. Early training is
on distance, no matter how slowly we go. Speed can come
later. Not only running, but other aerobic exercises would
be paced in the same way, beginning slowly, with emphasis
on endurance.

A beginning plan was devised by William Bowerman and
W.E. Harris, cardiologist, in their book, *Jogging, A Physical
Fitness Program for All Ages*. They offer progressive plans
to match adult levels of physical fitness. Plan A is for the
totally sedentary, for those just recovered from illness and
for the obese. Plan B is for the majority of people of all ages
while Plan C is for the 10% who desire to reach and maintain a high-level of fitness. These plans are based on alternate slow-fast paces, jogging at different speeds and
distances interspersed with walking.

Kenneth Cooper, who made "aerobic" a household
word, and his wife outline an exercise plan in their books,
The New Aerobics and *Aerobics for Women*. They offer a

graduated system of exercise adjusted to age and sex, where we are expected to average 30 points per week from several forms of exercise, including walking, running, cycling, swimming, stationary running, handball, basketball and squash, rope-skiping and stair-climbing.

In the near future the services of an organization called the S.M.A.R.T. Clinics should be available. Being developed by Dr. Tom Fahey, physiologist at the Human Performance Laboratories of DeAnza College in Cupertino, California, the system determines physical fitness with computers. The energetics of exercising at different speeds and levels, the information on how the body improves with training and all other known facts are fed into the computer.

The individual is fitness tested, then asked what type of exercise and sport he enjoys. His program is set up on a daily basis, indicating what he should do and for how long and how hard.

Fitness is very specific according to Dr. Fahey. That is why they put together the individual and the sport and the computer devises an exact, day-by-day exercise program, maximizing what the individual is capable of and likes without pushing him too far. This allows a person to improve without injuries or undue stress.

Whatever the exercise program we choose the overriding guideline is "Train, don't strain". Slow improvement is the key. We'll improve just as quickly if we take it fairly easy rather than continually flogging ourselves to go farther and faster before we are ready. We'll also be more likely to stick with the program.

Most importantly, do something, regularly! One can't expect to modify jet stress or any other kind of stress when the body isn't in good condition. Exercise can go a long way towards helping the body cope with stress.

Work is not an excuse not to exercise. Even if you have a

lot of physical exertion on the job it has been proven that physical exertion during leisure hours is more beneficial, and exertion on the job is rarely aerobic.

Nor is lack of time an excuse, though most non-exercising Americans use it as an excuse for not exercising. There is always the minitram, jumping rope, running in place, or the Exer-Cor. Not very exciting perhaps, but neither is not feeling well.

If you really believe you should exercise you will find some form that you will make into a habit and it will devlop a high priority in your lifestyle.

The choice is yours. So are the consequences.

NOTES FOR THE PROFESSIONAL TRAVELER

A.   "Today we are convinced of a correlation between inactivity and disease of the circulatory system," states Dr. Boyer. A moderate level of physical activity throughout life appears to inhibit the degeneration of arteries and veins, characheristic in coronary heart disease.

B.   The least-physically active has twice the chance of having his first heart attack than the one who follows an active exercise program. Between the ages of 40 and 60, sedentary workers have 40% greater fatality from heart attacks than workers doing heavy physical labor. *(Physical Activity and Coronary Heart Disease)*
In a 3-year survey of 110,000 people it was discovered that physically active men had only half the number of heart attacks that the inactive ones had, and in the most active there were only one-eighth the number of deaths. *(Newsletter, Metabology)*

C.   In a study done on dogs where an artificial heart attack was produced by tying off coronary arteries the resulting damage to the heart muscle was overcome by exercise, while rest wasn't able to do that. Many more "back-up" vessels grew to replace those damaged. *(Complete Book of Running)* Note: These bypasses are probably an enlargement of already existing, smaller arteries and capillaries.

D.   A recent Stanford University study showed that long-distance runners have extremely high levels of HDL as compared to the national average. They also have a much lower risk of cardiovascular disease. A new Orleans study of medical students who jogged, cycled and performed calisthenics for 30 to 40 minutes, 4 times weekly showed that after 7 to 10 days HDL levels began to climb. Conclusion was that exercise on a regular basis is very important.

E.   The usual 9 to 15% decline in our ability to do physical work that occurs when we are between 45 and 55 years old has been forestalled by regular cardio-respiratory endurance exercise programs. Those studied maintained a relatively constant body weight, resting heart rate and blood pressure, and had better lung ventilation besides.

F.   In a study group of 90 subjects, divided into one group of 20 to 30-year olds, and another group of 60 to 70-year olds, researchers Spirduso and Clifford showed that the active, older men responded far better than their sedentary counterparts, and even matched the performance of sedentary men 40 years younger.

G.   The American Association of Health, Physical Education and Recreation reported that golf played by sedentary, middle-aged men doesn't improve fitness to any great extent. In a time and motion study on golfers who played an average of 54 holes a week little more than 1/3 of the time was spent walking.

H.   There are both aerobic and anaerobic exercises. Tennis doubles and golf, for instance, would be considered anaerobic since they require short, sudden bursts of activity, using energy from a body sugar called glycogen.
    Aerobic exercise is both continuous and strenuous, so that energy comes not only from glycogen but the breakdown of lactic acid, a by-product of glycogen metabolism. When the glycogen is broken down into energy it leaves a metabolic ash called lactic acid. Oxygen

supplied to this lactic acid "burns" the lactic acid for energy. Since oxygen is required to get this energy the process is called "aerobic", meaning with oxygen. Anaerobic, on the other hand, means without oxygen.

I. Hypnosis expert, author and lecturer Dick Sutphen explains this effect on him. "Once I was past the self-critical phase of my running and was covering 5 to 10 miles without effort I found I was "tripping out" about the second mile. My eyes were open, and I was totally aware of my surroundings, but ideas and creative concepts poured into my consciousness the same way they do when I purposely seek knowledge in hypnosis. I began to run long distances early in the morning and found that I would write in my mind while running, what I would transfer to paper upon my return home." *(Self-Help Update,* Jan/Mar 1979)

J. Dr. Gordon Falknor, a Chicago physician, has discovered what he calls "jogger's ankle". "The symptoms are similar to traumatis and tendonitis of the achilles tendon just above its attachment to the heel bone," he reported to a meeting of the Illinois Podiatry Society. "Tissue of the feet and ankle take a terrific pounding from jogging on concrete and blacktop. This leads to the eventual breakdown of these tissues." *(Complete Book of Running)*

K. To determine just what effect running has on the musculo-skeletal system Dr. Roger Mann, orthopedic surgeon at the University of California, is doing studies on force-stress effect on the various parts of the body and the electrical activity in muscle groups. He hopes to document what the impact is at the time the foot stikes, how this is telegraphed up the body, and what instantaneous effect it has on the muscluo-skeletal system.

L.　In a study of 3 groups where one ran 15 minutes 5 days a week and the other two 30 and 45 minutes respectively, the 15-minute group improved only in running while the 30 and 45-minute groups reduced blood cholesterol and body fat significantly. Changes were in direct proportion to the duration of exercise.

M.　Where we start in an exercise program depends. on our present physical condition. Dr. Getchell suggests that middle-aged beginning runners ease into running by walking until they can continue briskly for an hour without shortness of breath, dizziness, chest pains or extreme fatigue.

Chapter Nine

Additional Help For
The Professional Traveler

We certainly don't have all the answers on how to cope with jet stress, so we have to do the best with what we know today until researchers come up with more definitive solutions. Besides getting and keeping ourselves as physically fit as possible with good food and good exercise, we can consider the following suggestions of various experts from a great variety of fields of health care.

ADRENAL CORTEX EXTRACT (A.C.E.)

A.C.E. is the raw extract of adrenal glands, used when our own adrenals are exhausted from trying to counter too much stress. the raw, glandular extract gives the adrenals a chance to rest and recuperate so they can return to adequate functioning again.

The adrenals are two little endocrine glands that lie just above the kidneys. Each has two parts: the central medulla and the outer cortex. Together they manufacture over 50 different hormones. Under stress so many are produced that they pour over into the urine. Doctors can measure the quantity of these corticosteroids like noradrenalin, adrenalin and aldosterone in the urine to determine how much stress the body is meeting. Needless to say, these are found in large quantities in the urine of persons experiencing flight stress.

The hormones from the adrenal medulla stimulate the sympathetic nervous system. When there is too much stress, too many are produced. The sympathetic system becomes overdominant and overstimulated. The result is that the parasympathetic, which must remain in balance with it, is forced to take a back seat. If the two systems remain out of balance too long, digestion and peristalsis, the contractions that move food through the digestive tract, become impaired. We start having gastric problems like indigestion, ulcers and constipation.

Hormones from the cortex of the adrenals control water balance, metabolism of foods and the amount of salt in the body. When it is overstressed, carbohydrate metabolism becomes impaired and symptoms of hypoglycemia or diabetes appear. It is also likely that the bloating we experience while in flight comes from the stress reaction of the cortex which controls the sodium and water balance. There is a very delicate balance between the sodium outside each cell and potassium inside the cell. Under stress the cortex releases hormones that make us retain sodium. The sodium gets out of balance with the potassium so we tend to retain water and excrete the potassium. This loss of potassium influences muscle activity, expecially of the heart, and can produce a strain on the heart.

Bloating, constipation, stomach disorders and craving for sweets are signs that our bodies are coping with stress. When the stress has been satisfactorily dealt with, or it goes away, the symptoms also go away. But if the stress is continual the entire adrenal gland can become so tired that it can't cope adequately. Both the sympathetic and parasympathetic systems get out of balance and remain out of balance. These symptoms become a chronic condition which doctors call adrenal insufficiency.

Catabolism, as well, can occur if enough of these hormones are produced. In a study of persons on an extended airborn alert, the elevated urea and cortico-steroids found in the urine showed that stress was causing catabolism. The cortisone was breaking down the basic protein of the body. If catabolism continues it causes protein deficiency, leading eventually to stress ulcers, ulcerative colitis, skin disorders and mucous membrane diseases of the sinuses, lungs, stomach and mouth, and intractible edema. An inefficient adrenal gland may also contribute to hypoxia of the central nervous system so that we don't take in and can't use as much oxygen as we would otherwise.

A.C.E. is a natural substances that gives this overworked gland a short rest, allowing it to recuperate so it can rebuild itself and function better on its own. Synthetic adrenal hormones like cortisone, on the other hand, often have serious side-effects, and the body starts to rely on them rather than making its own. A.C.E. doesn't have these drawbacks. It has been available for over 30 years for treating chronic adrenal insufficiency and has no known side effects. It is safe and harmless. [A]

SPECIAL SUPPLEMENTS

Certain vitamins are especially helpful for combating stress, among these vitamins E, C and the B-Complex-- expecially B-6 and B-15. All except vitamin E are water- soluble so what the body doesn't immediately use will be eliminated through the urine.

Potassium and Magnesium

To make up for the potassium which is lost from the body when we are under stress there are mineral combinations of potassium and magnesium. When this additional potassium replaces what the body excretes the sodium in the body tends to balance out, reducing the amount of bloating and water retention we normally suffer with when we are stressed. The potassium acts as a diuretic.

Potassium and magnesium salts are good for the functioning of the heart. They also have a anti-fatiguing effect.[B]

Digestive Enzymes

The afore-mentioned digestive enzyme supplements which contain enzymes from the pancreas as well can reduce the tendency of our blood cells to get sticky, which could lead to clotting. The presence of an overbalance of positive air ions as well as sitting for long periods without moving contribute to this "stickiness".

Inositol

A protein amino aicd, inositol may help us sleep. Dr. Robert Atkins, leading nutritionist, cardiologist and writer, considers inositol an effective "sleeping pill" without the harmful side effects and addictive qualitites of drugs when taken is dosage of 2,000 mg.

L-Tryptophan

Another amino acid called L-tryptophan is being studied for its effect on sleep. As yet researchers don't know how it works but suspect that when the pineal gland makes the hormone, melatonin, this melatonin in turn opens the blood-brain barrier to L-tryptophan. Then then L-tryptophan is used to manufacture serotonin, another hormone involved with sleep.

If it's light when you're trying to get to sleep L-tryptophan may not be all that effective. Since melatonin must be present for the L-tryptophan to work in helping us sleep, and since melatonin production slows down when there is light around us, the light may prevent enough melatonin from beng produced so that the L-tryptophan can't go to where it needs to be to be useful for sleep. c

Since sleep and L-tryptophan are correlated, and meat, cheese and other "heavy" proteins contain quantities of L-tryptophan, it is probably a good idea to avoid eating such foods when you need to be awake and alert-- especially during the dark hours, and especially between eleven at night and 7 in the morning. On the other hand, if you're trying to get to sleep, that age-old advice to drink a glass of warm milk may actually help.

As little as 1 gram of L-tryptophan can clearly improve sleep in some patients, according to Dr. Peter Hauri, Director of the Dartmouth-Hitchcock Sleep Center in Hanover, New Hampshire. He adds that aspirin may help L-tryptophan to work better. Aspirin seems to increase the amount of free L-tryptophan in the blood which can bind to the transport protein to cross the blood-brain barrier. Thus aspirin may directly improve sleep by increasing brain serotonin levels. *

---

* Some pilots have found that using vitamin E with tryptophan makes the tryptophan work even better for them.

Acidophilus tablets

Sickness during traveling adds to the stress of travel while obviously lowering our ability to cope with jet stress. Acidophilus tablets provide live lactobacillus acidophilus bacteria, or "bugs". These intestinal bacteria are very important to our health, but are easily destroyed in our bodies, especially when we take antibiotics. As an added caution and preventative acidophilus tablets may be a good idea.[D]

Superoxide dismutase (S.O.D.)

A cellular enzyme, produced naturally in the blood of mammals and found in all normal mammalian cells, superoxide dismutase is the body's natural weapon against the free radical,[E]   superoxide.* Superoxide derives from many forms of radiation, both natural like the sunlight and artificial like from cobalt, radium and X-rays, including waves from television and microwaves. Superoxide radicals are also produced in our bodies by our own disease-fighting cells called phagocytes because they are very useful in killing bacteria that might cause infections or disease.

These immune cells, the phagocytes, are not harmed by the superoxide radical because they contain goodly amounts of superoxide dismutase (S.O.D.) to protect them. This enzyme speeds up the deactivation, or "dismutation" of the radical into less toxic forms. With fewer superoxide radicals there is less destructive oxidation going on in the body. Oxidation is believed to cause us to age more quickly and to be a contributor to degenerative disease.[F]

**   Superoxide is an oxygen molecule with one rather than two electrons.

Researchers have used S.O.D. to counter depression, to improve memory and alertness, and to protect cells from carcinogens. Some are chewing supplemental S.O.D. while flying, believing it helps them counter jet lag.[*]

DRINKING ENOUGH OF THE RIGHT FLUIDS

To counter the tremendous dehydration to our bodies by the super-dry air inside the airplane we should consume great quantities of liquid--up to 4 quarts on a 15-hour flight. Juices, herb teas and mineral water are good. Hot water with lemon is good. On the other hand caffeine-containing tea, coffee, soft drinks and chocolate are harmful, adding more stress on an already-stressed body. Coffee has a dehydrating effect--for every cup you drink you will lose up to 1½ cups of fluid.

SPECIAL CLOTHING CONSIDERATIONS

Flight attendants stand for long hours while passengers and pilots sit for those long hours. Both can lead to varicose veins. Besides moving around as much as we can we should not wear tight garters, girdles, vests or other restrictive clothing. Girdles, especially, are made for the standing woman.

Sitting tends to press down and tightly constrict the big veins of the legs. This is countered somewhat by support hosiery, which is available to both men and women. Men can find knee-high support stockings in conservative black, navy and beige in department stores and drug stores.

[*] There have been no official studies on the use of S.O.D. for jet lag.

If there should be an accident fire would be an imminent danger. Synthetic clothing tends to melt into the body in the heat of the fire. Natural fiber clothing is preferable. (Ladies, if there is time to do so remove nylon stockings and lingerie before a crash landing.)

USING AGE-PROVEN BOTANICAL MEDICINE

Herbs help us counter some of the stresses of flight. They have been used for thousands of years and until the turn of the 20th Century were the major basis of medicine. Then their popularity decreased, more for religious and political than medical reasons.

Hippocrates, whose work forms the basis of today's medicine, used herbs along with diet and exercise to restore the body to health. He believed that the body has within itself the power to heal. herbs contain many vitamins and minerals so they can feed, regulate and cleanse the body, helping it to heal itself. Because herbs are primarily used to nourish the body rather than to kill germs, small doses are usually sufficient.

Ginseng

Ginseng is considered the king of all the kingly herbs.* The word ginseng comes from Greek meaning "all-healing" and Chinese meaning "man-like", referring to the shape of the root which resembles the body of a man.

Almost totally ignored in Western civilizations, ginseng

---

* Kingly herbs are at the top of the heirarchy of herbs, characterized by being mild in their effect and harmless even in large doses.

has been used for centuries by Oriental civilizations to treat diabetes, tuberculosis and diseases of the heart, kidneys and nervous and circulatory systems. It's been used to prevent tiredness, headaches, exhaustion, amnesia, impotency and the debilitating effects of old age. It has been used to fight insomnia and depression, and to improve concentration. Ginseng has been used traditionally to build our body's resistance to disease, providing the energy, stamina and vitality to fight illness. It is also used to heal an already-ailing body back to health.

Ginseng is an adaptogen because it is non-specific in its action. It adapts to what the body needs, attempting to stabilize it and return it to normal, the establishing homeostasis. This is what gives ginseng its great value--its a single drug which can pick us up when we're tired or sedate us if we're over-excited, it can stabilize blood pressure and blood sugar levels regardless of whether they are too high or too low.

As a stimulant ginseng produces more energy, increases our capacity to work and makes the brain more efficient by stimulating the nervous system. We can work better with fewer mistakes. It helps us overcome tiredness and exhaustion from heavily-taxing chores. But in contrast to other stimulants ginseng doesn't put additional stress on the body nor does it disturb the equilibrium of brain processes, so we don't feel any excitement or "high" when we use it. It is not an excitant. G

On the other hand ginseng is ideally suited for use when we are exhausted from overwork or suffering from insomnia or overindulgence and need a sedative. It reduces the harmful effects of long-term stress while at the same time increasing our resistance to stress by making the body more able to absorb stressors.

Ginseng seems to help protect us against most forms of

stress. Called *"Nature's Answer to Stress"* by Richard Luca *, it increases our resistance to a remarkable variety of stressors. The biochemical changes that accompany stress have been prevented, reliably and distinctly. [H]

Ginseng is also good for combatting chronic, accumulated fatigue, which Dr. Julian Thomas describes as "a persistent physical and mental listlessness, weakness, sleepiness and tiredness at any time of the day from rising to bedtime." * * In such cases our body's cells don't get a chance to recharge because we haven't been able to rest, relax, sleep and eat well, nor eliminate the body's waste product adequately. Finally more energy is used than is restored, the cells grow weak and nervous fatigue sets in, so gradually that we consider our low energy state to be normal. Many researchers have found that ginseng can reverse this fatigue.

One way it does this is by conserving body energy, releasing it more economically and storing more energy-producing compounds in the liver.[I]

Ginseng works gradually and its effects are cumulative. The longer we take it the more longterm benefits we are likely to have. The more we need the herb the more it will help us. It is totally safe even when taken in large doses over a long period of time.* *

Ginseng may be a good herb for the jet traveler since it is useful not only for disease conditions but for healthy people who are overfatigued or who must work in difficult conditions unfavorable to the body.

---

* Eleuthero--Health Herb of Russia

* * Healthful Herb

* * * This has been proven in modern research.

There are many different qualities and types of ginseng so prices vary accordingly. Most Americans and Europeans buy a second-grade ginseng which is Chinese or Korean red or white roots, now commonly cultivated. The wild Manchrian imperial ginseng, the best there is, is never seen outside China. American ginseng is not as potent or valuable as the Asian types, though American ginseng is shipped to Asia.

Because ginseng is expensive and difficult to cultivate, yet so highly-valued in Russia for its great health-giving properties, Russians have discovered a substitute. Called eleuthero ginseng, it is of the same ginseng family, is easily cultivated and not only the root but also the leaves have medicinal qualities of ginseng, plus some extras. [J]

Eleuthero-ginseng can restore lost vigor and vitality, increase energy, strength and endurance, improve vision and hearing, and strengthen the body after illness, surgery or exhaustion due to chronic illness. It acts as a tonic to relieve brain fatigue, making us more mentally alert. It improves the coordination of bodily functions. It can protect against stress and toxins, normalize blood sugar and blood pressure, help functions nervous disorders and reduce high cholesterol levels in the blood. It can improve sleep, restore a sense of well-being and stimulate an interest in life and work. It has even protected against radiation. [K]

Ginseng can be drunk as a tea, the root can be chewed, or it can be taken in capsule or liquid form. [L]

Cayenne

Capsicum, better know as cayenne pepper, is one of the most useful and oldest herbal remedies known. While it is hot on the mouth and tongue it is soothing and healing inside the body.* Herbalists use it to heal colon and stomach ulcers and for hangovers, diabetes, menstrual cramps and kidney ailments. It is the strongest, purest stimulant known. Added to other medicines it makes them work better.

Traveling often brings with it infections. Cayenne can be a useful herb for combatting infection,** especially colds and upper respiratory illness. Equal parts of ginger and cayenne mixed into equal parts of honey and vinegar to a sipping consistency will coat the throat when sipped slowly. It cuts through the phlegm in the throat, healing the infection and preventing the need to cough. It cleans out bronchial tubes and sinus cavities, relieving congestion.

Natural Laxatives

Constipation can be a problem for the frequent traveler. It's important to correct constipation because poor elimination can contribute to disease. Disease bacterias find a pleasant home in the putrefying feces of a colon that can't keep clean. Residues of fecal matter become old and dried, nutrients can't pass through the intestinal walls to nourish the body, and the muscles of the colon can become almost paralyzed, to the point that they are unable to produce the peristaltic action needed to move the wastes out.

Most health authorities attribute constipation to poor diet, lack of exercise and stress. Stress inhibits the parasympathetic system that stimulates the entire digestive tract to work properly. At the same time the stress causes the sympathetic system to remain dominant. The parasympathetic

---

*   Cayenne, once heated, is an irritant to the body.

**   This may be due to its high content of vitamin C.

doesn't get a chance to do its work and constipation results.

We can't remove the stressors of flying. Even eating a high-fiber diet and trying to exercise while traveling may not be enough to prevent constipation. While some travelers resort to drug laxatives, there are better alternatives. Chemical laxatives cause complete evacuation of the bowels, often in an irritating and stressful way. After total evacuation it takes several days for a normal bowel movement. In the meantime people become concerned and take another laxative. The "laxative habit" begins. But the problem of why the cells of the colon are behaving that way is not addressed, and may even be aggravated.

Constipation, regardless of what the advertising media would have us believe, is not a normal condition of the body. It can and should be reversed by simple, natural means. A natural, high-fiber diet, daily exercise, relaxing, and drinking enough fluid can prevent constipation. Vitamin B-5, pantothenic acid, can be helpful if faulty nutrition is a cause of constipation.

Dr. Kurt W. Donsbach, an internationally-recognized authority on the natural approach to health, offers a special concoction he calls the Molecular Sponge Rotorooter to prevent constipation. It consists of ½ cup each of granola and raw miller's bran, 4 tablespoons of whipping cream, 2 tablespoons of full-fat yogurt, and water added for consistency.

Dr. John Christopher, best-known authority on herbs on this continent, suggests we use a combination of herbs called the "lower bowel tonic" or "naturalax". This powdered mixture comes in capsules and not only relieves constipation but detoxifies the liver where pollutants and waste products from our bodies tend to accumulate.[M]

Other herbs that counter constipation are flax seed, Psyllium seed, cascara sagrada, licorice tea and turkey rhubarb. In his book, *How to Get Well,* Dr. Airola recommends flax and psyllium seeds with whey powder, brewer's yeast, B-complex vitamins, yogurt and soaked prunes and figs.

Eye Wash for Dry Eyes

There is an herbal combination available consisting of cayenne and eyebright herb that can soothe and heal the eyes when they become dry and gritty during flight. Premixed as "Eyewash", it is added to distilled water and used to wash out the eyes. It is very inexpensive, safe to use, and very effective.

Garlic: Age-old Medicine for Modern Problems

While most Americans think of garlic as a seasoning for bread and Italian food, it has been used as a powerful herbal medicine for over 5000 years. The ancients believed it possessed great resources for physical strength and energy, and they seemed to have been correct.

Garlic contains a high quantity of vitamins and minerals, especially vitamins A and C and a special kind of B-1 called allithiamine*. It contains lots of magnesium, copper, iron, zinc, calcium, aluminum, chlorine and germanium.[N]   It is the best known source of selenium,[O]   an antioxidant that works like vitamin E by inhibiting free radicals** associated with aging, degenerative disease and

---

*   Indentified and named by Dr. Satosi Kitahara, medical science director of research for the Wakunaga Pharmaceutical Company of Japan.

**   See footnote E

atherosclerosis.*   Garlic is one of the best vegetable sources of organic sulfur, having 33 sulfur-containing products.

Garlic emits a peculiar type of ultra-violet radiation called mitogenetic radiations, or Gurwitch rays after their discoverer, Russian electrobiologist Professor Gurwitch. These rays stimulate cell growth and activity and rejuvenate all body functions.

Garlic is a natural bactericide. The sulfides and disulfides in garlic oil, especially the amino acid alliin, unite with the virulent forms of micro-organisms to inactivate them. [P]

These same sulfur-containing compounds help regulate sugar levels. This makes garlic useful to both the hypoglycemic and the diabetic.

Garlic is proving useful in heart and vascular disease. Large enough amounts have lowered high blood pressure by dilating blood vessels. It seems to contain anticoagulant factors. Garlic oils have reduced both cholesterol and triglyceride levels in human blood when given on a long-term, daily basis. [Q]

Garlic can relieve stubborn cases of chronic constipation if it is eaten regularly. In addition it has a calming effect on the stomach and intestines by delaying excessive motor activity in this area as occurs when the body is under stress.

Garlic can be used to fight off the effects of ozone toxicity. It has a special affinity for the respiratory tract, helping secretions in the bronchia. This quality lead Japanese researchers, under the direction of Dr. Katahara, to test its use to combat the heavy air pollution, especially ozone, that Japan struggles with. Results proved that garlic detoxifies ozone because of the sulfides in it. While clinical studies aren't complete, they are encouraging airline personnel suf

---

* The second most significant major deficiency in heart disease is selenium.

fering from headache, breathing difficulties and pains during transpacific flights to use garlic.

Because garlic can detoxify, removing poisonous waste products and chemicals in the body, it can be useful for countering fatigue. Without these waste products and unwanted chemicals in the cells the mitachondria of the cells are more able to carry oxygen into the cell and remove cellular wastes from it. This improves production of ATP, resulting in more energy.

Garlic is available in natural food stores in capsule form. [R]

BEE POLLEN: ENERGY AND ENDURANCE FOOD

While not an herb, bee pollen has been used for centuries as medicine and food. Spurred by its use by athletes, modern scientists are studying its effectiveness.

Pollen is collected from the reproductive spore of flowering plants by the female working bee while she is looking for nectar. With enzymes from her saliva she forms the pollen into tiny granules with a hard shell which protects the pollen grain and perserves its potency. It is stored in sacs attached to the knees of her hind leg. As she enters the hive, a trap set by the beekeeper brushes the pollen pellets from these sacs. This is collected, dried and stored by the beekeeper.

Bee pollen contains all the same substances that make up the human body. It has all 22 amino acids and is up to 36% protein, having more by weight than any other animal protein source. It contains perfect, natural blends of all water-soluble vitamins, essential sugars, minerals salts, enzymes, and 59 trace minerals in a highly digestable, organic form. In essence, pollen contains all the food we need for optimum health, endurance and performance.[S]

Russian and East European athletes use bee pollen to increase their energy and endurance, as does United States Olympic gold medalist, Steve Reddick. Known as "the world's fastest human," Reddick feels the bee pollen makes the body shift into a more powerful gear, with muscles responding faster and lasting lasting longer before tiring. Rather than giving just temporary energy it improves the body's metabolism.

Reddick's enthusiasm was passed onto Olympic coach, Alex Woodly,[T] who began studying the use of bee pollen on his athletes. "We have seen an increase of strength and endurance of up to 25%, and generally a better attitude."[*] Fatigue decreased because there was less buildup of lactic acid. Pulse rate went down so the heart and lungs didn't have to work so hard. Overall, the cardiovascular, respiratory, muscular and nervous systems improved.

This makes bee pollen a good anti-stress food. Clinical tests have proven that the body becomes stronger and more able to fight stress so that resistance to stress increases significantly.[U] Constipation is less a problem and we are able to get more natural sleep. Bee pollen acts as a digestive as well, self-digesting while helping us digest other foods.

Bee pollen has another benefit for the traveler. Besides reducing fatigue and stress it can help fight infections. It contains an active antibiotic factor which destroys bacteria on contact.

Bee pollen is selected for its quality and flavor. Taste and color vaires as it does with honey, according to the flowers it comes from. Meticulous handling is needed to produce high-quality bee pollen, which means that the better pollen

* *Let's Live Magazine* June, 1979.

is likely to cost more. It is available in granules or in capsules.ᵛ

It is a natural product, easily tolerated by the body, compatible with any other therapies, easy to ingest, and suitable for all ages. No ill side-effects have been found. Few medications are as nontoxic.

RESTORING THE BODY ENERGY, RHYTHMS AND HOMEOSTASIS

Acupuncture, Acupressure and Shiatsu

For centuries millions of people have believed that the Life Energy of the body flows through 12 pathways called meridians. These pathways are paired and each one relates to a specific body organ from which the meridian is named. If for some reason that energy is blocked the associated organ or tissues may suffer.

Acupuncture, acupressure, shiatsu and electrostimulation attempt to prevent or clean such blockages by increasing circulation to the organs, removing toxic waste products and generally assuring a strong, healthy flow of energy along the meridians.

Acupuncture is the most precise of these techniques. Needles placed in specific points along the meridians balance the energy flow in the associated organ and muscle. The needles may be rotated, twisted in, vibrated or moved up and down. Tiny, pin-like needles are inserted with electroacupuncture, also called "transcutaneous electric nerve stimulation." The procedure is generally painless.

The general effect of acupuncture is to improve and normalize the workings of the endocrine and autonomic nervous system. The result is that internal organ pain ceases, functioning of internal organs, appetite and bowel movements normalize, sound sleep becomes possible, blood pressure normalizes, normal sex drive is restored and there is new, over-all body vigor.

Western medicine is beginning to study acupuncture scientifically and seriously. The Sixth World Congress of Psychiatry (Honolulu, 1977) reported that acupuncture points have been found to exist as small areas of altered skin electrical potential, measurable in millivolts. Needles placed in these points caused physiological changes. When stimulated by a pulsating, direct electrical current, these changes were even greater.

This latter technique is called electroacupuncture, used in the U.S. since the late 1960's by some neurosurgeons for treatment of chronic pain. It has reduced cold-pressor pain as effectively as 10 milligrams of morphine sulfate given intramuscularly in an experimental situation. Scientists have found that naturally-occurring substances called endophins, released in the body from acupuncture stimulation are similar to morphine.

No one knows just how acupuncture works. Dr. Philip M Toyama of the Stress Therapy Clinic, Greensboro, North Carolina, believes that the thalamus is involved. [W]

Toyama theorizes that messages are sent from the points of needle insertion to the thalamus in the brain by way of the endocrine and the automatic nervous systems (ANS). The ANS, reacting directly to the needle, sends normal neural messages to the thalamus. At the same time the needle causes the body to release chemically-active substances that move through humoral or endocrine routes to the thalamus. The thalamus regulates both ANS function and endocrine function. As acupuncture messages reach the thalamus it causes a series of chain reactions which influence the ANS, hypothalamus, pituitary and adrenal glands. This gives the body the optimum chance to adapt to the problems occurring. Internal organs operate at maximum efficiency.

Under stress the body naturally increases its ability to counter stress. The adrenal glands make stress-producing hormones, especially glucocorticoids, to replace used-up stores of carbohydrates and to protect our cells against injury that may result when the body responds to stress. Acupuncture stimulates these natural body defense mechanisms so they produce large quantities of ACTH*, cortisone and other like substances to combat stress. In short, acupuncture helps the body raise its level of resistance to stress.

Besides helping the traveler counter stress, acupuncture can stengthen the immune system, which is weakened whenever we encounter stress.x   It can also relax us, which may help us sleep. After acupuncture most people have a strong feeling of relaxation and well-being because the body's homeostasis, or normal balance, is restored by the antistress hormones produced in the body with acupuncture stimulation.

What else acupuncture can do for the traveler is speculative. Perhaps stimulation of the pineal gland would speed reestablishment of sleep patterns. Appropriate stimulation may rebalance the two cerebral hemispheres of the brain, strengthening the entire body while helping us rephase basic body rhythms disrupted with travel. Specific stimulation to the thymus, the gland most reponsive to stress, might strenghten that gland. Likewise for the adrenal glands. This would be interesting research.

Acupressure works by the same principle meridians are stimulated with the hands and fingers. Because these sur-

---

* Adrenocorticotropic hormone similar to corisol.

faces are broader and less fine than a needle point acupressure isn't so precise as acupuncture, but it can be very effective.

Shiatsu is the Japanese version of acupressure. Acupressure is gaining public attention through an organization called Touch for Health. Classes and books are available on this subject, which is simply a new version of a very old technique.[Y]

Reflexology

Reflexology works much like acupuncture, sending energy flowing along body meridians. Here the trigger points are on the bottoms of the feet and around the ankles. These reflex points correspond to specific parts of the body. For example, where the toe joins the foot-proper there is a reflex point for the shoulders. The back of the neck is represented at the lower part of the big toe. The adrenal gland is right in the center and just below the ball of the foot. Massaging these areas should increase circulation to, and relax the shoulders and neck, while stimulating the adrenals to work better.

You can do reflexology on yourself. Massage is done in a circular motion with the finger tips or the eraser end of a pencil. There are "roller bars" of wood available in some natural food stores and at some wholistic health centers that you put under one foot at a time and roll the foot over it, while applying some body weight. Sandals are for sale which have numerous small rubber points of varying heights, like a rubber bed of nails, that you can wear around home of the hotel room. They are supposed to produce the desired reflex actions when you walk.

Does it work? Reflexology has worked for me when I've

taken the time to massage enough or have gone to a professional. I own a pair of sandals but there is no way for me to know if they help. They do feel good after a long day on my feet, though, and if I were still working as a flight attendant I would have the roller bar also, to help my feet recover from the hours of walking. Any reflexology benefits would be in addition.

Keeping positive body energy.

Whatever weakens the positive energy flow in the body weakens us and our ability to respond to stress. Oriental medicine believes that when metal crosses over the governing large vessel that runs through the middle of the body energy flow is reversed, preventing positive energy flow along body meridians. This causes an imbalance between the two cerebral hemispheres of the brain. Known as "switching", this decreses energy flow throughout the body.

Such things as metal-framed eye glasses, dental bridges and the like tend to weaken us since meridians are more concentrated in the head and neck regions. Necklaces are an exception since they make a full circle. At the waist the meridians are more widely separated so belt buckles would not have as much negative effect as the eyeglasses. Dr. Yiwen Tang, former FAA examining physician, explains that this is why Chinese women prefer to wear pearls and jade rather than gold.

Applied and behavioral kinesiology

Like acupuncture and acupressure, both Applied and Behavioral Kinesiology are based on the concept of body energy flowing along meridians. The concept of Applied Kinesiology was developed by Dr. George Goodheart, who found that there was a direct relationship between muscles and their meridians. A weak muscle, he found, was an indication that the organ associated with that muscle by meridian channels was also weak. Testing the muscle strength would determine the condition of the organ.

Dr. John Diamond, psychiatrist, took this basic concept, then studied how our emotional attitudes, physical environment, social relationships, food, posture and stress affect the relative strength or weakness of the muscle, which in turn reflects the health of the organs and the body as a whole. He found that negative thoughts, gestures and words can deplete body energy. Poor posture, certain foods and chemicals, synthetic clothes, some symbols, a frown, some rock music and noise above 80 dBA can weaken us, while sitting or standing straight and tall, waltz-like music, positive thoughts and images, a smile, arms held outward in welcome, a positive shake of the head, a landscape painting, rhythmic poetry, and the natural sounds of birds singing, a cat purring or a brook babbling, can revitalize the body, increasing its strength and the energy flowing within it. He combined this knowledge with the newest developments in preventive medicine, psychiatry, dentistry, nutrition, and homeopathy, added lifestyle retraining and stress reduction techniques, and called the whole Behavioral Kinesiology.

We want to keep our two cerebral hemispheres of our brain in balance. This centers the energy or the body, making us invulnerable to stress. When we don't manage this, when we aren't "centered", when the normal symmetry of these hemispheres breaks down, "switching' occurs and one half becomes dominant.

The major and first gland to be affected by stress, which

causes us to "switch", is the thymus gland, until recently believed to be of no use in the adult human. It is the major, controlling factor of our body health and energy, monitoring and regulating the energy flow throughout the meridian system. The word itself derives from Greek denoting life force, soul, and feeling or sensibility. In more ancient languages it referred to breath, spirit, the breath-soul, upon which man's energy and courage depended.

The thymus gland is also responsible for manufacturing and activating the T-cells, lymphocytes (white blood cells) crucial to our body's immune system. Under acute stress the thymus gland may shrivel to one half its size within 24 hours. We can imagine how that affects our ability to fight bacteria and viruses. In this shriveled condition it can't adequately conduct and regulate the flow energy throughout the body. We cease to be "centered", the cerebral hemispheres become unbalanced, and we "switch". As we have seen it is not only the physical environment that affects the thymus gland this way, but also stress caused by emotional attitudes, posture, social relationships and food. Imagine what traveling does to the thymus gland.

Dr. Diamond believes that when we keep the thymus gland strong we are not likely to be affected too much by stress because body energy will be strong enough to handle whatever stressors come our way. * We do this by admitting to negative thoughts but then changing them immediately to positive ones, by smiling as often as we can (the smile

---

* Since the strength of the thymus gland is so crucial, the reader may want to ask his doctor about the possibility of using a supplement of the natural tissue of the thymus gland. Also, bee propolis, resin secreted by tress and metabolized by bees, is being studied in clinical research in Russia, Denmark and Germany for its ability to activate the thymus gland.

muscle is directly related to the thymus gland), and by developing a "homing thought"--a vision, reflection, memory or fantasy that strengthens the thymus gland, as determined by testing the strength of the muscle while you are envisioning the thought. We can also do this by walking and sitting tall and proud, by reading poetry, listening to sounds of nature, to music (but not rock music), by looking at a favorite painting. We strengthen the thymus when we put the tip of the tongue about a quarter of an inch behind the upper, front teeth, on the "centering button". This reflexively stimulates the thymus, says Dr. Diamond.

One of Dr. Diamond's specific suggestions to combat jet stress is the "thymus thump". The thymus gland is just under the breast bone where the second rib joins it. When fully active it relieves most of the stress from the mind and body energy will be at its maximum. The thump stimulates the thymus gland. Firmly tap the upper half of the breastbone in a waltz-type rhythm-DA-da-da, DA-da-da. This imitates the natural, physiological rhythm of the large blood vessels of the body, including the arteries and even the heart. If we do this while we are flying, every 15 to 30 minutes for about 12 thumps each time, and not too vigorously, the thymus gland should remain adequately stimulated, says Dr. Diamond.

His other recommendation is simply sitting on a hard surface. "All your soft, comfortable chairs are lowering your Life Energy and causing some degree of stress. Firm chairs with straignt backs are eminently better. However, the most important feature of a chair is the seat itself. If you sit on a firm surface, your spine will automatically be straighter, your thymus will be strong, and switching will not occur." (Behavioral Kinesiology)

Dr. Diamond uses a clear, plastic cutting board he bought

in a kitchenware store--small enough to fit into a briefcase and unobtrusive when he leaves his airplane seat. The hard, plastic magazine binders that are often found on board the airplane will also do. "The two problems which we must concentrate on overcoming in plane travel are mental stress patterns as evidenced by the breakdown between the normal symmetrical activity of the two cerebral hemispheres of the brian, and the reduction in body energy. It can be demonstrated kinesiologically (with muscle testing) that both of these factors will be overcome if one sits straight, with the firm support as the recommended plastic board provides."

In general, he advises us to keep "centered" by getting "into the habit of taking an energy break several times a day. Read a few verses of a favorite poem, and enjoy a postcard-size reproduction of a painting that you can put in your pocket. Take a walk with arms swinging freely. If you feel stress building up, check your tongue position and thump your thymus. Your body will respond to these activities immediately." *(Behavioral Kinesiology)*

C.E.S. Therapy

Dr. Diamond has emphasized that when the two halves of the brain become out-of-balance with one another we have less energy, making us less able to withstand stress. If the confusion produced in the body when the circadian cycle is altered can cause such an imbalance then it would follow that whatever reestablished that balance between the two cerebral hemispheres would help combat jet stress, returning the body more quickly to its normal circadian rhythms.

C.E.S. therapy may do that. C.E.S. stands for cerebral electrostimulation. It is similar to acupuncture. Developed in 1949 by Liventsen in the Soviet Union, tens of thousands have been treated with C.E.S. therapy for tension and stress-related disorders caused by an imbalance of the nervous system. It works on the basic theory that when the normal, equalized firing patterns of the nerves of the brain are shifted out of balance the brain begins to fire the nerves in a one-sided manner. Stress results, inducing insomnia, gastrointestinal disturbances, irritability and loss of concentration. In therapy a small C.E.S. machine* is used that stimulates all parts of the brain equally. The biochemicals that stimulate the nerves of the brain to fire are produced in equal amounts. Brain firing patterns balance and return to a normal relationship with one another.[Z]

Like acupuncture C.E.S. therapy affects our feelings of well-being and relaxation. It is mostly used where the central or autonomic nervous systems are primarily involved, such as sleep and psychiatric disorders, alcohol and drug addiction, hypertension and gastrointestinal and cardiovascular disorders. Insomnia has been reduced or eliminated in many patients through use of C.E.S. therapy.* *[AA]

C.E.S. treatment is safe. The neurology Panel of Consultants to the F.D.A. have recommended C.E.S. as a nonharmful treatment for situational anxiety and stress. Also called electro-sleep therapy, it produces no serious side-effects and doesn't cause convulsions, analgesia,* * *

---

*   C.E.S. machines are available by prescription only. See Appendix.

* *   It has been as effective as 100 mg of phenobarbitol in producing sleep.

* * *   Absence of normal sense of pain.

or unconsciousness. Normal subjects report feeling more tranquil, more satisfied, and more energetic after treatment. It is used in 55 countries and 42 states in the United States. [BB]

It's possible C.E.S. could help reverse the effects of jet lag by helping us rephase more quickly to a normal 24-hour body cycle. "While we have not researched specifically the effects of C.E.S. on circadian rhythms." reports Dr. Ray Smith, Chief of Training and Research, Department of Human Resources in Washington, D.C., "our feeling at this point in our work is that C.E.S. would bring a disrupted rhythm back to homeostasis." Referring to a 1976 study by Wever showing artificial electrical fields influencing body systems and rhythms, Captain Frank Hawkins reported to the International Air Line Pilots Association, "Electrosleep, applied as a conditioning process, may be potentially useful in aviation."

MIND CONTROL FOR BODY CONTROL

The mind is fabulous. Yogis, Indians and Eastern healers have known for years what medical scientists are just now proving, that by conscious control we can influence blood flow, heart beat, blood pressure, glandular secretions and muscular tensions in all areas of our bodies. "Just as you can cause your arm to lift food to your mouth to eat," explains the *Well Body Book,* "you can also cause your muscles to completely relax. Just as you can tense your muscles through mental suggestions, you can also relax them."

We can learn to influence our bodies through mind control techniques. Such techniques include biofeedback, progressive relaxation, meditation, autogenic training and hypnosis conditioning. They are most successful for stress-related problems like anxiety and hypertension, where the sympathetic nervous sytems is overactive. The traveler would be especially interested in using one or several of these to be able to relax to refresh to body and to help him sleep.

Relaxation is as important to the body as exercise, according to Herbert Moss, teacher of Transcendental Meditation speaking at the Second International Symposium on the Management of Stress (1979, Monaco). We need both ends of the spectrum, explains Mr. Moss, both exercise and relaxation, in order to improve and maintain flexibility of the nervous system. Relaxation lowers the metabolism on a regular basis just as exercise speeds it up.

Many of us don't know what it is to feel relaxed. Relaxation is called the ability to be quiet, to allow subtle states-of consciousness, to let the mind move more closely to the source of thought. It is a state of body harmony. Metabolism slows down.

In his book-length report to the International Air Line Pilots Association* Captian Frank Hawkins carefully outlines the various and numerous relaxation techniques we can use to counter stress. All of them, he emphasizes, require learning and training. They are not like a pill. Skill comes with practice.

What these techniques might do is speed up resynchronization of body systems along with finding ways to sleep or at least to deeply relax while the rhythms are out-of-phase, says Hawkins. At best we need sufficient, high-quality sleep with a minimum of disturbance to overcome flight fatigue. At the least we need some relaxation that will

---

* Sleep and Body Rhythm Distrubance in Long Range Aviation, The problem, and a Search for Relief.

restore energy to the body, keeping it strong enough to tolerate the stresses of flying.

We don't know how sleep and deep relaxation differ in their abilities to restore the body. Deep relaxation techniques condition us to go into an alpha brain wave, presleep state at will. Even when such deep relaxation doesn't become sleep it seems to revitalize the body, improving the functioning of our body's own self-regulating mechanisms so that we feel somewhat refreshed. Then how well we sleep isn't quite so critical. CC

Biofeedback: East Meets West

Probably the best mind-control technique for the Westerner is biofeedback. Machines monitor our brain waves, muscle tension and other so-called "involuntary" impulses. We learn what we feel like when these impulses are happening in a particular way. Techniques are taught that help us alter these impulses. We watch the changes as they appear on the machine to judge how successful we are in controlling them. The machines give us instant feedback. Thus the name--biofeedback.

Still in its infancy, biofeedback has produced many excellent results. It is one of the simplest and fastest methods of learning a relaxation technique, and does the same thing for us as light meditation, only more quickly. After 1 or 2 sessions most people can reach an alpha brain wave state while still awake. *

As with any mind-control techniques, biofeedback won't work for everyone. You must be a suitable candidate, which means, essentially, that you are open to the concept and want to learn. DD

___

* Alpha range is 8 to 12 Hz. Sleep usually occurs at 12Hz.

Progressive relaxation

The method most often used to get the subject relaxed in biofeedback is progressive relaxation. By itself it is becoming a popular technique of many therapists.

Essentially progressive relaxation is accomplished by sitting comfortably or lying on your back with legs and arms uncreased. If you lie on your back, arms should be at a 45 degree angle out from the sides, palms up. Eyes are closed.

Begin by taking deep breathes, followed by a series of normal breathing. Then visualize each part of your body relaxing* , beginning with the toes, going to the ball of the foot, the arch, the heel, the ankle, the calf, the knee, the thigh, to the base of the spine, and up the spine to the neck and head. Relax the finger-tips, the wrists, the lower arms, upper arms and shoulder muscles. Even the muscles of the skull can relax.

The next sequence is to count backwards from ten, slowly, envisioning yourself moving down--a hill, a stairway, an elevator--whatever works best for you. With each count, each move downward you become more relaxed, sayng to yourself, "Number seven, down, down, down, deeper, deeper, deeper, Number, six," and so on. Repeat the sequence if needed.

You are deeply relaxed when your breathing is very slow, deep and rhythmical --audible like that of a person sleeping. You may feel like you are floating a few inches off the floor. Brain waves have slowed down. You enter an alpha state comparable to meditation.

A variation of this is to contract a muscle, note the contraction, then relax it. This is done progressively with each

---

*   Hypnotist Dick Sutphen suggests visualizing "the relaxing power moving slowly through each area, penetrating every muscle, every cell, every atom, until they are completely relaxed.

set of muscles.

This takes daily practice until it is learned, but it can be self-taught or learned with tapes.* Devised in the United States, progressive relaxation is used extensively in clinical work. To date, unfortunately, it has not been systematically used for body rhythm desychronization and/or sleep disturbance.

Meditation for anybody, including you.

Meditation is another method of mind control to alter body responses and relax. In meditation your brainwave patterns will compare with those of an awake and restfully alert person, but your metabolic rate is slower. Carbon dioxide is down by 20 % while blood lactic acid, an indicator of tiredness, is reduced by 30%. This is a state of consciousness different from wakefulness, sleeping, hypnosis or auto-suggestion.

Simple meditation can be done in three easy steps.* Sit in a comfortable position with back straight or supported, in a quiet room. Continuously concentrate on an object, a sound or a bodily process like breathing. When you find your mind wander, slowly repeat a soothing sound or focus again on the breathing. Do this twice daily for 15 or 20 minutes at a time.

In essence this is how Transcendental Meditation, popularly known as T.M., is done. The soothing sound is your mantra, specially chosen for each individual. T.M. is a modernized, partly westernized and somewhat commer-

---

*   As described in *Stress, Sanity and Survival*.

cialized version of the classic Hindu meditation. Concentration on the mantra, explains its developer Maharishi Mehesh Yogi, helps control the breath. With shallower breathing less carbon dioxide is produced. This lowers the energy needs of the body, bringing calm and restful contemplation.[EE]

Studies on the benefits of T.M.* show it reduces both physical and mental tension. It makes us more tranquil while increasing energy and capacity for concentrated work. T.M. has been effective treatment for insomnia.[FF]

Unlike yogic or zen meditation which takes much practice, discipline and time to perfect, T.M. is learned easily and quickly and requires no specific beliefs or lifestyle. Usually 2 or 3 sessions of one and a half hours are enough to learn the technique. After that you may attend group sessions once a month for a year. Daily practice is 20 minutes, twice a day.

Is meditation for you? That depends on you. Conditioning the mind, like conditioning the body, depends on repetition--making a ritual habit of the activity. Once developed you can relax with it at the first sign of tension. Relaxation through T.M. could, feels Captain Hawkins in his report to international Air Line Pilots Association, reduce the impact of aviation stresses. Not only can it reduce the stress while we are awake, calming the body, normalizing it and restoring some energy, it may help us get to sleep more easily.

Autogenic Training

Unlike zen and yoga, Autogenic Training (or A.T.) is

---

*   Work by Stanford University research, engineer, Emitri Kanellakos.

neither mystical nor sectarian, but like them it assumes the body has a self-regulating mechanism that helps it adjust and recover after emotional or physical stress. A.T. is designed to help the self-regulating mechanism, accomplish this.

The complete method includes a series of 6 standard exercises and 7 meditative ones, but the meditative ones are rarely used. Usually the first 2 standard exercises are sufficient.

Like other mind-control techniques A.T. requires regular practice to be effective. But unlike some of the others it is not a simple relaxation formula. It must be adapted to the individual under supervision of a qualified teacher. Once learned, though, it can be used for just a few seconds at a time to help the body recover from stress.

A.T. may have the greatest potential of all the so-called "relaxation methods", according to Captain Hawkins. It could increase our tolerances to the stresses of long-range flying and, as a side-effect, improve our ability to sleep when we might not otherwise be able to. GG   One airline, he points out, is offering A.T. group training to its flying staff at airline cost.

Hypnosis for modern man and woman.

For most of us hypnosis is a very relaxed state where we are aware of all that is going on around us, while at the same time the brain is in an alpha-state and open to suggestion. Under such conditions it is quite easy to condition the subconscious mind to believe and respond in a particular way. *

---

* Hypnotist Dick Sutphén describes the subconscious as a computer which operates as it is programmed. Just like a computer, that programming can be changed.

While many physicians are skeptical, there is extensive, detailed evidence that hypnosis and autohypnosis have been successful in treating stress-related disorders. Professional practitioners of hypnosis have expressed their opinion that auto-hypnosis can reduce the adverse effects of sleep and body rhythm disturbance and help us get to sleep.* *

Self-hypnosis can be taught by hypnotherapists. It can also be learned from any number of good cassette tapes available commercially.* * *

ION GNERATORS

We have discussed hypoxia, where the cells of the body don't get as much oxygen as they need, as one of the stressors causing jet stress. The air in the cabin of the plane has an oxygen content equal to 5,000 to 7,000 feet above sea level. The body's reaction to stress decreases the amount of oxygen that reaches each cell. Smoking in the cabin displaces oxygen in the body with carbon monoxide.

Another cause of hypoxia can be an excess of positive air ions with a lack of enough negative ions in the cabin air. With enough neg-ions we utilize oxygen better but without enough our resistance is lowered and we become mentally fatigued. If there isn't a proper ion balance we simply can't absorb the quantities of oxygen we need.[HH]

Respiratory infections that often strike us when we are under stress can be reduced with properly ionized air.[II] Neg-ions have the ability to kill airbourne germs and clean

---

* Wouldn't it be interesting to see if we could reprogram the subconscious to believe that it is in the new time zone we arrive in, and so recycle our bodies rapidly?

* * See Appendix XV.

the air, even of smoke. In the United States negative ion generators have been used in operating rooms and burn centers to lower infection.

Air pollution means there are few ions of either positive or negative charge, but the neg-ions are dramatically absent. Added to the air, neg-ions can clean it, removing airbourne particles of pollutants. This can be an important consideration for the traveler since airport air is usually polluted, as is the air of many of the cities we travel to and from.

Negative air ions have been called the "happy ions" because they make us feel good. Their sedative, calming effect is similar to the common tranquilizer reserpine*. Neg-ions produce high-amplitude alpha brain waves--the same level we find ourselves in during deep relaxation, meditation and just prior to falling asleep. Not surprising, then, that added to ion-depleted air neg-ions have lowered emotion stress of work and travel while helping us sleep better.

No one is sure how they work in the body.[JJ]   Neg-ions don't cure us of anything. They don't themselves heal, but they do seem to help the body repair itself. Mostly they're known for giving us more mental and physical energy and improving mental and physical well-being. "You can't see the effect, except that in a sense you can," explains a management spokesman for Standard Back of South Africa in Johannesburg. "You can see it in the improved standard of work and the improved feeling of the workers."

It is unlikely that the airlines will put negative air ion generators aboard the airplane until public demand is great enough. But the traveler can carry a small one with them to use in their hotel room. Many flight attendants are doing this, claiming it helps them sleep better.

---

*   Both reduce serotonin in the mid-brain.

Do they really? Hotel rooms with central heat and air will contain high levels of pos-ions with relatively few neg-ions, due to the friction caused by air passing through the air-ducts. Pos-ions appear to cause serotonin levels to rise in the body, which French researcher Jouvet found directly related to horrifying nightmares. Such high serotonin levels made his volunteers sleep poorly, always on the edge of consciousness so they didn't get properly rested. They awakened after only a few hours of sleep. These same sub-jects placed in a room containing a neg-ion generator slept better despite an excess of serotonin in their systems.

Imagination or not, if you sleep better that's what counts. Who can argue with success?

Ion generators come in sizes large enough to ionize a whole house or office building and small enough to put into a purse or briefcase. It should contain replaceable needles. There are many on the market--some good, some bad. They are sold officially in the United States as air cleaners and have no officially-recognized medical value.

There are other ways to get neg-ions. Energy in moving water generates lots of neg-ions. As water breaks up positive charged ions remain with the larger drop and the negative charge flies free with the fine spray. If you take showers or go to the seashore or near a waterfall or fountain you are likely to encounter some beneficial neg-ions. There are also more ions in the woods, more on a sunny day, and more where the ground is naturally-high-radioactive. Mountains are especially good for beneficial ions.

CHELATION THERAPY

"Chelation" comes from Greek referring to the claws of a crab. Occurring naturally and constantly in nature, chelation is when a substance can grasp, enclose or unite with another substance. While all biological processes are involved in chelation, its value in healing only recently emerged.

Developed in the 1950's for removing heavy lead and mercury poisoning, it consists of dripping a chelatiing substance* into the blood stream intravenously for 4 to 6 hours, repeating the procedure on consecutive days. As it passes through the blood stream it wraps itself around the heavy metals collecting in the arteries and body tissues, picking them up and carrying them out the body through the urinary tract, the liver and the colon.

Now doctors have discovered that the chelate EDTA will bind with ionic calcium, which is an important component of the cholesterol/triglyceride plaques that build up in the arteries, decreasing circulation and apparently leading to stroke and heart disease.** As the calcium is removed from the plaque, the plaque breaks down, much like removing mortar from a brick wall will make it fall apart.

As cholesterol plaques are removed from the arteries circulation improves in the entire system. KK   It appears that chelation can not only prevent, but reverse atherosclerosis.

Properly administered it is safe and effective, and used along with controlled and judicious eating, vitamin and mineral supplementation and a graduated regimen of exercise beneficial results are retained. Several FAA examining physicians have recommended that flight personnel have at least one chelation treatment a month to maintain good circulation and remove heavy, toxic metals from the blood.

---

* The most common chelate for this is EDTA--ethylenediaminetetraacete.

** Negatively-charged molecules of EDTA form a bond with positively-charged molecules of ionic minerals.

HYPERBARIC OXYGEN THERAPY

Often used in combination with chelation therapy hyperbaric oxygen is used most extensively in decompression sickness caused by diving accidents. Recently it is being used for a variety of disorders like atherosclerosis, pulmonary insufficiency, carbon monoxide poisoning and gastric ulcer. Any of these could be beneficial to the traveler. A treatment that supersaturates the body with oxygen would be welcome after the hypoxia of flight.

Hyperbaric means, literally, high pressure. You are placed in a specially-designed chamber and oxygen is administered under pressure equivalent to 33 to 66 feet below sea level.[LL] Body tissues are saturated with oxygen. The cells increase their metabolic rate influencing many health problems favorably and healing. Treatment usually ranges from 60 to 90 minutes daily for 10 to 15 days.

Hyperbaric oxygen treatment is considered experimental for all uses except treatment for tetanus and gangrene. It is available primarily through clinical investigational studies and is not readily available to the general public.

It is not without its risk but when properly administered under carefully-regulated conditions for a very limited treatment time oxygen toxicity is not a problem. Doctors using it claim the present system contains all the necessary safegards to protect the individual.

HOMOEOPATHY: MEDICAL TREATMENT
OF ROYALTY

Another resource for health is the homoeopathic physician. While treatment by a homoeopathic doctor is so specifically geared to the individual that we cannot offer general suggestions for countering stress and fatigue or for aid in sleeping, we would like to introduce you to this field of medicine in case you are interested in this approach.

Based on Hyppocrates' thesis that like produces like, the basic tenet is "Through the like disease is produced, and through the application of the like it is cured." First the doctor will find the substance that most closely produces the same symptoms you suffer. He will administer it in the smallest potency possible. The body cures itself, from the inside out.

The theory is that the body automatically reacts to any disturbance within itself, trying to reestablish normalcy. A substance is chosen which is natural to the body and which will have a similar effect upon it that the agent causing the disease has. In a very small dosage this "drug" will stimulate the body's own defense mechanism to restore physiological balance.

Though dosage is minute, homoeopathic drugs are very potent because of a process called "potentization". They are made from selected mineral, vegetable and animal sources, finely ground, repeatedly diluted and then succussed--hit vigorously to release energy from the substance. With a series of succussions the drug substance is greatly dispersed, increasing the surface area and thus the surface energy, much like salad herbs become more aromatic the finer they are ground.MM

Treatment is very individualized. A homoeopathic remedy is specifically diagnosed and customized to each patient. It's cost is ridiculously inexpensive.

If you are interested in pursuing such treatment for dealing with jet stress you can write for the Directory of United States Homoeopathic Physicians.* Before dismissing this area of health care remember that three generations of the Royal Family of Great Britain, including the present one, have a homoeopathic physician as their family physician. So did John D. Rockefeller, Sr., Henry Ford, Sr., and Pope Pius XII. Homoeopathic treatment is part of the health plan of Great Britain and the USSR. There is constant demand for homoeopathic remedies in the pharmacies of France and Germany. You would not be unique using this approach.

CHRONOBIOTICS TO RESET THE BODY CLOCK

A major portion of jet stress could be removed if there were something we could take to immediately reset body clocks. There are chemicals called chronobiotics that can reset the clocks forward and backward a predictable number of hours, depending upon when they are taken. Scientists are looking at these, both in foods and in drug form, as a basis for a "jet lag pill". Dr. Martin Moore-Ede, Harvard Medical School, is in the process of developing such a pill which may be available around 1984.

Researchers are studying pentobarbital and barbituates, but are most interested in the methyl xanthine group which are found naturally in tea, coffee, and some foods.[NN] However, these are not entirely safe. While they can clearly alter our biological time structure they seem to cause genetic changes in cells that can produce mutation and cancer. Dr. Charles F. Ehret, Chief Scientist of Research of Argonne National Laboratories believes that chronobiotics are carcinogens, that each time the circadian cycle of the cell is reset by such a drug or by any other cue giver we increase the risk of tumor-producing damage to the gene-action

---

* National Center for Homoeopathy, 6231 Leesburg Pike, Suite 506, Falls Church, Virginia 22044

machinery of the cell. "All chronobiotics may be oncogenic (tumor-producing) when taken at the vulnerable phase of the circadian cycle," he warns. [OO]

Nonetheless Dr. Ehret has devised a plan to help us recycle quickly into a new time zone by using a proper combination of "cue-givers" like light and mealtime, along with diet and chronobiotic drugs. He uses methylated xanthines like theophylline in tea and caffeine in coffee, along with food. When these are taken and in what quantity determines what they do for us. [PP]

This program is nearly completely useless for the flight attendant and pilot for obvious reasons. While it may be helpful to the occasional traveler it still has its drawbacks. There are considerable doubts about the overall value of using drugs like caffeine and theophylline. Dr. Ehret himself acknowledges the carcionoginic properties of presently-used substances. More hard facts and well-proven data on substances used is needed. Hopefully we'll discover substances natural to the body with no side-effects.

NOTES FOR THE PROFESSIONAL TRAVELER

A.   A.C.E. must be obtained through a doctor. It can be taken orally, intramuscularly or intravenously. The tablets are not as potent as the injections, with the I.V.'s being the best form. An I.V. injection usually contains 6 cc. of A.C.E. in a mixture of 200 mcg ACE per 1 cc. Often vitamins C, B-1, B-6 and B-12, plus the mineral calcium are added, making a total of 11 cc. per injection. Intramuscular shots are usually only a few cc's using 1000 mcg/1cc of A.C.E. solution. The tablets are only 1 to 1/100th as strong as these injections. During a trip we could take 6 to 9 a day to give the adrenal glands added support.

B.   Rats given potassium/magnesium aspartate, then forced to swim until exhausted managed to swim 40% longer than the rats not give the supplement.

One such combination is called Aspartine. Recommended dosage is 6 tablets, along with 1 gram of (1000 mg.) vitamin B-6. This is a natural, safe, but strong way to deal with internal water balance. Dr. Gary Gordon, President of the American Academy of Medical Preventics, claims, "This makes Diuril (a diuretic) look like it hasn't started."

C.   Melatonin is produced and released on a daily rhythm. Most of it is made between 11 o'clock at night and 7 o'clock in the morning. As light appears melatonin production and release slows down. For this reason it is more difficult to sleep when there is light.

This inhibiting effect of light can be counteracted under stress when the hormone norepinephrine (similar to adrenaline) is released by the sympathetic system to combat that stress.

Dr. C. Norman Shealy, M.D., Ph.D., of the Pain and

Health Rehabilitation Center in LaCrosse, Wisconsin, recommends 1 gram of tryptophan 3 times a day, or 3 grams at the time we want to sleep. An added B-Complex vitamin tablet of 100 mg can be added for each gram of tryptophan taken.

D.   Recommended dosage while traveling is 3 tablets a day upon arising, in order to prevent diarrhea. If we see any negative change in the stool we'd want to increase to 9 to 12 tablets daily, spaced throughout the day in 3 or 4 doses.

E.   A free radical is a molecule or a fraction of a molecule that has one single electron. The body needs electrons in pairs, called a chemical bond, which holds the molecule together, like a glue. A free radical, with one single electron, is unstable. It can cause damage to any one of the important biochemical structures in our body. It is like a bullet, bombarding our cells. Every time it causes some damage it forms a new bullet so that the damaging effects of the free radical can go on and on.

F.   Research results not yet published suggest that large amounts of SOD can double the life span of test animals.

G.   Research was done by Russians Petkov and Brekman on stress and ginseng.
   Russian soldiers take ginseng into battle to counter battle stress and cosmonauts use it to improve their endurance as well as to counter the stress of space flight.

H.   Soviet scientists concluded that people who find themselves in trying situations or who are engaged in any activity which taxes their endurance or stress their body

gastric ulcers. Dosage woul s the freeze-dried garlic. It is
boiled water, before breakfa B-1, which is a stimulant.
It contains 200mg. of ginse ould be from 3 to 6 capsules,
apsules for a prolonged flight,

M.   Dosage is 2 capsul y. More than 10 grams is not
too loose we cut down; if it e is infection present because
we increase dosage until discernible, indentifiable, ma-
formed. Dr. Christopher w cts after that dosage.
constipated they need up to d be 3 to 4 capsules of the
person, he says, may take f apsules of the oil, taken with
the old fecal matter and re ut no inbetween. Taken right
ciently that the muscles of th estions and detoxification.

d for its therapeutic value by
N.   The high germaniun Australia and has been ap-
garlic capable of retarding valent of the F.D.A. for both
humans. e. It is non-toxic and safe with
bad breath. Parsley, fresh if
O.   It may be the seleniu tablet form along with garlic
effect on dangerous metals li
that build up in the body.

aum Petrovitsch Joirisch of
P.   Work by Dr. Arthur viet Academy of Science in
llected pollen is the primorial
Q.   Reported by Dr. Aru fe on our planet--a treasure
sal in British medical journa erative power." In his article,
nity" he claims it's use on ag-
R.   There are many bra rale, a sense of well-being and
parsley as well to help deod and lifeless skin seemed to
Dr. Kitahara's special statitus, high blood pressure,
organically-grown garlic cur rgies, distrubances of the en-
without the use of heat. In th nervous disorders responded
much of the odor is lost. The s studied.
be put into capsules, into a c
or into a tablet. ch and executive director of

the Educational Athletic Club in Philadelphia, which trains only 20 athletes but boasts 8 national champions and 7 gold medals from the 1976 Olympics. For the past 2 years he has studied the use of bee pollen on his athletes. They take 3 tablets daily while Woodly carefully monitors and records pulse rates and dosage times.

U.   Results of documented clinical tests on animals and humans.

V.   Dosage is normally 1 to 3 capsules or 2 to 3 tablespoons of granules daily. Reddick uses 7 tablets a day, and up to 14 if he is under a heavy competition schedule.

Granules are delicious added to peanut butter. Some add a touch of honey as well. Bee pollen cakes are available in some natural food stores that contain wheat germ, honey, peanut butter and a day's supply of pollen. They are topped with carob frosting. These might be handy, energy-building snacks during flight.

W.   This opinion is based on independent reports from researchers in Russia and China who found that electroencephalographic studies of normal adult subjects after acupuncture showed a predominance of alpha brain waves with an increase in their amplitude. Since alpha waves originate in the thalamus they concluded that acupuncture arouses thalamic function.

X.   Acupuncture raises the levels in the body of both glucocorticoids and catecholamines. Beta-adrenergic catecholamines stimulate and increase in production of AMP, adenosine monophosphate, which is closely involved in regulating the immune response. Glucocorticoids inhibit the release of histamine from cells, normalize capillary permeability, stabilize cell membranes and lysozyme, and inhibit the migration of neutrophils--all important for immunity.

Y.   Touch for Health, 1175 N. Lake Ave., Pasadena, CA 91104

Z.   The C.E.S. machines use the same stimulator that is used in electroacupuncture. Impulses are sent through electrodes placed over the eyes or on the eyelids and on the mastoid area behind the ears. About the size of a heavy-duty, portable radio, it is solid-state, transistorized and battery-operated, using sine or rectangular waves in pulse widths of 2 to 4 milliseconds or less, and from 10 to 150 Hertz on a 12 to 120 volt source. The series of low-intensity pulses in the microamp range of specific frequencies stimulate subcortical regions of the brain to bring the central nervous system and the autonomic nervous system back into normal homeostasis or equilibrium. Treatment lasts from 30 minutes to 1 hour and usually is comfortable and quite relaxing.

AA.   In tests gastric hyperacidity has been reduced in both man and animals. Continually-stressed rats had a decrease in gastric acid secretion in spite of the stress and they continued to perform well.
    C.E.S. therapy has reduced blood pressure in many hypertensive patients, producing relaxation, influencing vascular conditioning, altering neuronal firing and bringing about better emotional and mental functioning. Most students in a University of Mississippi test became both psychologically and physically healthier, less schizoid, less neurotic and showed lower blood pressure and pulse rates. Alcoholics showed lower recidivism, better attitudes, im-

proved moods and less memory loss. They became less
neurotic, required less medication and were more reponsive to treatment.

C.E.S. therapy has produced a "state of consciousness
grossly indistinguishable from ordinary sleep". Produced by
the direct action of a weak, rhythmic current on the brain, it
has been as effective as 100 mg of phenobarbitol in producing sleep. In a double blind study patients got to sleep faster,
spent more time in Stage 1 sleep, had more total Delta
Sleep time and spent less time awake in bed.

BB. Dr. Ray Smith, Chief of Training and Research,
Department of Human Resources, Washington, D.C.,
predicts that in the next 10 years there will be far more prac-
tical, clinical use of C.E.S. by physicians than there will be
research on its use, since effective research isn't likely to
begin until C.E.S. effects are obtained on actual patients.
"C.E.S. has an effective, safe and legitimate place in
medical practice," asserts Dr. Smith, "and is no doubt here
to stay." (Use of Electrostimulation.)

CC. Captain Hawkins feels it is reasonable to assume
that if a pilot cannot obtain proper sleep before a flight, then
deep relaxation is a substitute to some degree. To carry that
one step further, it could be suggested that to avoid sleeping
during flight pilots schedule 10-minute meditation periods
every hour, especially during long, night flights, to revive
the body to some degree.

Hawkins suggests all crew members be offered training in
scientifically-developed relaxation techniques early in their
careers.

DD. Hawkins reports a study done in 1974 using
biofeedback in the aviation environment, but results were

not conclusive. In his opinion further experimental work is justified.

EE. In studying T.M. subjects at the University of California, Irvine, Wallace found brain waves similar to those of Zen monks, as well as a decreased metabolic rate, indicated by the fact that the body was using less oxygen. They had shallower breathing, increased skin resistance to electrical current and a drastic drop in blood lactate levels. Both high levels of blood lactate and low skin resistance are associated with nervous tension, stress, anxiety neuroses, chronic anxiety symptoms and hypertension.

T.M. practitioners told Wallace they felt their health improved overall, especially in stress related areas like mental health, headaches and blood pressure. The drug abusers among them reported less need and desire for drugs.

FF. Used in treating insomnia, T.M. has been officially defined as "a specific method of allowing the activity of the mind to settle down while one sits comfortably with eyes closed. This mental process automatically triggers a physiological response conducive to both deep rest and increased wakefulness." (Reported in *Fatigue in Safety Equation*).

In a study, T.M. meditators returned more quickly to normal levels of functioning and required less compensatory REM sleep to make up for lost sleep than did the non-meditators.

GG. For effectiveness, Hawkins believes we would need a series of 5 to 10 sessions of an hour each of Autogenic Training, with private daily practice in between to be able to counter effects of body rhythm dyschronism and sleep deprivation.

HH.   Excessive amounts of pos-ions decreases the partial pressure oxygen in the alveoli of the lungs. This impairs the normal exchange of oxygen and carbon dioxide in the lung, which lowers our resistance and contributes to mental fatigue. The fewer the ions the lower the efficiency of mind and body. When enough neg-ions are present we utilize oxygen better. In a study at the Air Ion Laboratory in Berkeley, California, animals placed in deionized air died within 2 weeks because they couldn't use oxygen properly without the ions. Apparently, scientists concluded, we simply can't absorb the quantities of oxygen we need to live.

In a human test volunteers breathed overdoses of pos-ions for only 2 minutes. They developed dry throats, husky voices, headaches, and itchy or obstructed noses. Their breathing capacity was reduced by 30%. The pos-ions had made breathing more difficult.

Brazilian hospitals use ion generators as common treatment for breathing problems. In East Germany factories where lung disease was a serious problem have set up their own neg-ion clinics for the workers. An East German doctor, after treating more than 11,000 workers by 1975, reported that neg-ion therapy worked with "monotonous regularity."

II.   A Swiss bank cut work loss days from 16 to 1 by installing neg-ion generators in the bank. A Swiss textile mill reduced time loss by 92.5% by the same means.

JJ.   *The Journal of General Physiology* theorized that "an excess of pos-ions caused the overproduction of serotonin in mammals and that, initially at least, this causes hyperacitivity which rapidly leads to exhaustion, anxiety and perhaps depression." (1960) Pos-ions have made even the timid rabbit aggressive. They provoke a sensation of discomfort, headache and nausea.

In a Russian test neg-ions had no important effect on blood pressure, pulse rate and perspiration but brought considerable improvement in the general physical and mental "tone", cheerfulness, energy, appetite and the ability to sleep soundly. The body absorbed vitamin C better.

We noted that neg-ions have a calming effect similar to the tranquilizer reserpine. Both reduce the amount of serotonin in the mid-brain.

KK.   Chelation eliminates calcium that is not in normal cells and bones with a catalytic power far beyond the dose of medicine given. Thermograms taken before and after treatment show the effectiveness of chelation treatment on arteriosclerosis, coronary heart disease, heart block, gangrene of the extremities and strokes. It has reduced blood cholesterol deposits in the liver, the incidence of heart arrythmias, and heart valve calcification.

LL.   Oxygen under pressure is administered either by mask or directly into the chamber, which may vary from a small one-person unit to a large multiple-place unit capable of housing an entire surgical team.

The partial pressure of oxygen that comes in contact with the alveolar capillaries of the lungs increases, which in turn forces more oxygen than normal into solution in the blood. From there it goes into the plasma with the result that body tissues become saturated with oxygen.

For more information contact: Life and Health Medical Group, Box 465, Loma Linda, CA 92354.

MM.   This surface energy determines how well the cell can absorb the drug--the diffusion, speed of chemical reaction, electrical potential and catalytic action that occur between cell and drug. All drug actions work this way, which is why a small dose can be highly effective without risking toxicity that can occur with high doses of regular drugs.

Dr. Neil Pruzzo of Richardson, Texas, describes homoeopathic medicine as an energy pattern without the original substance.

Usually one drop of the actual substance used for healing would be placed in 99 drops of spirit. After mechanically shaking this mixture one drop is removed from the new mixture, placed with another 99 parts spirit, and so on--for 6 or 12 times. The bottle is marked 6x or 12x, indicating the number of dilutions. the more diluted the material, the greater the effect on the body's own healing forces.

NN. Continuous use of theophylline found in tea and caffeine causes a dramatic lengthening of the circadian period of our cells, while chronic use of phenobarbital in the diet of rats has kept them from resychronizing, even when given in low doses. Constant use of these chronobiotics seems to keep the body in a constant state of disarray, which may be what causes the mutagenesis.

OO. In mentioning the vulnerable phase of the circadian cycle Dr. Ehret is reminding us that the effectiveness of any drug varies over the 24-hour period, depending upon when it is taken during the day or night. An antihistamine taken at seven in the morning lasts 15 to 17 hours, but only 6 to 8 hours taken at seven in the evening. Adrenal hormones, glucocorticoids, are more effective and have fewer side-effects when they are taken early in the day. Appetite depressants, epilepsy medicine, aspirin and cold remedies and medication for diabetes all show circadian variables. Some drugs can be helpful at one time of the day, harmful at another and ineffective at still another time.

The time we are exposed to a potentially noxious substance could mean the difference between life and death. Taken when the body or target organ is most susceptible it could cause death. Taken in a less-susceptible cycle it could be helpful with no risk. Whether or not it is toxic depends upon where the body is in its daily cycle of absorption, metabolism, inactivation and exretion, and how much fluid is in the tissue where the drug will be distributed, as well as how susceptible the target tissue will be to the drug in any particular cycle.

PP. Using Dr. Whret's program, going eastbound when we are arriving at a place that is seven hours ahead of our time we would try to advance body cycles. Eating habits are modified beginning 4 days before flight. Assuming a Wednesday departure, Sunday and Tuesday are "fast" days and Monday and Wednesday are "feast" days. Fasting means eating lightly in order to deplete glycogen reserves (sugar stored in the liver) but not to the point of becoming overly-famished or hypoglycemic.

On Wednesday we would avoid caffeine entirely because it causes a phase delay. But Wednesday night between 7 and midnight, new local time, we drink 3 to 5 cups of black coffee without sugar or cream, or else strong tea. This further depletes glycogen reserves to induce the phase advance.

We rest as much as possible that night, not eating, not watching a movie, not talking. We avoid bright lights and all things that might make one think he should be up rather than asleep. When the hour arrives that breakfast is being eaten at our destination it is time to eat our breakfast on the plane.

We give the body all the cues that tell it it should be up and about. We turn on the lights, clap our hands, talk enthusiastically and eat a large, high-protein high-calorie breakfast to replenish the energy reserves we have worked so hard to deplete. Lunch and supper will also be heavy and eaten on schedule according to normal mealtimes at our destination. Lunch should be high-protein, but dinner high-carbohydrate, low-protein. We go to bed early and continue to operate completely within the new time zone.

Returning westbound we feast the day before we leave and fast the day of the flight. We are trying to delay our cycle--lengthen it. We can drink lots of coffee and tea until noon, local time, but then have none during the afternoon and evening. Nor any alcohol. Inflight we break the fast with a high-protein, high-calorie breakfast, eaten when breakfast would normally be eaten at our destination. This program has been used successfully on flights to Japan, China and the Orient.

While in the process of rephasing we try to live completely in synchrony with the new time zone. When it's daylight we remain awake and active, eating at normal hours. When night comes we avoid lights, socializing, work--anything that could make the body think it should be up rather than slowing down to sleep.

It is important that breakfast and lunch be high-protein meals. This helps us make catecholamines which we need lots of during our active wake-cycle. Supper which is low-protein but high carbohydrate helps us manufacture serotonin, which needs to be high during our inactive, rest-cycle. (When this sequence was reversed in rats and they were give low-protein breakfasts and high-protein suppers, phase shifts were very sluggish.)

Chapter Ten

Smoking, Drugs andAlcohol--And Flying: They Don't Mix

Repeated changing of our body cycles causes tremendous physical and biochemical stress on the body. Gradually health worsens and fatigue sets in. When we feel poorly it's not unusual for us to resort to stimulants to keep us going, depressants to help us sleep, and alcohol, and/or smoking for momentary relaxation and stimulus.

DRINKING AND FLYING

Alcoholic beverages do nothing to counter jet stress. If anything they make the stress of flying more difficult for the body to handle. Yet many drink when traveling, including flight personnel. [A]   Using alcohol when you're traveling to feel better and to be able to sleep can lead to alcoholism if the conditions are right.

Recent research is relating alcoholism to malnutrition, hypoglycemia and food-allergy-additions. Alcoholism seems to be primarily biochemical in its origin--physically rather than emotionally caused.[*] When these physical,

---

[*] Except to the extent that emotional upset causes physical changes in the body which make it crave alcohol.

biochemical preconditions are present and we face unusal or heavy psychological pressures the small amount of alcohol we take to alleviate the accompanying tension can, with time, become larger to alleviate the tension, until alcoholism becomes a learned habit in a psychological sense. It's primary cause, though, is biochemical--malnutrition of the brain cells. "While psychological influences can help to create the alcoholic," categorically states Dr. Roger Williams, reknown biochemist and discoverer of vitamin B-5, "no one who follows good nutritional practices ever becomes an alcoholic."

Malnutrition has always been associated with alcoholism. Doctors felt alcoholism caused the malnutrition. Now these doctors see malnutrition as the cause. The body has a mechanism that controls metabolism. It is very sensitive to important nutrients. When these are missing, a biological thirst for alcohol is created. Dr. Williams has proven that diets deficient in essential nutrients encourage alcohol consumption in animals but the drinking habits can be reversed by adding the missing nutrients to their food.

That an allergy to a food substance could cause alcoholism is a revolutionary idea. The alcoholic may be allergic to--and thereby addicted to--either the alcohol itself or the traces in it of the grains, sugars or other foods from which it was made. This type of allergy is called a cerebral allergy. In such cases alcohol isn't needed to relieve or neutralize a hangover. Watery extracts of yeast or the food that is fermented for the beverage can get rid of the hangover. The morning-after miseries of too much imbibing are actually the withdrawal phase of food and yeast addiction, which results from a chronic allergic state.

"If the next time you over-indulge in drinking and wake up the next morning with a hangover, don't seek out the 'hair of the dog', an additional drink of what you were swallowing last night," advises *Let's Live Magazine* *. "Instead, take a bite of food made from the same fermentable food substance present in the alcoholic beverage. Eat rye toast if it was rye whiskey. Take a slice of whole wheat bread if it was blended whiskey. Suck some sugar if it was rum. Your hangover may disappear that way and you'll recognize that you have an allergic addiction to that food."

Hypoglycemia is also a factor in alcholism. It exists in 70 to 80% of all alcoholics. It may initiate or prolong addictions. Ex-alcoholics report that they craved alcohol, caffeine, nicotine or sweets when their blood sugar was low. Correcting the hypoglycemic condition brought quick recovery. * * Advises Dr. Charleton Fredericks, well-known nutritionist, "If it takes very little liquor to intoxicate the drinker we grow suspicious of low blood sugar (hypoglycemia) or an allergy, one possibly causing or aggravating the other." * * *

Considering these possible causes of alcoholism doctors have devised a new approach to its treatment which is showing great promise. Basically nutritional, it corrects metabolic and biochemical imbalances within the body that produce cravings for alcohol. Included is a basically hypoglycemic diet of unrefined, high-fiber foods, mostly raw and mostly complex carbohydrates. Caffeine is avoided, including chocolate, certain medications, strong tea, cola and cola beverages. Smoking is also prohibited. Caffeine and nicotine significantly hinder recovery, contribute to hypoglycemia, and add one more addiction. * * * *

* August, 1978

* * If alcoholism is suspected or confirmed there should be a 6-hour glucose tolerance test for hypoglycemia.

* * * *Psychodietetics*

* * * * Nicotine prevents the absorption of the vitamin C needed for recovery.

Megadoses of specific nutrients are used. The most important ones are niacin (vitamin B-3) and vitamin C. Niacin reduces the swings in mood and the insomnia common in alcoholics. It stabilizes behavior making other treatments more effective. It also reduces or changes the effect alcohol has on the body, to the point where there is neither the high nor the usual drug withdrawal. Drinking simply becomes less rewarding.

Hard-core, "revolving door" type alcoholic boys were put on this program with an 86% success rate. Dr. Russell . Smith, medical director of Michigan State Boys' Training School, added to this program a total of 5000 alcoholics in all stages of the disease. All are showing improvement in every area.

One reason for such success is that no will power is required. Patients remain sober because drinking becomes less rewarding. There is little physical or psychological distress in stopping. "The change in eating habits and the vitamins leveled me out, made life seem easier," explains a recovered alcoholic. "I no longer think of grabbing a drink when the going gets rough. I have a lot more energy. For the first time in years I'm sleeping well--and really enjoying myself when I'm awake."* *

Another testified, "I didn't make any vows--I just went on a diet and six weeks later realized that I hadn't had a drink in a week--for the first time in forty years--and didn't want one--for the first time in forty years. I am off liquor now for more than three years, after striking out with Antabuse, psychiatric treatments, shock therapy and tranquilizers."*

If the treatment is so successful then the cause of alcholism may be accurate. [B]   This is especially interesting

---

*   Psychodietetics

** Psychonutrition

to the traveler who can become hypoglycemic and who may not be able to supply all the nutrients the body needs because of jet stress. Aviation flight personnel tend towards dipsomania which has periods of compulsion to drink to excess with periods of complete sobriety. Could fight-induced or fatigue-induced hypoglycemia be a cause?

Sleeping pills

If you are continually crossing time zones or required to shift your work/rest cycle, sleep problems become a major concern for you. Many travelers attempt to get sleep by using sleeping pills. No less than 46% of the flight crew members interviewed in one study admitted to occasionally using sleeping drugs before long flights. Usually the flight crews don't use them at home because they don't seem to have any sleep problems, but they used them more than most of us realize while they are on a trip.

Nitrazapan (Mogadon) is the one most commonly used by the flight crews interviewed. The most common sleeping pill for the general American public is fluazapan (Dalmane), which is similar to Valium and Librium. These are less addictive and more effective than barbiturates which were the more popular sleeping pills in the past. [C]

Sleeping pills, even the commonly-used ones, seem to stop being effective when they are used for more than 10 to 14 days. Sleep can be worse after taking them for awhile than it was before starting. What sleep is produced with sleeping pills differs radically from normal sleep because there is much less REM (Rapid Eye Movement) sleep. "The same pills people take to regulate their sleep profoundly disturb sleep," warns Dr. William Dement, specialist in sleep disorders. "Chronic ingestion of hypnotics can cause insomnia from dependency for the drug. D ¡BBB Once withdrawal from sleeping pills is complete patients feel better and sleep much better."*

There is another problem with using hypnotic drugs. Some will work well during night sleep but may not work during daytime sleep. We don't know how long the drug will remain in the body to affect our performance when we must be awake and alert. If 10 mg of valium is taken in the daytime it affects our performance for the next 14 hours. Others may last much longer or not as long. Effects are relative to the circadian cycle of the body. We just don't know.

Non-prescription sleeping pills contain antihistamine methapyrilene to cause drowsiness. It is relatively harmless in small doses unless you are trying to perform skilled tasks. But if you mix them with alcohol they can make you dizzy, blur your vision and intoxicate you. They also commonly contain scopplamine from the belladonna plant. This also causes drowsiness but brain waves indicate abnormal rest and sleep patterns.

Hypnotics are not the solution for getting good sleep. They are addictive, they affect our performance even after they have seemingly "worn off", they are diuretic where dehydration of flight is already a problem, they may stimulate rather than put us to sleep, and even when they do help us sleep more quickly the second part of our sleep is disturbed.

Until something better is offered, however, most travelers will probably continue to take sleeping pills. If you are going to use them get the advice of an aviation doctor on what to use and how to use them. Know how your pill will affect your health and performance, how long it will stay in your

---

*   Of Iron Men and Wooden Ships

body, how effective, what the mean sleep was before they were used, what the level of sleep will be with chronic use, what the immediate withdrawal symptoms are and how long they will last, and what happens if you drink alcohol while they are still in your body.

Remember that used over months and years they can destroy sleep. Stop using them, warns Dr. Peter Hauri in his book *Current Concepts: the Sleep Disorders,* when the stressful situation that led you to use them in the first place is over, or after 2 to 4 weeks following the initial prescription. If you need to continually increase dosage and still sleep poorly stop using them. [E]

Stimulants, or "uppers".

On the other side of the coin are so-called "uppers" or stimulants you may take to help you get through the day when fatigue or lack of energy becomes overwhelming. These completely disrupt the normal life rythms of the body--hardly something the traveler needs to impose on rhythms already desyhncronized because of crossing time zones and staying up all night. Amphetamines, benzadrines, dexadrines and other "speed" drugs affect the central nervous system and virtually every cell. [F] [DD]

Also realize that drugs are studied under conditions of normal pressure (i.e. at sea level) in normal situations. Little research has been conducted on how they affect us when we're at higher altitudes or suffering jet stress. (*Crosscheck,* a Pan American Airways magazine, warns pilots that altitude will most likely accentuate drug effects dramatically.) Not only should we be careful with prescription drugs but over-the-counter drugs as well.

ALTERNATIVES TO DRUGS

Instead of drugs to get to sleep you could try mind control techniques like meditation, biofeedback or progressive relaxation, yoga exrcises, C.E.S. therapy, and/or particular nutrients like inositol, L-tryptophan or PABA. To counter fatigue vitamin C, dessicated liver, wheat germ oil, bee pollen and superoxide dismutase could help. So might a negative ion generator in your room.

SMOKING AND DEATH: A LOVE AFFAIR
(Or Cancer Cures Smoking)

"The cigarette is the single most lethal agent in America today," claims Dr. Hollis Ingraham. * Nicotine is one of the most toxic of all drugs, acting as rapidly as cyanide. Nearly 20 billion dollars are lost annually because of smoking, with direct health costs running close to 8 billion a year. Every year 81,000 Americans die of lung cancer with 75% of the cancer linked to smoking. The cigarette contains more than 30 known carcinogens. [G]   Cigarette smoking is defintely linked to chronic bronchitis and emphysema. Heart disease and smoking have been thoroughly linked. [H]

For the person who flies, smoking is even a greater threat to health. He will suffer a mild hypoxia because the cabin altitude is around 7,000 feet above sea level. Add to this the fact that smoke from one cigarette raises the carbon monoxide level of the blood to be equal to the hypoxia experienced at 7,000 feet. Two or more consecutively-smoked,

* *Public Health and Fitness*

raised the level to 10,000 feet. *

Smoke affects the body much the way sugar does. It can cause a rapid raise in blood sugar followed by just as rapid a drop shortly after the cigarette is put out. With hypoglycemia a potential reality while flying this added strain on the body's attempt to maintain a satisfactory blood sugar level is not needed.

Nicotine constricts the blood vessels, which are already constricted by the norepinephrine hormone secreted by the adrenal glands in their attempt to protect us against the stresses of flight. This increases blood pressure dramatically while blood flow into the arms, legs and brain is reduced. Smoking places a very heavy load on the vascular system and the heart.

NICOTINE IS A POTENT, ADDICTIVE DRUG

Nicotine is a potent drug which affects the entire body, every cell, in a way we can't control. It is both stimulant and depressant so its effect on us is complex and unpredictable. The central nervous system is stimulated. Nerve transmission at the junctions between cells is affected. Respiration is excited. Tremors and vomiting can occur. It can inhibit urination for 2 to 3 hours after just one cigarette. It seems to be the cause of many minor upper respiratory infections, difficult breathing, lack of normal response to hunger, increased salivation and heart palpitations, constriction of blood vessels and increased blood pressure. Nicotine decreases the amino acid content of the blood by 24 to 31%, which has the same effect, reports ascorbate resear-

---

* The carbon monoxide binds to the oxygen-carrying part of blood called hemoglobin, preventing it from carrying enough oxygen to satisfy the needs of the cells.

cher Dr. Irwin Stone, as increasing our chronological age by 40 years.

Nicotine is addictive. The cigarette smoker is addicted to a drug just like any other addict who, by definition, habitually uses chemical agents to avoid real or imagined physical and psychological consequences of not using the drug. The average smoker requires his drug not just every day but every hour, usually smoking at least one cigarette per waking hour. The dependent smoker craves nicotine every 30 to 60 minutes. When he tries to stop he has the normal withdrawal symptoms common to all drug addiction: nervousness, drowsiness, anxiety, headaches, energy loss, sweating, cramps, tremors and palpitations.

The smoker is a drug addict who endangers the lives of all those around him, smoker and non-smoker alike, far more than any junkie on dope. His smoke enters the air affecting everyone else who must breathe that air. It is not unfair to say that the cigarette addict is a contributing cause to heart disease and all the other smoke-related diseases, including cancer and emphysema, which are suffered by those who have to breathe his smoke.

SMOKING INSIDE THE AIRPLANE: IS IT DANGEROUS?

If it is dangerous for us in a normal environment under normal circumstances at sea level, it is bound to be dangerous for us inflight. It's toxic effects are increased. It adds cyanide and carbon monoxide to the air, increasing the problem of hypoxia. It removes negative air ions. It depletes our bodies of vitamin C which we need to counter stress. It causes blood pressure to rise, which may already be occurring in response to the stress of flight.

It's especially dangerous in the cockpit where it's affect on the blood pressure, heart and brain of the pilot can mean life and death to the passengers.

REHABILITATION FOR THE NICOTINE-ADDICT

Like the other forms of drug addiction, nicotine addiction can be resolved with diet and nutritional supplementation. Dr. Emanuel Cheraskin has used his Optimal Diet* on smokers to successfully break their habit. In his opinion, "The Optimal Diet will help overcome your dependence on nicotine, will lessen your craving for cigarettes and will neutralize some of the unpleasant side effects of withdrawal." He also uses megadoses of supplements along with lots of regular physical activity and going "cold turkey".

Hypnosis helps some addicts. Other find that fasting for from 3 to 10 days gives the body time to get rid of all the nicotine and other chemical by-products out of the blood so they don't crave a cigarette.

However if he chooses to break his addiction, the smoker must admit he is an addict, that he has a definite problem no matter how favorably advertising and society may look upon it. If he wants to be free of drug dependency, he can be.

The tragedy of smoking was strikingly and pathetcally commented upon by columnist Herb Caen in his article, "Get Off Your Butts": "I watch him walk away, wheezing slightly, and think about Humphrey Bogart. Every time you see Sam Spade light up on the late show you want to holler, 'Don't, Bogey! Put it out!' How sad it is."

---

*   Described in Cheraskin's book, *Psychodietetics*

NOTES FOR THE PROFESSIONAL TRAVELER

A.   Most drinking by flight personnel is done during layovers. Since alcohol is a drug, its effect on the body varies according to which cycle the body is in when it is consumed. It's possible that alcohol drunk on layover continues to affect the crew member when he reports to work.

Alcoholism is a problem among airline personnel. Airlines have joined with the Air Line Pilots Association in a jointly-supported rehabilitation program. They claim alcoholism is no more prevalent among airline personnel than the population in general, but even at that it is a problem. In the United States production loss because of alcoholism is over 20 billion dollars every year. Direct health costs run nearly 12 billion.

B.   There is another way of treating alcoholism that has worked remarkably well. The C.E.S. machine, mentioned earlier in Chapter Nine, was used along acupuncture points in the ear by British researchers. It eliminated the effects of withdrawal in both alcoholics and drug addicts. In another study 6 months of C.E.S. therapy brought improved mood, reduced short-term memory loss and found the patients less neurotic. Rate of recidivism after 7 months was 33% for the treatment group and 67% for the placebo group.

C.   Barbiturates vary greatly in what they can do, how long they stay in the body, and what their long-term effects on behavior might be. They depress everything in the body--every cell. They reduce consumption of oxygen by the cells and depress nerve activity, skeletal muscles and the heart muscle. They can produce sedation or coma in the central nervous system. They can lead to addiction and suicide. Rather than improve sleep over a period of time they tend to disrupt sleep patterns.

D.   These drugs include alcohol, methqualone, seconal, menbutal and benedryl.

E.   There are cases where patients have used low doses for years without undue side effects and without needing to increase dosage, reports Dr. Peter Hauri in his book *Current Concepts: The Sleep Disorders.* Apparently the placebo effect was enough to help them sleep.

F.   Even marijuana, considered safe by many, can affect the flying capabilities of a pilot. In a test, pilots who smoked a social dose of marijuana flew more poorly, making more major and minor errors, altitude and heading mistakes and radio navigation errors. The effects lasted for 2 to 6 hours after taking the drug. Marijuana decreases the amount of oxygen available in the body due to the carbon monoxide in the smoke.

G.   L-tryptophan is an amino acid we eat every day and one which can be used as a supplement to aid sleep. If it is mixed with tobacco smoke at a particular stage in its breakdown in the body it becomes a cancer-causing metabolite called orthoaminophenal.

H.   Cigarettes caused three-fourths of the heart attacks suffered by a group of otherwise healthy women under fifty in a study conducted at Boston University Medical School. Researchers reported in the *New England Journal of Medicine,* "some 75% of infarctions could be avoided if women did not smoke." Women who smoke also have 5.7 times more brain hemorrhages (strokes) than those who don't and if they take oral birth control they run a risk 21.9 times greater than the nonsmoker.

Chapter Eleven

HOW DO WE COPE WITH JET STRESS?

Jet stress is a real problem for the traveler. It encompasses more than the jet lag we feel when our body is forced into confusion and disharmony from crossing time zones and staying up when we should be sleeping. Conditions inside the airplane create more stress for us. Cabin air doesn't have as much oxygen as we are used to breathing. It is extremely dry, often contains toxic ozone gas and may be overloaded with positive air ions but depleted of the negative ions. Vibration and noise are additional stressors.

Even if some of these stressors were minor by themselves, when added together their cumulative effect is serious. Some are major stressors--especially the disruption of our body cycles and the resulting loss of adequate sleep.

We can prevent jet stress by not flying--an absurd answer for most of us.

But we can learn to cope with jet stress. First we should try to remove as many stressors as possible. Improving the atmosphere inside the airplane by increasing the humidity, increasing available negative air ions and decreasing ozone gas would help. Ear plugs against noise would help. Certain supplements may help us use better what oxygen is available. No smoking, no drinking of alcoholic beverages and no overeating would help.

The most difficult problem we face is dealing with the

stress of dyschronosis--trying to get all the body clocks back in order so they once again work together harmoniously. Hopefully we will locate a master, internal biological body clock and the natural substance that controls it so we can synthesize the chemical to take like medicine when we want to alter body cycles. Dr. Martin C. Moore-Ede is working on something like that which he calls a "jet lag pill".

In the meantime we can try some other things. A combination of certain foods, beverages, activities and drugs can alter body cycles. Dr. Charles F. Ehret has devised a complicated diet and activity regimen to delay or advance body clocks. Others speculate that using acupuncture or a C.E.S. machine could help rebalance brain waves, which would help the body recycle more rapidly.

If we could get enough good sleep the fatigue from jet stress would be much, much less. Lack of it is a major stressor in and of itself. We haven't found the body's natural substance that triggers sleep. Once found, it too can be synthesized, to be used like medicine when we need to sleep. It would help the body sleep even when it wasn't in a sleep cycle.

In the meantime we can self-experiment with proven-safe substances and techniques. Exercise, hot baths and massage can reduce tension in the body, preparing it for sleep. Relaxation techniques like biofeedback, progressive relaxation, autogenic training, self-hypnosis and post-hypnotic suggestion, meditation and yoga can help some people. Supplements of the amino acid L-tryptophan or inositol (sometimes combined with Vitamin E or aspirin) sometimes work. Eating a light snack to get back to sleep when you wake up after only a few hours of rest sometimes helps, especially if you're hypoglycemic.

Using hypnotics like alcohol, sleeping pills, Valium, barbiturates and antihistamines can work for a short time but after awhile they make sleep problems worse. Most have undesirable side-effects. They are not the solution, especially for the pilot since they may remain in the body while he is trying to fly the airplane. When used they should be prescribed by a physician and you should know just what to expect from them.

The healthier you are the better you will withstand jet stress. To be physically fit you need nutritious food and good exercise. "Good physical fitness means diet, exercise and not smoking at all," says Dr. Stanley Mohler, internationally-known aerospace medical specialist. "The diet should include all the essential food nutrients we find in raw fruits and raw vegetables, lean meat and fish. No junk food." Exercise, he suggests, would be aerobic like running, swimming or racquetball combined with some form of stretching and limbering activity like karate, judo, yoga or tai chi.

Since its doubtful we could eat enough food to get all the nutrients we need when we are under stress we should supplement our diet with vitamins, minerals, raw glandulars, herbs, and any other products natural to the body that can strengthen it. Vitamins C and B-complex combat stress. Vitamins A and E, along with garlic, can protect somewhat against ozone toxicity. Vitamin E and B-15 can reduce hypoxia.

Stress reduces our immunity to disease. Overall resistance goes down because the adrenal glands get tired and the thymus gland shrinks. Raw glandular tissue of the adrenal gland and the thymus gland will help our own glands recuperate and rebuild. Vitamins C and A also bolster the immune system. So will garlic and ginseng.

Fatigue can be reduced if we take whole food supplements of desiccated liver and wheat germ. Food yeast is a high-protein, anti-stress food. Bee pollen, ginseng and garlic can increase our resistance to disease, provide energy and generally build and strengthen our bodies if they are used over a period of time.

The problem of jet stress is complex and so are the solutions. There are no simple nor absolute answers. Nothing in health is simplistic and this is no exception. What works well for you may not work well for someone else. Or it may work fine for you sometimes, but not always.

The best you can do is understand where the stress comes from and how your body responds to it. Then you can work with your doctor to find which of the techniques and nutrients we have mentioned work best for you. Your active participation is crucial to your success since in the final analysis only you can tell how your body is responding.

You can also apply pressure on the airlines to serve better food, add humidifiers and ozone filtration systems (and to the airplanes.) You can force them to acknowledge that fatigue is a real and dangerous problem in flight safety. You can demand they look for solutions to reduce this fatigue in the pilots flying your plane and the flight attendants who will get you out of the plane safely in a crash.

Chapter Twelve

APPENDICES

I Offer the following information to the reader as an aid, and nothing more. Neither are the products mentioned the only ones available, nor is there any intention of endorsement of these products. No recommendations are made. There are many excellent products available that I haven't listed, for want of space and sufficient information. You can probably find these products in your local health food or natural food store, or ask them to order them for you.

I reiterrate, this is not an advertisement. I am not attempting to evaluate or sell the products of anyone. I apologize to those companies and manufacturers that I have not been able to list.

APPENDIX I
HYPOGLYCEMIA AND THE GLUCOSE
TOLERANCE TEST

In their book, *Psychodietetics*, Drs. Cheraskin and Ringsdorf provide a self-administered questionnaire to help you prediagnose hypoglycemia. Especially if you feel any three or more of the following symptoms, they warn that you probably suffer some sugar intolerance.

1. Chronic fatigue

2. Chronic nervous exhaustion
3. Eat often or get hunger pains or faintness
4. Faintness if meals delayed
5. Fatigue, eating relieves
6. Get shaky when hungry
7. Sleepy after meals
8. Sleepy during day

Dr. Paavo Airola clearly and thoroughly explains what the glucose tolerance test entails and how to read it yourself, in his book, Hypoglycemia: A Better Approach. It pays to know this yourself, since all doctors have not been trained in how to interpret this test correctly. It also helps you understand your physical condition just that much better, and thereby be able to control it better.

APPENDIX II
HERBS

Health food stores will carry at least one brand of herbal products. If they don't they will be able to order them for you, or give you the address of a reputable herbal company. You might also check advertisements in health magazines.

APPENDIX III
EXERCISE EQUIPMENT

The Exer-Cor machine is sold by distributors, many of whom have booths at health conventions and meetings like the National Health Federation Conventions held annually in major cities.

For the name of a distributor nearest you, write:

Health & Education Services
2442 West Irving Park Road
Chicago, Illinois 60618

Minitrampolines are sold at many health food stores, or they can tell you where to send for them. They are also sold at health conventions, through mail order and by some chiropractic clinics. Some are advertised in health magazines.

APPENDIX IV
HOMOEOPATHY

A Directory of United States Homoeopathic Physicians is available from the National Center for Homoeopathy. So are Homoeopathic First Aid Kits. They would have a listing of other retailers of these kits, as well as pharmacies carrying homoeopathic medicines. This information is also printed in the February issue (1979) of Let's Live Magazine in an article by Gregory Vlamis.

6231 Leesburg Pike, Suite 506
Falls Church, Virginia 22044
(703) 534-4363

APPENDIX V
DIET AND METABOLIC TYPES

An optimal diet varies with each of us, depending upon our metabolic type, according to Dr. William Kelley. For information on this thesis, and metabolic testing, write one of the following:

The Kelley Foundation of Life
Castle Avenue
Winthrop, Washington 98862
(509) 996-2214

The Nutrition Academy
P.O. Box 345
Des Plaines, Illinois 60016

APPENDIX VI
SLEEP DISORDER CENTERS

The following is a list of fully-accredited members of the Association of Sleep Disorders Centers.

Sleep-Wake Disorders Unit, Montefiore Hospital
111 E. 210th Street, Bronx, NY 10467 (212) 920-4841

Sleep Disorders Center, Cincinnati General Hospital
Cincinnati, OH 45267 (513) 861-3100

Sleep Clinic, Dept. Psychiatry, Ohio State University
Columbus, OH 43210 (614) 422-5982

Sleep Disorders Center, Henry Ford Hospital
2799 W. Grand Blvd. Detroit, MI 48202 (313) 876-2233

Sleep Clinic, Baylor College of Medicine
Houston, TX 77030 (713) 790-4886

BMH Sleep Disorders Center, Baptist Memorial Hospital
Memphis, TN 38146 (901) 522-5651

Sleep Disorders Center, Mt. Sinai Medical Center
4300 Alton Road, Miami Beach. FL 33140 (305) 674-2613

There are other sleep clinics around the nation. If you are
looking for one closer to where you live, any of the above
clinics should be able to send you a roster of centers belonging to the above association.

APPENDIX VII
ION GENERATORS

The following list offers a variety of models of ion
generators. The list is not inclusive, and apologies go to
manufacturers who are not listed. Generators are becoming
available more and more in health food stores. Some are
advertised in newspapers and health magazines as air
cleaners. You will want to check and compare all sources.

Energy Master, Inc.
3188 Airway Avenue, Building "F"
Costa Mesa, California 92626

Environmental Sciences Corporation
P.O. box 7907
Charlotesville, Virginia 22906

Medion International, Inc.
261 Hamilton Avenue #320
Palo Alto, California 94301

Ion Systems, Inc.
P.O. Box 601
San Leandro, California 94577

Dev Industries
5721 Arapaho Avenue
Boulder, Colorado 80303

Environmental Integrity Systems
P.O. Box 928
Capitola, California 95010

Paradise Marketing
1870 Chris Lane
Anaheim, California 92805

APPENDIX VIII
EAR PLUGS

Hocks Laboratories
935 N.E. Couch Street
Portland, Oregon 97214

APPENDIX IX
C.E.S. MACHINES

These machines are available through prescription only. For information, write:

Neuro Systems, Inc.
2709 National Drive
Garland, Texas 75041

(214) 271-5418

Biotronic Corporation
55 Glendale Road
Glenbrook, Connecticut 06906
(203) 348-9725

APPENDIX X
FORMULA FOR REST

The following is the travel-time formula for determining rest periods needed to reduce the effects of travel. It was devised for the International Civil Aviation Organization with headquarters in Montreal, Canada by the late Dr. L.E. Buley, Chief of Aviation Medicine for ICAO.

BULEY'S FORMULA

$$\text{Rest period (in tenths of days)} = \frac{\text{Travel Time (in hours)}}{2} + \text{Time Zones in excess of 4}$$

$$+ \text{ Departure time coefficient (local time)} + \text{Arrival time coefficient (local time)}$$

Departure and Arrival Coefficients

Period	Dep. Coef.	Arrival Coef.
0800-1159	0	4
1200-1759	1	2
1800-2159	3	0
2200-0059	4	1
0100-0800	3	3

In using this formula, consider the following fine points:

1. If fewer than 4 time zones are crossed, that part is eliminated from the formula.

2. The answer in tenths of days will be rounded to the nearest higher half day. Rest stops that total less than one day before rounding, unless the journey involved an overnight flight, are not considered.

3. Travel hours are the number of hours of elapsed time required for the journey, according to published schedules of the airline, rounded off to the nearest hour.

4. Time zones are computed in increments of 15 degrees of longitude from Greenwich.

5. Departure and arrival times are local.

(This formula printed with permission from the ICAO as it appeared in the November, 1972 issue of the ICAO Bulletin.)

APPENDIX XI
ORTHOMOLECULAR MEDICINE: LISTS OF PRACTICING PHYSICIANS

Orthomolecular medicine attempts to discover what natural constituents of our bodies we are low in, high in, or lacking, and then to balance body chemistry by giving large amounts of the substances needed. The object is to normalize the body's metabolism with substances natural to the body, enabling it to maintain an adequate supply of healthy replacement tissue to any one, or any group of organs or bodily function.

Testing usually includes a hair analysis for mineral and metal content of the body, a blood "wet-mount" test under a dark field microscope to see how the body handles fat, a complete blood lipid and chemistry panel, vital capacity testing for detecting early lung disease, and a glucose tolerance test. Often included are thermography and plethysmograph tests for measuring blood flow and circulation. Allergy testing is normally done. EKG's are given where needed.

Lists of practicing doctors may be obtained from:

Huxley Institute for Biosocial Research
1114 First Avenue
New York, New York 10021
(212) 759-9554

International Academy of Metabology
2236 Suree Ellen Lane
Altadena, California 91001

International College of Applied Nutrition
Box 386
La Habra, California 90631

International Academy of Preventive Medicine
871 Frostwood Drive,
Houston, Texas 77024

APPENDIX XII
CEREBRAL ALLERGY/ADDICTION

For more information on food allergies that cause addiction to the food, thus affecting both body and mind, write:

The Society for Clinical Ecology
Robert Collier, M.D.
4045 Wadsworth Boulevard
Wheat Ridge, Colorado 80033

APPENDIX XIII
BEHAVIORAL KINESIOLOGY

Institute of Behavioral Kinesiology
376 Jeffrey Place
Valley Cottage, New York 10989
(914) 268-7883

APPENDIX XIV
SPORTS MEDICINE SPECIALISTS

For a listing, write to:

American Physical Therapy Association
Sports Medicine Section
c/o George J. Davies
2036 Cowley Hall
University of Wisconsin
La Crosse, Wisconsin 54601

Sports Medicine Division

Canadian Physiotherapy Association
Att: Linda L. Mason
13020 113th Avenue
Edmonton, Alberta, Canada T5M 2XL

APPENDIX XV
TAPES FOR SELF-RELAXATION AND
SELF-HYPMOSIS

Usually you can buy these tapes through mail order and at health conventions. You can ask about them at your health food store, wholistic health center and at offices of hypnotherapists and pain clinics. If you can't get help from these places you might write to the following addresses. Again, my apologies to the companies not listed. I simply cannot know about all of you.

Valley of the Sun
Box 4276
Scottsdale, Arizona 85258

Halpern Sounds
602 Taylor Way #14
Belmont, California 94002

BIBLIOGRAPHY

Abrahamson, E.M., A.W. Pezet. Body, Mind and Sugar. New York: Pyramid Books, 1971.

Aging. H.E.W. Publication, April, 1976.

Airola, Paavo.
Are You Confused? 1976.
Hypoglycemia: A Better Approach. 1977.
How To Get Well. 1976.
Miracle of Garlic. 1978.
Phoenix, Arizona: Health Plus Publishers. (P.O. Box 22001, 85028).

ASHA Reports. "Effects of Noise on Psychological State". pp. 74-86. No. 4. 1969.

Atkins, Robert. Let's Live Magazine. Vol. 46, No. 10. Oct. 1978.

Atkinson, D.T. "Malnutrition as an Etiological Factor in Senile Cataract". The Eye, Ear, Nose and Throat Monthly. pp. 79-83. Vol. 31. 1952.

Aviation Medical Bulletin. P.O. Box 20787. Atlanta Airport, Georgia 30320. Jan 1977/ Feb. 1978/ Oct 1978/ July 1978/ May 1979.

Barron, Charles. Interview.

Bennett, G. "Ozone Contamination of High Altitude Aircraft Cabins". Aerospace Medicine. pp. 969-973. Vol. 33, No. 8.

Bischof, Walter. "Ozone Measuarements in Jet Airliner Cabin Air". Water, Air and Soil Pollution. pp. 3-14. Vol. 2. 1973.

Blanc, C.J., R. Digo, P. Moroni. "Psychopathology of Airline Stewardesses". Aerospace Medicine. pp. 184-187. Feb 1969.

Bohlen, Joseph G. "Health and Work Shifts: Discussion I." Health Consequences of Shift Work. Nat Institute Occupational Safety & Health (NIOSH). 4676 Columbia Parkway, Cincinnati, Ohio 45226.

Boyer, John M. "Effects of Chronic Exercise on Cardiovascular Function." Physical Fitness Research Digest. Series 2, No. 3. July 1972.

Brabets, Robert I., et. al. "Ozone Measurement Survey in Commercial Jet Aircraft." J. Aircraft. Vol. 4, No. 1. Jan/Feb 1967.

Buckley, Robert E. Negative Air Ions: Vitamins of the Air. Paper presented Orthomolecular Medicine Society Meeting, San Francisco. Jan 22, 1978.

Caen, Herb. "Get Off Your Butts". San Francisco Chronicle. April 1978.

Cantrell, Geo. K., Ralph Trimble, Bryce O. Hartman. Longterm Aircrew Effectiveness--A Literature Survey. U.S.A.F. Sch of Aerospace Med. Brooks A.F. Base, Texas. April 1971. (Also avail in Aeromedical Reviews)

Carruthers, Malcolm, A.E. Arguelles, Abraham Mosovich. "Man in Transit: Biochemical & Physiological Changes During Intercontinental Flights". Av, Sp & Envir Med. Sept 1977.

Catlett, G.F., G.J. Kidera. "Detection & Management of Latent Diabetes in Commercial Pilots." Aerospace Med. pp. 545-551. Vol 37, No. 6. June 1966.

Challem, Jack J. "Cholesterol: Discerning Myth from Fact." Let's Live. Vol. 46, No. 10. Oct 1978.

Cheraskin, E., W.M. Ringsdorf. Psychodietetics. New York: Bantam Books. 1976.

Chiles, W. Dean.
"Effects of Ionized Air on Decision Making and Vigilance Performance." 1962.
"A Study of the Effects of Ionized Air on Behavior." 1960.
Behavioral Sciences Lab. Wright-Patterson A.F. Base, Ohio.

Christensen, Carl L., et. al. "Effects of Three Kinds of Hypoxieas on Vigilance Performance." Av, Sp & Env Med. pp. 491-495. Vol. 48, No. 6 June 1977.

Christopher, John R.
The Healing Herbs, 1972.
Dr. Christopher's Three-Day Cleansing Program and Mucousless Diet, 1978.
Interview in Healthview Newsletter, No. 18.
Box 352, Provo, Utah 84601.

Colquhoun, W.P. "Accidents, Injuries & Shift Work." Shift Work & Health -- A Symposium. Washington, D.C. Supt of Documents, U.S. Gov Printing Office, Wash, D.C. 20402. July 1976.

Consumer's Digest, "Megavitamins, New Hope for the Mentally Ill." Nov/Dec 1973.

Cooper, Kenneth H. The New Aerobics. New York: M. Evans & Co. 1970.

Cooper, Midred, Kenneth Cooper. Aerobics for Women. New York: M. Evans & Co. 1972.

Crane, James E.
How to Become the Oldest Retired Pilot. (A paper) "Heart Attack." Air Line Pilot. June 1967. "Low Humidity and Dehydration in Jets." Air Line Pilot. pp. 12-18. Jan 1966.

Crosscheck. Pan American World Airways. Flight Safety Analysis & Information. J.F.K. Int'l Airport. Hangar 14, Room 350. Jamaica, N.Y. 11430. Vol 5, No. 5. May 1978, and June, 1979, pp. 6-7.

Day, Nancy R. "Fatigue in the Safety Equation." Business & Commercial Aviation. pp. 151-160. Sept 1976.

Deaf Smith Country Cookbook. New York: Collier, Macmillan. 1977.

Diamond, John. Behavioral Kinesiology. New York: Harper & Row. 1979.

Donsbach, Kurt. Cholesterol. Huntington Beach, CA 92646: Int'l Inst Nat Health Science. Box 5550.

Dufty, William. Sugar Blues. New York: Warner Books. 1976.

Ehret, Charles F.
  & Kenneth Dobra. "The Oncogenic Implications of Chronobiotics in the Synchronization of Mamalian Circadian Rhythms: Barbiturates and Methylated Xanthines." Proceedings of 3rd Int'l Symposium on Detection & Prevention of Cancer. pp. 1101-1104. Ed. H. E. Nieburgs. New York: Marcel Dekker, 1977.

  & Kenneth R. Groh, John C. Meinert. Circadian Dyschronism & Chronotypic Ecophilia as Factors in Aging & Longevity. Argonne National Lab, 9700 South Cass Ave, Argonne, Ill. 60439.

The Clockwatcher's & World Traveler's Diet. Argonne Lab, Ill.

The Sense of Time: Evidence for Its Molecular Basis in the Eukaryotic Gene-Action System. Argonne Lab, Ill.

  & Van R. Potter, Kenneth W. Dobra. "Cronotypic Action of Theophylline and of Pentobarbital as Circadian Zeitgebers in the Rat." Science. pp. 1212-1215. Vol 188. June 1975.

  & John C. Meinert, Kenneth R. Groh. Chronopharmacology and Orthochronal Use of L-DOPA: Implications for Orthochronal Therapy in the Prevention of Circadian Dyschronism. Argonne Lab, Ill.

Feltman, John. "Vitamins from A to Z." Let's Live. pp. 115-122. Feb 1978.

Fishbein, William & Baruch M. Gutwein. "Paradoxical Sleep and Memory Storage Processes." Behavioral Biology. pp. 465-475. Vol. 19. 1977.

Fixx, James F. The Complete Book of Running. New York: Random House. 1977.

Fox, Samuel M. & John L. Boyer. "Physical Activity & Coronary Heart Disease." Physical Fitness Research Digest. Series 2, No. 2. April 1972.

Frank, Benjamin S. "The Molecular Indications of Nucleic Acid Therapy." Int'l Academy Metabology Newsletter. Jan/June 1978.

Fredericks, Carlton. Psychonutrition. New York: Grosset & Dunlap. 1976.

Fryer, Lee & Annette Dickinson. A Dictionary of Food Supplements. New York: Mason/Charter. 1975.

Fulder, Stephen. About Genseng, the Magical Herb of the East. Wellingobrough, Northamptonshire, England: Thorsons Publ. 1977.

George, Graham. Pollen Power. (A paper)

Gilmer, J. Ray. Cerebral Electrostimulation Overview. (A paper)

Glaubman, Hanayah, et. al. "REM Deprivation and Divergent Thinking." Psychophysiology. pp. 75-79. Vol. 15, No. 1. Jan 1978.

Glines, C.V., "The Report of the I-Team", pp 14-16. "Flight Time/Duty Time: A New Approach" pp. 6-10. 55. Air Line Pilot, May 1979.

Goldberg. Vicki. "What Can We Do About Jet Lag?" Psychology Today. pp. 69-72. Aug 1977.

Goodman, Louis S., et. al., Editors. The Pharmacological Basis of Therapeutics. Fourth Ed. New York: Macmillan.

Green, Julia Minerva. The Heart of Homoeopathy. National Center for Homoeopathy. 6231 Leesburg Pike, Suite 506, Falls Church, VA 22044

Greenberg, Daniel S. "Those Witch Doctors in White Coats." Washington Post. Friday, Aug 19, 1977.

Halcomb, Charles G., Robert E. Kirk. "Effects of Air Ionization Upon the Performance of a Vigilance Task." J. Engineering Psychology. pp. 120-130. Vol 4. 1965.

Halstead, Bruce W. Hyperbaric Oxygen Therapy. American Academy of Med. Preventics. 1976.

Harland, Barbara, & Annabel Hecht. "Grandma Called It Roughage." Aviation Med Bulletin. Feb 1978.

Harper, C.R., & G.J. Kidera. PHYpoglycemia in Airline Pilots." Aerospace Medicine. pp. 769-771. July 1973.

Harper, Harold. Chelation: Light on the Medical Horizon. (A paper)

Harris, Raymond. Guide to Fitness After Fifty. New York: Plenum Press. 1977.

Harvard Medical School Health Letter. Vol 3, No. 8. June 1978.

Hauri, Peter. Current Concepts: The Sleep Disorders, Upjohn Company, Kalamazoo, Michigan. 1977.

Haus, Erhard. "Pharmachological and Toxicological Correlates of Circadian Sychronization and Desynchronization." Shift Work & Health--a Symposium. pp 87-117. U.S. Gov. Printing Office. July 1976.

Hawkins, Frank H. Sleep & Body Rhythm Disturbance in Long-Range Aviation: the Problem & a Search for Relief. Amsterdam, Netherlands: Dutch Air Line Pilots Assoc. 1978.
Sleep in the Long-Range Aviation Environment. Londn: Sept 1978. (Available: Dutch ALPA, Vereniging van Nederlandse Verkeersviliegers, Charlotte van Montpensierdaan 28, Amstelveen, Nederland: US $7, plus postage and handling.)

Henderson, James L. & Dixie J. Church, A. Eugene Lee. Using Electrosleep Therapy with University Couseling Center Clients: A Preliminary Study presented Rocky Mt. Psychological Assn. Las Vegas, May 9, 1973.

Hittleman, Richard. Hittleman's Yoga 28-Day Exercise Program. New York: Bantam Books. 1973.

Hoffer, Abram & Morton Walker. Orthomolecular Nutrition. New Canaan, Conn: Keats Pub. 1978. Holistic Way to Health & Happiness: A New Approach to Complete Lifetime Wellness. Simon & Schuster. 1978.

Honorof, Ida. "A Report to the Consumer." Int'l Acad Metabology Newsletter. Jan/June 1978.

Houston Post. "Study Questions Advantage of Bypass Surgery." Sept 23, 1977. (Also reported in N. Eng. J. Med.)

Howitt, J.S., et. al. "Workload & Fatigue-in-Flight EEG Changes." Av, Sp & En Med. pp. 1197-1202. Oct 1978.

Howlett, L., & R.J. Shepard. "Carbon Monoxide as a Hazard in Aviation." J. Occupational Med. pp. 874-877. Vol. 15, no. 11. Nov 1973.

Huemer, Richard P. "A Theory of Diagnosis for Orthomolecular Medicine." Int'l Acad Metabology Newsletter. Jan/June 1978.

Huhlman, W., et. al. "Mutagenic Action of Caffeine." Cancer Research. pp. 2375-2389. Vol 28. Nov 1969.

Hunter, Beatrice Trum. The Great Nutrition Robbery. New York: Scribner's & Sons.

Hyland, Carl A. "Women & Minerals." Let's Live. Aug 1978; "Pick of the Books." Let's Live. Aug 1978; "A Vitamin Therapy for Drug Addicts." Let's Live pp. 24-27. Oct 1978.

Igraham, Hollis S. "Public Health & Fitness--the Outdoor Life & Other Antidotes to Enemies of Fitness." Guide to Fitness After Fifty. Ed. Raymond Harris. pp 39-44. New York: Pleanum Press. 1977.

Int'l Academy Metabology Newsletter, "The Molecular Indications of Nucleic Acid Therapy." Available 1000 E. Walnut St., Pasadena, CA 91105, Jan/June 1978.

I.U.F.A. Health & Safety Report. 1860 El Camino Real Burlingame, CA 94010. Jan 1979.

Jaffe, L.D., & H.D. Estes. "Ozone Toxicity Hazard in Cabins of High Altitude Aircraft--A Review & Current Program" Aerospace Med. pp. 633-643. July, 1963.

Janowsky, D.S., et. al. "Simulated Flying Performance After Marihuana Intoxication." Av, Sp & Envir Med. pp 124-128. Vol 47, No. 2. Feb 1976.

Jensen, Ned. "Raw Glandulars--the Adrenals." Let's Live. pp. 83-128. Vol 47, No. 2. Feb 1979.

Johnston, A.M. "Behavioral Problems & the Air Line Pilot." Crosscheck. pp 3-6. Jan 1978.

Jones, Susan Smith, & Torney Smith. "Exercise for Reducing Stress & Lifting Spirits." Let's Live. pp. 121-128. June 1979.

Keelor, Richard. Aging. H.E.W. Publication. April 1976.

KPIX-TV, The Human Factor: A Report on the FAA's Air Crew Rest Rules, Channel 5, San Francisco, California. Aired December 5, 1978.

Klein, Karl E., et. al. "Air Oerations & Circadian Performance Rhythms." Av, Sp & Envir Med. pp. 221-230. Vol. 47. No. 3 1976.

Koester, William S. "Steve Reddick: It's All in the Pollen." Let's Live. pp. 57-62. June 1979.

Kornblueh, Igho H. Air Ions & Human Health. Presented at Seminar on Human Biometerorology. et. al. "Relief from Pollinosis in Negatively Ionized Rooms." Amer J. Physcial Med. 1958.
& James Griffin. Aftifical Air Ionization in Phsycal Medicine--a Preliminary Report. Dept Phys Med & Rehab. Grad Hosp U. Penn.

Krueger, Albert Paul. The Case for Air Ions as a Psychosomatic Factor. A Paper. Ach Public Health, U.C. Berkley. CA 94720.
& Eddie James Reed. "Biological Impact of Small Air Ions." Science. pp. 1209-1211. Vol 193, Sept 1976.
"Are Negative Ions Good For You?" New Scientist. pp. 668-670. Vol 58, No. 850. June 14, 1973.
& Richard F. Smith. "The Biological Mechanisms of Air Ion Action." J. General Physiology. pp. 533-540. Vol 43. 1969.

Kugler, Hans J. "A Healthier Way of Life." Let's Live. Aug 1978.

LaFontaine, E., et. al. "Influence of Air Travel East-West & Vice-versa on Circadian Rhythms of Urinary Elimination of Potassium and 17-Hydroxycorticosteroids." Aerospace Medicine. pp 944-947. Vol 38, No. 9. Sept 1967.

Law, Donald. Guide to Alternative Medicine. Dolphin. 1976.

Leonard, Jon N., & J.L. Hofer, N. Pritikin. Live Longer Now. New York: Grosset & Dunlap. 1976.

Let's Live. "The Concept of Holistic Health." pp. 98-103. Oct 1978.

Levine, Howard. "Health and Work Shifts." Shift Work & Health--a Symposium. pp. 57-67. U.S. Gov Printing Office. July 1976.

Libby, A.F. & I. Stone. Orthomolecular Psychiatry. pp. 300. Vol 6. 1977.

Luca, Richard. Eleuthero-Siberian Ginseng: Health Herb of Russia. Spokane, WA: R&M Books, box 7703, 99208. 1973.

Machta, L., & W.D. Komhyr. "Ozone in Aircraft Cabins." WMO Bulletin. pp. 222-226. Vol 22. Oct 1973.

Malstrom, Stan. Own Your Own Body. Bell Press. 1977 Herbal Remedies. Family Press

Martin, Paul. "How to Beat Pollution." Let's Live. pp 24-29. Jan 1978.
"Arthritis & the Natural Treatment." Let's Live. Oct 1978.

Mayer, Jean. Overweight: Causes, Cost & Control, Reported in Physical Fitness Research Digest. Series 7, No. 2. April 1977.

McFarland, Ross A. "Influence of Changing Time Zones on Air Crews and Passengers." Aerospace Med. pp 655-658. June 1974.

Miller, James D. "Effects of Noise on People." J. Accoustical Soc Am. pp. 729-762. Vol. 56, No. 3. Sept 1974.

Miller, S., & R. Ehrlich. "Susceptiblity to Respiratory Infections of Animals Exposed to Ozone." J. Infectious Diseases. pp. 145-149. Vol 103. Oct 1958.

Millman, Marcia. "Bypass Surgery: Does Anybody Need It But the Surgeons?" Medicine. Sept 13, 1976. Adapted from the Unkindest Cut: Life in the Backrooms of Medicine. Wm. Morrow & Co. Jan 1977.

Mohler, Stanley R. Fatigue in Aviation Activities. Office of Aviation Medicine, FAA AM 65-14. March 1965.
"Modern Concepts in Pilot Aging." Human Factors Bulletin. Avail: Flight Safety Found., 5510 Columbia Pike, Arlington, Virginia 22204. Nov/Dec 1978.
"Physiological Index as an Aid in Developing Airline Pilot Scheduling Patterns." Av, Sp & Envir Med. pp 238-247. Vol 47, No. 3. 1976.

Moore-Ede, Martin D. "Circadian Rhythms in Drug Effectiveness & Toxicity in Shift Workers: Discussion II. " Shift Work and Health--A Symposium. U.S. Gov Printing Office. pp. 140-144. 1976.

M.R.C. Perceptual and Cognitive Performance Unit Progress Report. "Effects on Performance Efficiency of Alterations in Sleep/Waking Schedules Occasinged by Shift work and Time-Zone Changes." England: Dept Employment, Commission No. 187, Brighton, Sussex. 197501978.

National Institute of Safety & Health. Health Aspects of Smoking in Transport Aircraft. Washington D.C. Dec. 1971.

National Health Federation Bulletin. Monrovia, CA 91016. Oct 1978.

National Medical Bulletin. Aug 8, 1978.

Neldner, Kenneth. Int'l Ac Metabology Newsletter. Jan/Mar 1977.

Null, Gary. Biofeedback, Fasting & Meditation. New York: Pyramid Pub. Harcourt, Brace Jovanovich. 1976.
"How to Cope with Stress." Let's Live. pp 81-86. Jan 1978.

Nutrition Almanac. New York: McGraw-Hill. 1975.

Nutrition Journal. Vol 1. No. 2., Fall 1978.

Ogden Standard-Examiner. "Bypass Surgery Overused." Wed. March 24, 1976.

O'Neill, Tom. National Bulletin. Vol. 15, No. 21. Sept 27, 1976.

Organic Consumer Report. Vol. 58, No. 36, Sept 5, 1978; No. 37, Sept 12, 1978; No. 46, Nov 1978.

Oxford & Carter. "Examination of the Airline Pilot." Av, Sp & Envir Med. Feb 1976.

Pauling, Linus. Science. pp. 265-271. Vol. 160. April 19, 1978.

Parrett, Owen S. Why I Don't Eat Meat. (A Paper)

Patrick, Jay. "Vitamin C & Potassium." Let's Live. pp. 72-76, 132-139. Aug 1978.

Passwater, Richard A. "Dieting with Protein." Let's Live. p 51. Jan 1978.

Pfeiffer, Carl C. Zinc and Other Micro-Nutrients. New Canaan, Conn: Keats Pub. 1978.

Physical Fitness Research Digest. Series 1, No. 1. Series 4, No. 2, & Series 7, Nos. 1, 2, & 6. (Available: Pres Council Physcial Fitness & Sports, Wash D.C. 20201).

Pike, Arnold, "American Youth and the Electronic Addiction to Junk Foods." Let's Live. p 104. Jan 1978.

Pilot's Physiological Index. pp 238-242.

Preston, F.S. "Sleep Loss in Air Cabin Crew." Aerospace Med. pp 930-935. Aug 1973.
et. al. "Effects of Time Zone Changes on Performance & Physiology of Airline Personnel." Av, Sp & Envir Med. pp. 763-769. July, 1976.
"Further Sleep Problems in Airline Pilots on World-Wide Schedules." Aerospace Medicine. pp 775-782. July 1973.
& S.C. Bateman. "Effect of Time Zone Changes on the Sleep Patterns of BOAC B-707 Crews on World-Wide Schedules." Aerospace Med. pp. 1409-15. Dec 1970.

Prevention Magazine. p 23. Jan 1979.

Price, William J. "Sleep Loss & the Pilot." Of Iron men & Wooden Ships. Air Line Pilots Assoc. Burlingame, CA Nov. 29, 1977.
Report of Attendance at Sleep Research Clinic. UAL Master Executive Counsil, ALAP Report. Mar 25, 1977.
Report to United Airlines Master Executive Council. Jan 15, 1979.
"Task Force on Pilot Fatigue." The Leading Edge. UAL-MEC Newsletter. Oct 1977.
UAL-MEC Task Force on Pilot Fatigue, 1979.

Psychology Today. "Jet Lag". p 69. Aug 1977.

Public Scrutiny. "Vitamin C Advocate Hits Medical 'Myths'". Aug 1, 1978.

Rosen, Stephen. "Deep Weather." Prevention. pp. 103-110. Jan 1979.

Ross, Harvey M. "Vitamin Pills for Schizophrenics." Psychology Today. Apr 1974.

Ross, R. S. "Ischemic Heart Disease: An Overview." Amer J. Cardiology. pp. 496-505. Vol. 36, Oct 1975.

Ryan, Joseph J., & Gary T. Souheaver. "The Role of Sleep in Electrosleep Therapy for Anxiety." Diseases of the Nervous System. pp 515-517. Vol.

38, No. 7. July 1977.

Scheving, Lawrence E. "Chronobiology & How It Might Apply to the Problems of Shift Work." Shift Work & Health--a Symposium. U.S. Gov. Printing Office. July, 1976.

Samuels, Mike, & Hal Bennett. The Well-Body Book. New York: Random House. 1975.

Science. "A Damaging Source of Air Pollution." Vol. 158, No. 3808. Dec 22, 1967.

Seigel , Peter V., & Seigfried J. Geratherwohl, Stanley R. Mohler. "Time-Zone Effects." Science. pp. 1249-1255. Vol. 164. June 13, 1969.

Sekiguchi, Chiharu, et. al. "The Effects of Rapid Round Trips Against Time Displacement on Adrenal Cortical Medullary Circadian Rhythms." Av. Sp & Evir Med. pp. 1101-06. Oct 1976.

Siliger, Susan. "Living: How to Stop Killing Yourself." San Francisco Chronicle. Tues. Sept 26, 1978.

Selye, Hans. The Stress of Life. New York: McGraw-Hill. 1978.

Sevelius, Gunar. Int'l Ac Metabology Newsletter. Jan/Mar 1977.

Scheer, James F. "The Awesome Ascorbates." Let's Live. pp. 57-62. Jan 1978.

Science Digest. "B-15". Sept 1978.

Sharp, Charles R. Air Ions: A Summary of the Biological, Medical, & Psychological Aspects of Air Ionization. Presented at Int'l Conf on Ionization of the Air, Franklin Inst., Philadelphia, Penn. Oct 16-17, 1961.

Shore, Robert M. The Layman Speaks. Nat Center for Homeoeopathy. Vol 30, No. 12. Dec. 1977.

Silver, Diane, "Snobs & Slobs Get A Bang Out of Rancquetball." Moneysworth. Sept 1978.

Silverman, Daniel, & Igho H. Kornblueh. "Effect of Artificial Ionization of the Air on the Electroencephalogram, Preliminary Report." Am J. Physical Med. Vold 36, 1957.

Smith, James C. Int'l Ac Metabology Newsletter. Jan/Mar 1977.

Smith, Ray B. & Glen Rowinski, Kathleen K.

Gerstein. "Evidence of Chronopathology in Alcholism from the Rehabilitation Center for Alcholics." Annals of the District of Columbia. Vol 43, No. 2. Feb 1973.

Smith, Ray H. Use of Cerebral Electrostimulation in the Treatment of Alcohol Addiction. Presented Winter Conf on Brian Research. Keystone, Col. Jan. 1977.

Stamler, Jeremiah. As quoted in Live Longer Now. pp. 140-141.

Stone, Irwin. The Healing Factor: Vitamin C Against Disease. New York: Grosset & Dunlap 1977.
"Smokers Scurvy--Orthomolecular Preventive Medicine in Cigarette Smoking." J. Orthomolecular Psychiatry. pp. 35-43. Vol 5, No. 1. 1976.
"My Daily Megascorbic Regime for Full Health & Long Life." Better Nutrition. Dec 1977.

Storm, William F., et. al. Effect of Low Humidity on Human Performance. USAF Document Task #7930 - 09-01. Environmental Sciences Division. Dec 7, 1972.

Sullivan, Ann. "Some Fats Found Helpful in Fight Against Cholesterol." The Sunday Oregonian. April 2, 1978.

Sutphen, Dick Self-Help Update. No. 6. Jan/Mar 1979.

Tasto, Donald L., & Michael J. Colligan, Eric W. Skjei, Susan J. Polly. Health Consequences of Shift Work. U.S. Gov. Printing Office. March 1978.

Toyama, Philip M., M.D. The Mechanism of Action of Acupuncture, Moxibustion and Electric Nerve Stimulation Therapy. Reprints available: Friendship Center Office Park, Suite 500, Greensboro, North Carolina 27409.

Udabe, R. Ucha, & R. Kertesz, I. Franceschetti. "Utilization of Negative Ions in Disease of the Nervous System." Bioclimatology, Biometerology, & Aeroionotherapy. Ed. R. Gualtierotti, I. Kornblueh, C. Sirtori. Carlo Erba Foundation, Via Cerva 44, 20122, Milano, Italy. 1968.

Ulett, George A. "Acupuncture: Pricking the Bubble of Skepticism: Biological Psychiatry. pp. 159-161. Vol. 13., No. 2. 1978.

U.S.H.E.W. publication: Air Ions, A Summary of the Biological, Medical & Psychological Aspects of Air Ionization. Presented to Int'l Conf. Ionizatin of the Air. Franklin Institute, Philadelphia, Penn. Oct 16-17, 1961.

van Heusden, S. & G. J. Mans. "Alternating Measurement of Ambient and Cabin Ozone Concentrations in Commercial Jet Aircraft." Av. Sp & Envir Med. pp. 1056-1061. Sept 1978.

Vargo, Kay. What is Homoeopathy? Nat. Center for Homoeopathy.

Viellefond, et. al. "Characteristics in the Atmosphere of Long-Range Transport Aircraft Cabins." Av, Sp & Envir Med. pp. 503-507. June 1977.

Volle, Robert L. & George B. Koelle. "Ganglionic Stimulating & Blocking Agents." The Pharmocological Basis of Therapeutics. 4th Ed. Macmillan. pp. 585-592.

Wallach, Charles. "Clarifying Airions & Their Effects on Quality of Life." National Exchange. Vol. 3, No. 4/5. Dec. 1978.

Walsh, Michael. "Sugar Symposium: An Appraisal." J. So. Cal. Dental Assoc. pp. 18-24. Vol 17, Dec 1950.

Wamsley, James R. "Cockpit Dehydration." Combat Crew. pp 8-10. June 1966.

Wasserman, Donald E. "A Theory of Biological Cell Resonance & Its Relationship to Health & Occupational Shift Work." Shift Work & Health--a Symposium. 1976.

Weitzman, Elliot D. "Circadian Rhythms.: Discussion." Shift Work & Health--a Symposium. July, 1976.

Wurtman, Richard J. "The Efects on Light on the Human Body." Scientific American. pp. 66-77. vol. 233, No. 1. July 1975.
"The Effects of Light on Man & Other Mammals." Annual Review of Physiology.pp 467-483. Vol. 37. 1975.
& Michael A. Moskowitz. "The Pineal Organ." N. Eng. J. Med. Part I: pp 1329-1333. Vol. 296, No. 23, Part II: pp. 1383-1386. Vol. 296. No. 24. 1977.

Young, W.A., et. al. "Presence of Ozone in Aircraft Flying at 35,000 Feet." Aerospace Med. pp. 311-318. March 1962.

INDEX